THE DIAGHILEV BALLET
1909–1929

D1601417

PLATE I

SERGE DIAGHILEV

THE
DIAGHILEV
BALLET
1909-1929

BY

S. L. GRIGORIEV

TRANSLATED AND EDITED BY

VERA BOWEN

A DANCE HORIZONS REPUBLICATION

One of a series of republications by Dance Horizons,
1801 East 26th Street, Brooklyn, N.Y. 11229

This is an unabridged republication of the first edition
published in 1953 by Constable and Company Ltd., London,
England

Standard Book Number 87127-047-1

Library of Congress Catalog Card No. 74-76556

Printed in the United States of America

CONTENTS

LIST OF ILLUSTRATIONS

vii

EDITOR'S NOTE

'SERGE LEONIDOVICH GRIGORIEV is probably the only man living who knows the history of the [Diaghilev] troupe from its first performance to its last. . . . It is extremely unlikely that he will ever write his memoirs. . . .'

So, in 1940, wrote Mr. C. W. Beaumont in his excellent *The Diaghilev Ballet in London* about the author of this book. He judged Monsieur Grigoriev to be both too discreet and too uncommunicative to place his experiences of the Diaghilev Ballet on record. Happily, however, Mr. Beaumont has now been proved mistaken. In 1950, when Monsieur Grigoriev was living at Louveciennes, on looking through some old note-books in which he had carefully summarized information relating to all the seasons ever given by the Diaghilev Ballet, he decided to carry out a project he had long had in mind and, by using these and other records in his possession to revive his memory, construct a short history of that famous company in the form of annals.

The resultant work was written in Russian; and this book is an English version of it, somewhat shorter than the original and with a certain rearrangement of the matter in places.

The book is, of course, full of Russian names; and the question was how to spell them. I decided that it was best not to attempt adopting any system of transliteration, but simply to use the spellings that have become most familiar. Most of these Russian names, therefore, appear in what amounts more or less to a French transliteration; and though this may give English readers a false idea of how the names are really pronounced, I thought it better to risk this result than possibly to cause confusion by giving such famous names as, say, Chaliapine and Massine what in English transliteration would be the strange spellings Shalyapin and Myasin. This applies chiefly to surnames. But the dancers were inclined also to use, when abroad, the French forms of their Christian names, where these existed; and so I have kept Michel for Mikhail, Serge for Sergey and Léon for Lyev, except in certain

ix

contexts. Finally, I have used the French names for all the ballets but three, all of which had English names originally. The author and I have to thank Mr. Richardson of the *Dancing Times* and many former members of the Diaghilev Ballet for kindly lending us photographs for use as illustrations.

V. B.

PROLOGUE

I SAW Diaghilev for the first time in 1900. I had just finished my training at the Imperial Theatre School and had been admitted into the permanent company of the *Mariinsky* Theatre at St. Petersburg, which was devoted to opera and ballet. Diaghilev was on the stage, wearing the uniform of an official. He was tall and rather solid, with a large head and an interesting face. He had a small black moustache and thick dark hair, and on the right side of his head there was a white streak, which gave him an unusual air. He had been attached to the Director of the theatre in an official capacity. He did not appear very often, but when he did he always attracted attention by his imposing looks.

One day, in the middle of the season, we heard that Diaghilev had been dismissed 'without leave to appeal'. Everyone was amazed: to be dismissed 'without leave to appeal' meant that he could never again be officially employed. It appeared that the Director, Prince Volkonsky, had asked Diaghilev to supervise the production of a new ballet— *Sylvia*, with music by Delibes. Diaghilev had begun work on the production but had been unable to get on with the other people concerned in it; and since he depended on their approval, no progress had been made. They disliked his artistic ideas and his modern outlook. They considered that he was undermining the academic traditions of the Imperial Theatres. Prince Volkonsky, who had himself been appointed Director only a short time before and had no great experience of theatre management, was influenced by these criticisms and asked Diaghilev to relinquish the production. Diaghilev was naturally much offended and irritated by this demand, and not only retired from the production of the ballet but also refused to continue editing the annual report on the theatre's activities. He had edited this report for some time and done it extremely well. Prince Volkonsky would not hear of his giving it up and said that if he insisted on doing so, he had better resign altogether. This Diaghilev declined to do; whereupon Prince Volkonsky dismissed him 'without leave to appeal'.

This incident produced quite a sensation in Petersburg. The Emperor came to hear of it, and in spite of the manner in which

I

The Diaghilev Ballet

Diaghilev had been dismissed, and although he remained under a cloud as far as the Imperial Theatres were concerned, gave orders that he should be attached to his own household. In later years Diaghilev used to delight in recalling this episode.

Before his appointment to the staff of the Imperial Theatres, Diaghilev had founded a magazine called *The World of Art*, which he edited himself. He had also begun arranging yearly exhibitions of contemporary painting in St. Petersburg. The magazine survived till the beginning of 1905, when it ceased publication; but in the same year he organized an important exhibition of portraits by Russian painters, which he collected from all over the country. The exhibition was held in the Tavrida Palace. I went to it; and it was there that I saw Diaghilev for the second time. He had scarcely changed since leaving the *Mariinsky* five years before, and looked as impressive as ever.

Three years later, in the spring of 1908, it became known that Diaghilev was taking Moussorgsky's opera *Boris Godounov* to Paris. The *Mariinsky* company were much excited. The performances began in May with Chaliapine as Boris; and their success was immense. Russian newspapers reporting the event pointed out that this was Diaghilev's third Parisian venture: in 1906 he had taken over an exhibition of Russian paintings; in 1907 he had organized a series of concerts of Russian music by Rimsky-Korsakov, Glazounov, Rachmaninov and Scriabine, conducted by Arthur Nikisch; and now in 1908 he had given Paris its first experience of Russian opera. All three undertakings had been enormously successful; and Diaghilev's name was now celebrated in the whole art world of Paris.

CHAPTER ONE

1909

AFTER his success with *Boris Godounov* Diaghilev had decided that in the spring of 1909 he would arrange another season of opera in Paris. He did not at first intend to include ballets in this programme. Indeed he was not then particularly interested in ballet. But his great friend and collaborator on *The World of Art*, Alexandre Benois, was an enthusiast for it: he considered ballet a most interesting art form, which by some miracle had survived in Russia, whereas it had died out everywhere else; and he at first suggested, and later insisted, that Diaghilev should show not only operas but also ballets during his spring season in Paris. Benois was able to support his argument by pointing to two particular features of ballet in Russia at this time. First, there was the existence in the *Mariinsky* ballet company of a number of exceptionally brilliant male and female dancers, including a young man named Nijinsky, who had only just completed his training. Secondly, there appeared to have dawned a new era in choreography with the succession to the venerable *maestro* Marius Petipa, on his retirement, of Michel Fokine, the latest of whose new and highly successful ballets was *Le Pavillon d'Armide*, with music by Nicolas Tchérépnine. The result of Benois's persuasions was that Diaghilev began appearing at performances of Fokine's ballets—to the intense interest of the company, who were always rather excited at seeing the man who had once been the subject of a rumpus in the theatre and had now scored such a series of triumphs in Paris. The Fokine ballets seemed to appeal to Diaghilev. Yet it was only after considerable hesitation that, under continued pressure from Benois and other friends of his who were equally interested in ballet, he at length made up his mind and agreed.

Many rumours of Diaghilev's plans reached the company by way of his friends and acquaintances; but I did not expect that they would affect me personally. One day at rehearsal, however, Fokine, with

3

whom I was great friends, told me that Diaghilev had not only at last decided to give ballets as well as operas during his Paris season, but had invited him, Fokine, to become his *maître de ballet*. Fokine said he was delighted at this offer, which he had accepted: he liked the idea of working with Diaghilev and his friends and also of showing his ballets abroad. And then, a few days later, Fokine said that Diaghilev wished to know whether I too would join them, as *régisseur*.

It appeared that they had already made two unsuccessful attempts at filling this post. The first candidate, a certain Medalinsky, who like myself was a member of the *Mariinsky* ballet company, had resigned on being criticized by Diaghilev for incompetence. Diaghilev had then invited the *régisseur* of the *Mariinsky* itself, Ivan Ivanov, to join him for the season; but the management had advised Ivanov against accepting the offer. At his next meeting with Diaghilev and his friends, accordingly, Fokine, on being consulted by them again, had put forward my name, telling them that just because we *were* great friends he had considered it awkward to do so before; but that he had always worked with me; that I had helped him in arranging various ballet performances in the past; and that he considered me a suitable person for the post. Diaghilev's two chief advisers, General Bezobrazov and the writer and critic Valérien Svetlov, had both supported my candidature; with the result that Diaghilev had asked Fokine to talk the suggestion over with me and, if I welcomed it, to send me to see him.

When Fokine gave me Diaghilev's message, I was elated and did not hesitate a moment. I was both flattered at receiving the offer and interested in the prospect that it presented: to become Diaghilev's *régisseur*, with Fokine as his choreographer, was very clearly a chance not to be missed.

I went to see Diaghilev in a great state of excitement. Eight years had gone by since I had first seen him and heard his name; but it had never entered my head that I should work for him. I rang the bell of his flat with a certain trepidation. The door was opened by a man with a little beard, who asked me to come in and said that Diaghilev would like me to wait for him. I was rather glad of the delay, which gave me the chance to calm down. I started looking round the room I was shown into. The walls were covered with a wide-striped paper. There were three or four good pictures and an open grand piano with music on it. A large Delft vase with a bunch of flowers stood on the table, and over the door hung the death-mask of Beethoven. Everything was simple and severe. But I had hardly finished my inspection when Diaghilev came in, and after shaking hands, asked me to sit down. Our interview was very brief. He said that Fokine had recommended me as a *régisseur*; that if I agreed he would pay me so much; and that my first duty would be to sign contracts with the artists. I agreed to his terms and he handed me the contracts. He asked me to be as quick as I could, and gave me the list of the artists who were to form his company. We shook hands again and he added that he hoped I would justify Fokine's recommendation. He gave me a curious smile: his mouth alone smiled, the rest of his face remaining entirely serious. In time to come I often noticed this peculiar smile on Diaghilev's face, polite but cold, and reserved for people he knew but slightly. Thus it was that I first made Diaghilev's acquaintance. On leaving him I felt happy: our meeting, his offer to me, and the coming visit to Paris, had completely changed my life. For the moment everything seemed interesting, eventful and full of meaning.

★   ★   ★

I began to carry out Diaghilev's orders. It was comparatively easy to do so, since he had already written to the artists proposing the conditions on which they were to be engaged for the Paris season. I had all the contracts signed within a week. I was eager to justify Fokine's recommendation and show Diaghilev how far I was capable. When all the contracts were signed, I went to see him again. He seemed very pleased. He did not keep me long and asked me to call again with Fokine to discuss various points concerning the season. Next day Fokine and I arrived at the flat at the appointed hour. 'Diaghilev's committee', as I called the gathering of his friends, was in full session. They were sitting in the dining-room, a small room with an oval table. On the table to Diaghilev's right stood a *samovar*, and his valet, Vasili, poured out tea. There were biscuits and jam on the table, and several plates of Russian sweets. In front of every member of the company lay a sheet of paper and a pencil. Diaghilev had a large exercise book in front of him. He presided over the meeting. Fokine and I were introduced to everybody.

Of all those present the only person I knew was Benois. He was short, with a beard and moustache, and wore pince-nez. His movements were gentle and quiet; and what he said was usually accompanied by a charming smile. On my right sat a man with curly red hair, very carefully brushed, with lively, slightly laughing eyes and clean-shaven cheeks. He was elegantly dressed and smelt of scent. When speaking to him Diaghilev called him 'Lyovushka' and looked at him affectionately. This was Léon Bakst, also a painter. He spoke with a curious accent, giving his r's a guttural pronunciation. As I noticed later, he greatly amused Diaghilev, especially by his accent.

Next to him sat one of my sponsors, His Excellency General Bezobrazov, a Privy Councillor and one of the greatest connoisseurs of ballet in St. Petersburg, a very old man of heavy build with an amiable face, completely round. He looked most imposing and followed all Diaghilev said with close attention. Now and again he would comment in a deep bass voice in short monosyllables: 'good', 'right'. Further away sat my other sponsor, Valérien Svetlov, a grey-haired man, bearded and moustached and elegant. The two of them were the 'patriarchs' of the ballet and as such deeply respected.

The next person was a small man. He walked up and down the room making witty remarks, slightly sarcastic, at which he was always the first to laugh. He had a peculiar laugh like a siphon discharging soda-water. At each of these witty remarks Diaghilev used to turn round to him and say, 'Just a minute, Valechka'. This was Valentine Nouvel, an official of the Imperial Court and a friend of Diaghilev from their University days. He was very musical, and although quite indifferent to ballet was considered a great authority on it. He did not wish to have anything to do with the business side of Diaghilev's scheme, hated being worried, and wished only to enjoy a quiet and regular life.

There was yet one more person, a young man, modest and attractive. His name was Mavrine: he was Diaghilev's secretary. Fokine and I completed the 'committee'. But it was by no means a closed circle. Any friend of Diaghilev who happened to call during the sittings was made welcome and took part in the discussion, expressing his opinion and giving his advice. Diaghilev took notice of what everyone had to say. The famous portrait painter, B. A. Serov, used to call occasionally. He spoke rarely and very briefly, but his opinions were always interesting and convincing. Prince V. N. Argutinsky-Dolgorukov, who was a great connoisseur of painting and ballet, a true *grand seigneur* with charming manners, used often to call. So did Dr. Botkin, the Tsar's physician and another friend of Diaghilev; so did the composer, N. N. Tchérépnine, and several other painters, composers, writers and critics—in fact the *élite* of the Petersburg world of art.

In the course of the first meeting, at which I was present, we discussed the question of the *répertoire*. It had already been decided to include Fokine's latest work, *Le Pavillon d'Armide*; but two more ballets were required to make up a whole evening's performance. Fokine suggested his *Chopiniana*, a romantic ballet to the music of Chopin, which had proved very popular. Diaghilev agreed, but said that he did not care for the name *Chopiniana* and would like to call it *Les Sylphides*. No-one objected except Fokine, who was reluctant to forgo the title he had chosen, but in the end he too consented. There was also an argument about the overture: at the *Mariinsky* they had used a Polonaise by Chopin; but Diaghilev considered this unsuitable in style and suggested that *Les Sylphides* should instead be preceded by one of Chopin's preludes. Everyone agreed. He further declared that he did not care for the orchestration as it stood and that the music ought to be reorchestrated by a good composer. He also argued about the prelude used in the ballet itself, in the course of which it was played three times, suggesting that Fokine should cut one of the repeats. But Fokine objected. He said that if this were done, he would lose some of the best groups, the circles round the ballerinas, and he was very unwilling to part with them. On this occasion Diaghilev agreed, and the ballet was included in the programme as it stood. Benois was asked to design the scenery and costumes.

We then tackled the question of a third Fokine ballet, called *Egyptian Nights*, to music by Arensky. Diaghilev immediately said that in its present form he could not possibly show it in Paris and that it must be considerably altered. Arensky's music must be reorchestrated and in places cut. The title also was inappropriate and must be changed. So must the *finale*. 'I am going to consider all these changes,' he said, 'and put suggestions to you when next we meet.' Thus ended the business part of our meeting. The conversation then turned to concerts and various incidents in the life of St. Petersburg; so Fokine and I said goodbye and left. Diaghilev saw us off, saying he would let me know about the next meeting.

This next meeting of the 'committee' took place a week later, the composer Tchérépnine being present. Diaghilev opened the discussion by saying that the ballet *Egyptian Nights*, about which we had not had the time to go into details on the last occasion, was to be called *Cléopâtre*. The sound of this title appealed to everyone. Diaghilev then proceeded to explain the alterations to the music. The overture by Arensky must be dropped and replaced by an overture to the opera *Orestia* by Taneev. Cleopatra's entrance must be planned to music from

The Diaghilev Ballet

the opera *Mlada* by Rimsky-Korsakov. What was needed for the *Bacchanale* was some music by Glazounov, already used very successfully by Fokine. Finally, he wished Fokine to compose a grand *finale* on music by Moussorgsky from the opera *Khovanshchina*. He paused here for a moment, looking at our astonished faces, then smiled and continued: 'Then the end of the ballet is banal. It must be changed. The youth poisoned by Cleopatra, instead of coming to life again, must be killed for good, and his bride must sob over his lifeless body as the curtain falls. And since we have no music for such a dramatic scene, I will ask our dear Nikolay Nikolayevich [Tchérépnine] to write this music for us.' Tchérépnine was astounded. This was entirely unexpected; and he remained speechless. We all indeed sat silent, till at last Fokine spoke, 'Well,' he said, 'with so many changes—it will be an entirely new ballet!'

'That does not matter,' said Diaghilev. 'What I want to know is whether you like the idea.'

We all said yes, and he continued, 'As for you, Lyovushka [Bakst], you will have to paint us a lovely *décor*.'

Lyovushka instantly began tracing the plan of the scene as he visualized it and describing it in his curious guttural accent. 'There will be a huge temple on the banks of the Nile. Columns; a sultry day; the scent of the East and a great many lovely women with beautiful bodies. . . .'

Diaghilev shook his head, as if at an incorrigible child; and we all laughed. Bakst then tried to think of an effective entrance for Cleopatra; it had to be original and unexpected. We all listened with great interest until Diaghilev interrupted him and asked us all to go into the next room, where he sat at the piano with Nouvel next to him and asked us to listen to the altered score.

I did not know that Diaghilev could play the piano and watched him doing so. He played very well, biting his tongue the whole time, especially when he came to difficult bits. He would frequently stop and explain to Fokine the passages in the score that had been altered. Fokine sat holding the score and marking them. When the playing was over, everyone started talking and going into the details of the ballet. Nouvel laughed in his peculiar way, remarking that what we had just heard was just a mediocre *salade russe*. Diaghilev replied that this was unavoidable; he required a third ballet; and this was the only music available. He dismissed Nouvel's criticism almost without considering it.

8

At that time such musical *mélanges* did not shock anyone. Moreover, Diaghilev's chief interest was centred on the opera, the performances of which were to be the main event of the season; the ballet was no more than an extra. His opera programme was by now complete. It consisted of *The Maid of Pskov* by Rimsky-Korsakov, renamed for the occasion *Ivan the Terrible*; *Prince Igor* by Borodin; *Ruslan and Liudmila* by Glinka, *Judith* by Serov and *Boris Godounov* by Moussorgsky. The three ballets accepted and approved by the 'committee' were *Les Sylphides*, *Le Pavillon d'Armide* and *Cléopâtre*.

★ ★ ★

Having settled the question of the *répertoire*, Diaghilev proceeded to the engagement of the principal dancers. He proposed to show Paris the cream of both the Petersburg and the Moscow companies. At that time there was a galaxy of talent on the stage of the *Mariinsky*, headed by the ballerinas Mathilde Kchessinska and Anna Pavlova. Fokine had worked with Pavlova in a number of his ballets, since she was in sympathy with his modern ideas. Kchessinska, on the other hand, was less appreciative and had not taken part in them. Diaghilev wanted both of them to appear in the Paris season and announced at the committee meeting that he had invited both Pavlova and Kchessinska; to which Fokine objected, 'But what is Kchessinska going to dance in the projected *répertoire?*' Diaghilev replied that she could dance *Le Pavillon d'Armide* and could also take part in *Les Sylphides*; but Fokine argued that she was not suited to his ballets and since she did not show any wish to appear in them it would be much better to leave her out.

A lively discussion followed. Some of the committee agreed with Fokine, others supported Diaghilev. In the end Fokine agreed as a compromise that Kchessinska should appear in *Le Pavillon d'Armide*, but refused to have her in *Les Sylphides*. There was no difference of opinion regarding Pavlova. She was to be given the leading role in *Les Sylphides*; and Fokine was eager that she should also dance the part of Tabor in *Cléopâtre*, with which Diaghilev agreed. Tamara Karsavina was to appear as soloist in all three ballets, and so were Baldina and Smirnova. There still remained the part of Cleopatra to cast. No-one liked the dancer who had taken it at the *Mariinsky*. But Fokine said he had a private pupil, Ida Rubinstein. 'She is tall, beautiful and plastic in her movements; and I consider her most suitable for the part.'

9

The Diaghilev Ballet

Bakst, who knew Ida Rubinstein well, shared Fokine's opinion; and the rest of the committee were inclined to agree, except His Excellency General Bezobrazov. Being a very strict *balletomane*, he considered that no-one except professionals should be admitted into the company, and disapproved of amateurs. The committee tried to point out that there was unfortunately no suitable dancer for the part at the *Mariinsky*; but he was not convinced and went on grumbling for some time.

The question of ballerinas being settled, we began to consider male dancers. It went without saying that Fokine was to be *premier danseur* as well as choreographer. He was to fill the leading role in the Le Pavillon *d'Armide*, and also to dance Amoun in *Cléopâtre*. Then there was Nijinsky, the young dancer who had just finished his training and was renowned for his remarkable *élévation*. He had already danced the slave in *Le Pavillon d'Armide*, and was to be given a similar part in *Cléopâtre*; and Diaghilev considered that he should also take the romantic part of the poet in *Les Sylphides*. It was further decided to invite Adolf Bolm for the part of the chief warrior in the Polovtsian Dances in the opera *Prince Igor*, and also the dancers Kozlov and Rozay, who were both excellent; while for the role of the *Marquis* in *Le Pavillon d'Armide* Diaghilev was determined to have Pavel Gerdt, who held the rank of 'Soloist to His Imperial Majesty', the highest distinction an artist in Russia could reach.

As soon as our casting was completed, Diaghilev proceeded to the signing of contracts—over which there was no difficulty, since everyone was keen to appear in Paris. He then left for Moscow, intending to collect some more artists there, and returned after about ten days, when we forgathered again at his flat to hear the result of his expedition. We found him in a particularly good mood. He was charming to everyone. He announced that he was delighted with what he had accomplished in Moscow. He was wicked enough, however, first to tell us at great length whom he had commissioned to do *décors* for the operas, what singers and chorus he had engaged, etc. For the committee, as he knew, were pretty well indifferent to opera and only really wished to hear his ballet news. Moreover, when he eventually came to this, he began by saying that he had invited Koralli, a ballerina of the Moscow *Bolshoy* Theatre —an announcement that was met with little enthusiasm, since none of us cared for her, least of all Fokine. Diaghilev, however, defended her: he maintained that, being a notable beauty, she would look most effective in the part of Armida. He had also, he said, invited Sophie

Fedorova, who was famous in Moscow as a character dancer, and, as for men, he had been lucky in securing Mordkine, a great favourite, as well as various other men and women for the *ensemble*.

It was evident that the committee were not much impressed with the results of Diaghilev's visit to Moscow. The fact was that there existed a strong prejudice in St. Petersburg against the Moscow school of dancing; and the committee would no doubt have preferred to confine our cast to dancers from the *Mariinsky*. However, Diaghilev remained quite unmoved by their lack of enthusiasm and insisted that his wish was to show Paris the best artists available, whether they came from Petersburg or Moscow.

★   ★   ★

The Paris season was to be presented under the patronage of the Grand Duke Vladimir, an uncle of the Emperor, who was President of the Academy of Fine Arts. He knew Diaghilev well and was greatly impressed by his success in arousing interest in Russian art abroad. Thanks to the Grand Duke's influence, Diaghilev was to receive a large subsidy from the Imperial Treasury, and had also been promised the loan of scenery and costumes from the *Mariinsky* for some of the operas and ballets.

Though Diaghilev had never mentioned finance when discussing the projected season at our meetings, we all knew that the Grand Duke was at the back of it. We also gathered that Diaghilev was counting as well on the support of some wealthy people, patrons of the arts, and hoped that receipts from the performances would meet a large part of the expenses.

So far all our preparations had gone smoothly. Diaghilev attacked them with immense energy and never doubted that the season would prove a great success. But having at length settled all urgent business in St. Petersburg, he left for Paris to make final arrangements there; and during his absence there occurred certain events which all but wrecked the whole enterprise. The Grand Duke Vladimir suddenly died, and Diaghilev lost in him his chief support.

For in spite of all that Diaghilev had achieved in Paris before, some of the officials of the Imperial Theatres, and certain members of the *Mariinsky* company itself, were ill-disposed toward his new venture. They maintained that instead of the Fokine ballets, what he should show in Paris were the big classical ballets of Petipa. They regarded

The Diaghilev Ballet

Fokine as far too modern and his collaborators as almost decadent. They argued, in fact, that Diaghilev's policy would fail to do justice to Russian Ballet.

As long as the Grand Duke Vladimir was alive and continued to lend Diaghilev his support, no-one dared criticize him and everyone kept quiet. But no sooner was he dead than Diaghilev's enemies raised their voices and started a savage campaign against him. Some of his ill-wishers had great influence at Court; and this they now used to hamper the realization of his scheme.

Before leaving for Paris, Diaghilev had not only signed contracts with members of the Company, but had arranged with Kchessinska that she too should appear in Paris. The first thing he was met with on his return to Petersburg was a refusal on her part to keep her promise. No-one knew the exact reason, but it was supposed that as she was to appear in one ballet only, namely the *Le Pavillon d'Armide*, for which she anyhow did not particularly care, she probably considered an appearance in Paris not worth her while. She may also have thought that she might fail to meet there with the success she was used to at the *Mariinsky* in the old classical ballets that Diaghilev did not wish to show in Paris. Or possibly she thought it beneath her to appear in Fokine's ballets or to be associated with Diaghilev's enterprise altogether.

Whatever it was that made her refuse, refuse she did, and she was followed by Gerdt, the 'Soloist to His Imperial Majesty' and a notable 'diplomat' of the ballet world. The refusal of these two artists was a bad sign. They were both influential at Court; and it became clear to Diaghilev that his enemies were determined to wreck his project.

Diaghilev told us all this at a meeting of the committee after his return. We were all greatly upset; and I had never seen him so agitated as he was on that occasion. He had just received a letter, which he read out to us, from the Imperial Secretariat. It was to the effect that by the Emperor's order the subsidy granted for the Paris season was to be cancelled. Having read the letter out to us, he put it in front of him, and banging the table with his fist, said, 'I am most indignant that the Emperor should act in such a way!' We were all silent; there was nothing to be said. We all shared his indignation at such base intrigues by people in high places. Diaghilev was the first to break the silence. 'This alters our whole position,' he said. 'I shall have to think it all over and find some way out. One thing is clear, though, we can no longer rely on help from above. And I should refuse it now, even if it were offered.'

We said goodbye; and he asked us to come again in a few days. We were greatly depressed. At the same time it seemed inconceivable that a venture that had started so auspiciously should so suddenly founder. Personally I felt very miserable. I had grown used to the idea of going to Paris; and now it was not to be. I was very young; I did not know Diaghilev; and now it seemed to me that without the money he had been promised he could not possibly carry on with his season and would have to undo the work that had already been done.

I went to see him a few days later, still feeling much dejected. He had not yet returned when I arrived, and his valet Vasili engaged me in conversation while I was waiting. He told me that the *Barin* (Master), as he called Diaghilev, was very cheerful, and seeing my dejected face, added with a smile that he was sure we were going to spend the spring in Paris after all. I looked at him intently. I had noticed by now that Vasili was extremely well informed regarding Diaghilev's affairs; and this filled me with hope.

Diaghilev arrived looking very spry and animated; and the usual members of the 'committee' soon assembled. He declared that in spite of the reverse we had suffered from on high, he had thought of a way out. He had been in touch with his friends in Paris, and now found that a season would be possible after all, though unfortunately it would have to be replanned on a smaller scale. In view of the reduced budget, we should only be able to give one opera in its entirety, namely *Ivan the Terrible*, and only one act of each of the two others, *Ruslan and Liudmila* and *Prince Igor*. Each of these acts would be given on separate nights, and each followed by two ballets to make up full performances. But since we had only three ballets decided on so far, *Le Pavillon d'Armide*, *Cléopâtre* and *Les Sylphides*, we were still one short. What he had in mind as a fourth to complete three programmes was a *grand divertissement*.

We all welcomed his decision except Nouvel, who said that since we could not show the operas as intended, and since the ballet would not really impress Paris sufficiently, it would be better to give up the whole season. Diaghilev got very angry with him at this and said he could not possibly cancel the season. He had signed too many contracts in Petersburg, Moscow and Paris itself. If Nouvel was not satisfied, perhaps he would raise enough backing for us to carry out the scheme as originally planned. This argument silenced Nouvel. Besides, no-one took his objection seriously. We all thought Diaghilev was getting out of his difficulties brilliantly and rejoiced on his behalf.

13

The Diaghilev Ballet

When winding up the meeting, Diaghilev said that everything now depended on Paris, but that he was convinced that things would be settled satisfactorily. He left for Paris a few days later; and there was a lull till he came back.

One night, three weeks later, I got a note from him saying that he had returned and would I and Fokine call at the flat the next day? I went wondering what news he had to give us, and must confess felt somewhat nervous. On this occasion I arrived last, having been kept by a rehearsal at the *Mariinsky*. The 'committee' had already assembled and Diaghilev was reporting on his visit.

It appeared he had been able to do what he wanted. His great friends, Madame Edwards (afterwards Madame Sert) and the Comtesse de Greffulhe, had given him all the help they could; and their efforts had been successful. They had formed a committee of influential and wealthy people, under whose auspices Diaghilev had been able to announce his season. He had found an excellent impresario in the person of Gabriel Astruc, to whom he had handed over the administrative side of the business. He had also signed a contract with the theatre. Here Diaghilev paused and surveying our pleased and excited faces, said, 'Yes, I've signed a contract with the *Théâtre du Châtelet*.' We were all puzzled. We knew that on his first visit to Paris he had signed a contract with the *Grand Opéra*; but the explanation followed. 'When I told the management of the *Opéra* that I was unable to provide an opera season such as I had at first intended, but that instead there would be a mixed season of opera and ballet, the directors declared that considering the unique position of the *Opéra* as one of the French National Theatres, it could not possibly let it for mere ballet performances. Ballet was not art of the kind that could possibly be shown by itself at the *Opéra*, within whose precincts there was no place for such a thing.' It goes without saying that our committee were indignant at this attitude to ballet. Diaghilev fully expected this to be our reaction and after a pause said calmly, 'So that is why I have signed a contract with the *Châtelet* and cancelled the one with the *Opéra*.' The fact of appearing in a smaller and more modest theatre evidently did not worry him.

It was a happy evening for Fokine and myself. Everything was now settled; Diaghilev was cheerful; the theatre in Paris was fixed on; the programme chosen; the company organized; and the time approaching to begin rehearsals. Diaghilev seemed to guess what happy thoughts were in our minds, and speaking to the two of us (I sat next to Fokine), he said, 'And now I wish you to start rehearsals at once, so as to prepare the *répertoire* as well as you can'.

★　　★　　★

The winter had gone by almost without our noticing it, so that when Diaghilev told Fokine to begin rehearsals it was the end of March and only about a month was left till the opening of the Paris season.

Rehearsals began at the *Yekaterinsky* Theatre on the quay of the canal bearing the same name. A few days before we started Diaghilev, Fokine and myself distributed the parts in the various ballets and on April the 2nd at four o'clock in the afternoon there took place the first, and what may justly be called historic, rehearsal of the Diaghilev Ballet. The entire committee were present. After I had introduced every member of the company to Diaghilev, he addressed them in the following words, 'It gives me great pleasure to make your acquaintance. I trust that we are going to work together in harmony. I am delighted to be showing Paris the Russian Ballet for the first time. Ballet, to my mind, is one of the most lovely arts and it exists nowhere else in Europe. It will depend on you all to make it a success, and I greatly hope that you will do so.'

The speech was applauded; and Diaghilev was surrounded by the members of the company, eager to ask questions. He made a great impression on everyone by his distinguished looks and his little speech. The majority of the artists had never seen him, but had only heard of his activities. Now they had a chance to examine him at close quarters.

This first rehearsal was devoted to the planning of the Polovtsian Dances from *Prince Igor*—one of the most remarkable works of Borodin.

Thus began an enterprise that was destined to last twenty years; to create an enormous *répertoire*; to bring up several generations of wonderful dancers; to raise the art of ballet to great heights; and to diffuse it all over the world.

The composition of the Polovtsian Dances went ahead rapidly. Fokine invented the steps with great speed; the dancers rehearsed with enthusiasm and their execution was excellent. When the whole had been mapped out and danced right through, the entire company, as well as the members of the committee, were in ecstasy. They surrounded Fokine and gave him a great ovation.

The other ballets, having already been performed at the *Mariinsky*, did not take long to prepare, although *Cléopâtre*, owing to the changes

PLATE II

ANNA PAVLOVA

made by Diaghilev, gave Fokine a good deal of work and required more rehearsals than *Les Sylphides*.

In place of the fourth ballet required to complete our Paris programme, Diaghilev, as already mentioned, had decided to stage a *divertissement*. But he did not like to call it so and preferred to give it the shape of a ballet consisting of a suite of separate dances leading up to a grand *finale*. He therefore called it *Le Festin*. It was made up of numbers taken from various ballets and operas from the *Mariinsky*. All Fokine had had to do was to invent the *finale*, which was to be danced to music from Tchaikovsky's Second Symphony. Its object was to enable the whole company to appear together at the end. For some reason, however, it proved difficult to compose satisfactorily. Fokine spent much time and energy arranging and rearranging it; but it never really came off.

Once rehearsals started, the meetings of the committee ceased, since the main questions relating to the Paris season had been settled; and if there was anything to discuss it was usually done at rehearsals, at which not only Diaghilev himself but also most of the committee were always present.

Diaghilev was also kept busy supervising the painting of the scenery and the making of costumes and accessories. He would visit the studios and work-rooms daily to inspect colours and materials. He would frequently argue with the scene painters about a particular tone of colour in the scenery or with the costumiers about some stuff of which a costume was to be made, always obtaining what he wanted.

By the end of April we were ready. Having made arrangements about transport, etc., Diaghilev left for Paris, leaving General Bezobrazov in charge of the company.

The yearly season at the *Mariinsky* finished on May the 1st; and on the following day all those who had joined Diaghilev's enterprise were on their way to France.

As for myself, I left Petersburg in a happy and excited mood. Little did I know that the journey I then embarked on would last with brief intervals for twenty years!

★ ★ ★

We reached Paris in the early morning. Some of Diaghilev's staff were there to meet us; and one of them, Chausovsky, attached himself specially to me.

The Diaghilev Ballet

At Petersburg the weather had been cold and damp; the spring had been late; and we were quite surprised to find the sun warm in Paris and the trees in leaf. I took a room at a small hotel in the Boulevard Saint-Michel; and when I came out into the street and looked about, a wonderful feeling of happiness came over me, which was always to remain connected in my memory with this first visit of mine to Paris. I stopped for a few minutes at the corner of the street, gazing across a neighbouring garden. I could scarcely believe that my dream of seeing Paris had come true.

My first visit was to Diaghilev. He was delighted to see me, and wanted to know all about our journey. He told me that the Moscow dancers, headed by Mordkine and Koralli, were expected the day after, together with the chief machinist of the *Bolshoy* Theatre at Moscow, K. Waltz—who Diaghilev said was a wonderful old man. He also told me that the *Châtelet* was still occupied, but that we should be able to rehearse there.

Diaghilev was in great form and full of energy. It was obvious that things were going well. The Moscow dancers duly arrived; and as I had never met any of them before, Diaghilev introduced us. Mordkine, the *premier danseur*, was most affable and handsome, though to my mind his movements as a dancer were rather angular. He had a loud laugh and spoke very fast and disjointedly; but, on the whole, he made a pleasant impression on me. The ballerina Koralli was extremely good-looking; while Sophie Fedorova, who was a celebrity in Moscow, was very small, modestly dressed and rather untidy. The other girls and men of the Moscow group were mostly very young and attractive-looking. They had brought their own *régisseur*, Semenov.

The rehearsals duly began at the *Châtelet* two days after our arrival. The theatre was large but much neglected. Diaghilev set out to improve its appearance—no mean task in so short a time. He gave orders for carpets to be laid in the foyer and the corridors, for the lighting to be improved and for flowers and plants to be set in the entrance; with the result that within a few days the theatre became unrecognizable. To make room for a large orchestra he removed several rows of stalls, thereby much improving the appearance of the auditorium. The whole place was not only cleaned and scrubbed out, but also, where possible, even freshly painted. The stage had to be overhauled as well. The floor was uneven and knobbly, and, as it was, would have been unsafe to dance on. But it, too, was quickly put in order.

Fokine's first task was to familiarize the Moscow dancers with the ballets already rehearsed in Petersburg and so to achieve a smooth *ensemble* and an exact rendering of the choreography. Thanks to the eagerness with which the company rehearsed, this proved easy. The rehearsals were usually attended by a number of Diaghilev's Paris friends, who were amazed at our capacity for work and our adaptability to new conditions. These were certainly most uncomfortable for Fokine. The stage was usually occupied by carpenters, either repairing it and moving bits of scenery, or opening large packing cases newly arrived from Russia. This hardly helped rehearsals; but Fokine was wonderful—though he did occasionally lose his temper. Diaghilev's friends often got on his nerves. He much resented their talking to the dancers and distracting their attention. Diaghilev asked me to keep an eye on them and stop them whenever I could. But this was by no means easy; and one day, when one of the visitors insisted on talking to a ballerina, Fokine flew into a rage and told him to leave the theatre. Unfortunately the visitor happened to be Robert Brussel, a celebrated critic and a friend of Diaghilev. He was much offended and complained to Diaghilev; but Diaghilev was merely amused and made a joke of it. Evidently the people in charge of the rehearsal, he said, did not realize that Monsieur Brussel had special permission to distract the dancers!

Our first night was to be on May the 19th, with a *répétition générale* the day before; and since in the meantime rumours had spread through Paris of the wonders of our company and the ballets Diaghilev was to show, the theatre at the *répétition générale* was filled, not only with Diaghilev's personal friends, but with all the most eminent journalists, writers, musicians and painters.

The *répétition* started with *Le Pavillon d'Armide*; and its strange story, invented by Benois, and his beautiful *décor*, harmonized perfectly both with Tchérépnine's music and Fokine's choreography. Although in Fokine's *Pavillon d'Armide* the influence of Petipa was still evident enough, he combined in it the good points of the old tradition with his own fresh ideas. In his later works Fokine freed himself from the influence of Petipa and became entirely original.

The part of Armida was to be danced at the first public performance by Pavlova, the *Marquis* by Fokine and the favourite slave by Nijinsky; the ballet being conducted by the composer. But to save the energies of Pavlova and Fokine for the next night, their places were taken at the *répétition générale* by Koralli and Mordkine.

The Diaghilev Ballet

The ballet went very well. It was followed by one act of the opera *Prince Igor*, conducted by Émile Cooper of the Moscow Opera House. As I said before, Diaghilev had been anxious to show this remarkable opera in its entirety, but circumstances had made it impossible. So on this occasion we gave only the act which is set in the Polovtsian camp. The part of the Khan was sung by Chaliapine, who was tremendous; and the act ended with the Polovtsian Dances, again arranged by Fokine. The *répétition générale* concluded with the *divertissement Le Festin*. This gave Diaghilev a chance to show some of Petipa's choreography and in particular his famous *pas de quatre* from *Raymonde*, one of the *chefs-d'œuvre* of his invention. This dress rehearsal made a great impression on all who saw it; and Diaghilev seemed delighted with the result.

★   ★   ★

May the 19th, 1909, was a great day in the history of the Russian Ballet of Sergey Pavlovich Diaghilev; for it was on that day that it gave its first public performance.

All of us, Diaghilev included, were at the theatre from early morning, and all in a feverish state. Our aim was to correct any defects we had noticed at the dress rehearsal, whether in the dancing, the setting of the scenery, the lighting or any detail of the costumes. K. Waltz, who was in charge of the stage, rushed up and down, taking tiny steps, determined, above all, that in *Le Pavillon d'Armide* the scene changes and the trap-doors should work without a hitch. For the hundredth time Diaghilev checked the lighting; Fokine corrected passages in the dancing; and I inspected the costumes, wigs and accessories. We spent the whole day going over and over various points. I shall never forget with what tremendous concentration we all considered every detail.

But it was time to start. The house was packed. There was not one empty seat. A few minutes before the curtain went up, Diaghilev appeared on the stage to address the dancers, who were all assembled. All Paris, he said, was there to see them and he wished them luck. Then, after asking me whether everything was ready, and being assured it was, he ordered the house lights to be dimmed; and the performance began.

We stood in the wings, watching anxiously for the reaction of the public to what they were witnessing on the stage. As the ballet proceeded, the dancers began to feel that with every moment the interest in their performance was growing, till it reached a climax with Nijinsky's great *variation*. It was clear that no-one had dreamt of seeing such a dancer: the applause was deafening, both at the end of this variation and when the curtain fell. In the interval the excitement was intense; everyone discussing who was best: Pavlova, Fokine or Nijinsky. They were amazed by Nijinsky's *élévation* and compared him with Vestris. It was on that night that Nijinsky made his name, which was destined to become so famous. The public were also enchanted with the dancer Rozay, who performed the very difficult virtuoso part of a buffoon.

After the interval the house was again filled with a most excited public. The curtain went up on Roerich's lovely scene of the south Russian steppe, beautifully lighted by Diaghilev. This was the Polovtsian camp in *Prince Igor*, with Chaliapine, as I said, singing the chief part. Then, at the end of the act, came the dances, to the accompaniment of the full orchestra and a huge chorus from the Opera at Moscow. The impression produced by this spectacle and the music was so overwhelming that the public constantly interrupted the performance with wild applause, and when the curtain came down the pandemonium was indescribable. Such were the cries of delight that even Chaliapine was forgotten for the time. The part of the chief warrior in the dances was taken by Adolf Bolm; and no-one in after years ever danced it so well. Sophie Fedorova danced the Polovtsian girl with tremendous fire; and the whole company surpassed themselves.

The third item, *Le Festin*, was also highly successful. It served as a kind of parade in which the dancers could show themselves in both classical and character numbers.

When the performance was over, it was clear that the audience had enormously enjoyed it and were deeply impressed by it as a remarkable spectacle. On that night Diaghilev had been able in fact to show Paris, what had so long been forgotten, that ballet could be a truly wonderful art. This first night was undoubtedly a revelation to the Paris public, and marked a resurrection of the ballet in the world outside Russia.

On the following day the papers were full of laudatory notices, the critics lavishing their praises on Pavlova, Fedorova, Fokine, Bolm, Rozay and Nijinsky. The last, in particular, seemed to have astounded everyone by his wonderful dancing. The Russian Ballet was the talk of Paris. Our first night happened to coincide with a storm in the French

The Diaghilev Ballet

Parliament; and a full-page portrait of Nijinsky appeared in *L'Illustration* with the caption: 'Dancer Nijinsky more talked of than the debates in the *Chambre*'. In discussing Fokine all agreed that he was a great choreographer, and singled out the *Danses Polovtsiennes* for particular praise. Their creation undoubtedly showed how outstanding was his talent: they were something entirely new. He was evidently a master of pattern and able with comparatively simple means to achieve a work of great originality. The solos were perfectly welded into the *ensemble*, and the whole work was saturated with such force and passion as to make of it a real *chef-d'œuvre*. Nor were the critics less full of admiration for the stirring music and the wonderful *décor*, the like of which had never before been seen.

After this, there was an interval of six days before the next first night, to which we now looked forward with no little impatience.

★   ★   ★

On May the 24th Diaghilev presented the opera *Ivan the Terrible* by Rimsky-Korsakov, with Chaliapine and a wonderful cast of singers. The *mise en scène* was by A. Sanine, who came from the Moscow Art Theatre and the *Alexandrinsky* at St. Petersburg. Incidentally, he had been one of my instructors at the Theatre School. He was a most talented *régisseur* and an excellent teacher; and I remember him with gratitude.

This second *première* was also a great event, though no such revelation as the first, since the year before Diaghilev had already acquainted Paris with Russian opera by bringing over *Boris Godounov*. There is no ballet in *Ivan the Terrible*; so we had plenty of time to prepare for our next appearance. This was again preceded by a *répétition générale*, which was even more largely attended than that of May the 18th. The first night was on June the 2nd. Once again the *Châtelet* was filled with a distinguished audience. They now knew what to expect of the Russian Ballet and could hardly wait to see our second programme. We began with one act from the opera *Ruslan and Liudmila* by Glinka, the father of Russian music. From the first bars of the lovely overture the spectators felt that once more they were in for a feast. The overture was loudly applauded; and the curtain rose on a most attractive *décor* by the painter Korovine, representing a medieval Russian palace built of wood. The singers were the same as in *Ivan the Terrible*: headed by Lipkovska,

Zbroueva, Kastorsky, Sharonov and Davidov. This first act of *Ruslan and Liudmila* is musically perfect and could not fail to please.

After the interval came *Les Sylphides*, by Fokine. This romantic ballet, now so well known, had of course no plot; but the dances were so skilfully combined that they formed a whole, each following the other as if inevitably. The female dancers taking part were all dressed alike in long skirts à la Taglioni. The only male part was danced by Nijinsky, and the leading female parts by Pavlova, Karsavina and Baldina. Anna Pavlova was at her best in this ballet. She was the very essence of the romantic, ethereal and unearthly, a Sylphide incarnate; and if Nijinsky was compared to Vestris, Pavlova in the opinion of all who saw her was a second Taglioni. The second Sylphide was Tamara Karsavina, tender and poetic, dancing with exquisite charm and enchanting the audience. Alexandra Baldina was delightfully graceful, young and attractive. Nijinsky created an unforgettable image as the youthful poet. His dancing was faultless, and the rendering of the valse by him and Pavlova truly incomparable. The groupings of the *ensemble* were simple and beautiful. The *décor* by Benois; the music by Chopin, orchestrated by the best Russian composers; the original choreography; the *mise en scène*; and the collaboration of such magnificent dancers, created a dream of poetry. *Les Sylphides* was a renaissance of the romantic ballet in all its charm. The public were genuinely moved and enchanted.

The last ballet at that performance was *Cléopâtre*. Diaghilev was right in so naming it: the title alone roused the interest of the audience. After the overture the curtain rose to reveal the interior of an Egyptian temple overlooking the Nile, with a distant horizon seen through a long colonnade. The *décor* by Bakst was in reds and pinks—extremely effective.

Cléopâtre was a dramatic ballet, which allowed the dancers to exhibit their acting powers. Cleopatra was played, as I have mentioned, by Ida Rubinstein, for whom Bakst had devised a highly effective entrance. She was carried on to the centre of the stage in a closed sarcophagus, from which she was lifted, wrapped like a mummy in veils. These her attendants removed one by one, till she emerged from the innermost clothed in magnificent Egyptian robes. Ida Rubinstein was most decorative in this 'plastic' part. Tall and lovely, her mime and gestures were beautiful, and her interpretation most striking.

Pavlova danced Tabor; and her acting was superb. It was impossible to recognize in her the ethereal nymph who in the ballet before had

PLATE III

MICHEL FOKINE

seemed to float across the stage. In the last scene, when Tabor finds
Amoun, her lover, murdered, and sobs over his dead body, the effect
was tremendous. Fokine as Amoun looked extremely handsome and
interpreted his part with great style; and even more effective was
Nijinsky, in the much smaller part of Cleopatra's black slave: his *pas de
deux* with Karsavina was entrancing. Almost the greatest success of all,
however, fell to the '*Bacchanale*', danced by a group of men round two
Bacchantes (Sophie Fedorova and Vera Fokina), which excited the
audience wildly. The whole ballet indeed was much to the taste of the
Paris public. The choreography, the *décor*, the *ensemble*, the solos: all
were highly praised. Nor was a word said against the musical hotch-
potch of the score, about which we had been so nervous. We could
breathe, on this account, again.

★   ★   ★

We still had another first night to come—but one of comparatively
minor importance. The programme on this occasion consisted of one
act of the opera *Judith* by Serov, with the celebrated soprano, Félia
Litvine, and a performance of *Le Pavillon d'Armide* with Koralli and
Mordkine in the parts first taken by Pavlova and Fokine.

We were nearing our final performances in Paris when we were
suddenly invited by the Quai d'Orsay to give *Les Sylphides* at a reception
for the *Corps Diplomatique*. This performance took place in the presence
of the President of the Republic and the leaders of Parisian society. As
usual the success was immense; and the principal dancers were presented, as a souvenir, with gold medals inscribed with their names.
We were also invited by Baron de Rothschild to give an outdoor performance of *Les Sylphides*. But Diaghilev's greatest ambition was to
end the season with a performance on the stage of the *Grand Opéra*; and
this, owing to our outstanding success, he was now able to realize. So on
June the 19th we gave two acts of *Boris Godounov*, *Les Sylphides* and a
divertissement—thus ending in a blaze of glory.

Looking back on our weeks in Paris, all of us, Diaghilev included,
could scarcely believe that what had happened was true. We all lived in
an unreal and enchanted world, which was shared not only by those in
close touch with us but even by the public, over whom we seemed to
have cast a spell. Needless to say, the Diaghilev committee, who had all
assembled in Paris, were elated by our success. Svetlov wrote this about
it: 'The first season of the Diaghilev Ballet must be commemorated in

letters of gold in the annals of the Russian Ballet. To say that it was successful is to say nothing. It was a revelation, a major event in the artistic life of Paris. Pavlova, Fokine and Nijinsky were the heroes of the day. The effect of the *ensemble* dancing was indescribable. Until the appearance of this company Paris had never seen male dancers, and their being here the equals of the ballerinas completely revolutionized the current conception of ballet. Fokine deprived the ballerina of her exclusive importance and made her share her position with the rest of the company. The *corps de ballet* became as it were a collective actor in its own right. It was made to live on the stage, to act, to interpret the psychology of the crowd, to possess its own individuality.' Svetlov's opinion was fully endorsed by the other critics.

On taking leave of the company Diaghilev said that the results of the season had surpassed all his expectations and that he was delighted and very happy. He thanked us all for our devotion to our work, and then, raising his voice, announced that the French Government had awarded the *Palmes Académiques* to Pavlova, Fokine, Nijinsky and Grigoriev. The whole company applauded loudly; and this naturally pleased us very much.

★　　★　　★

The result of our first Paris season was highly satisfactory both artistically and financially. Thanks to the excellent business we had done, Diaghilev managed not only to cover the enormous expenditure involved, but also to repay all the money that had been advanced to him. He accordingly felt sure that if he wished to return to Paris the next year, we should find everything much easier to arrange. Before he left Paris I went to say goodbye to him and asked him if he in fact intended to give another Paris season. Instead of answering he asked me whether I would care to join him again.

'Not only I, but all of us, would like to,' I replied.

He thought for a while. Then, 'I cannot yet say,' he said. 'I must first pause and collect myself, and think over all that has happened to us in the course of this year. Then we shall see, we shall see.' I left him feeling more than ever that our Paris adventure had been a fairy tale, a kind of dream, which might not recur.

CHAPTER TWO

1910

IN the autumn of 1909 the usual season at the *Mariinsky* was in progress. The ballet company was buzzing with tales of Diaghilev's great season, and he was referred to as the Conqueror of Paris. He arrived back in St. Petersburg at the beginning of the winter; and our ant-heap was thrown into a commotion. Everyone was wondering what he would do next, and I myself waited impatiently for some sign from him. It came at last in the form of a short note, giving me an appointment at his flat. 'You wished to know whether I intended giving another season in Paris,' he said on greeting me. 'Well—I can now answer your question in the affirmative. Tomorrow my friends, my committee, as you call them, are to meet here for a talk. I should like you to come too, and bring a list of the dancers you suggest, so that we may approach them at once and sign contracts.'

Before the committee met, as it duly did the next day, it had become generally known that Diaghilev had decided on another Paris season and that the committee were in favour of one. As soon as we were all seated round the table with the inevitable *samovar*, Diaghilev produced his large black exercise book and began thus: 'Before we start planning a second Paris season, I should like to impress on you that after the prodigious success we scored this summer, we must be especially careful in framing our new policy. The ballets we choose for next year must on no account be less interesting than this year's. But here we are faced with a problem. We could not possibly show Paris any of the ballets now given at the *Mariinsky*, or for that matter in Moscow. So, after thinking it over, I have come to the conclusion that we must invent new ones; and I shall begin by inviting my old professor of harmony, A. K. Liadov, to compose the music for a ballet on the Russian fairy tale of the Firebird.' We approved this suggestion. Nouvel, however, pointed out that Liadov composed very slowly and that it was doubtful whether

27

the score would be ready in time. 'At any rate I propose to see him and find out,' said Diaghilev. 'And for a second ballet I thought of Rimsky-Korsakov's symphonic poem *Schéhérazade*.' Here he paused a moment and then continued, 'My only doubt is over the third movement, which is unsuitable for dancing and anyhow not very interesting.' We all liked the idea of *Schéhérazade*, though some of the committee were shocked at the suggested cutting of any part of a work by Rimsky. Diaghilev, however, was quite definite about it; and after he and Nouvel had played the music through on the piano, in an arrangement for four hands, Fokine had to admit that he was right. This accounted, then, for two ballets. But there still remained two to choose; and Diaghilev asked us all to think our hardest. During a momentary lull in the conversation Benois observed in his quiet voice that it might be a good move to show *Giselle* in Paris. We might, he thought, make much of its being a French classical ballet with attractive music by Adam. For 'we must remember,' he said, 'that the Russian school of ballet dancing grew out of the French, and so in taking *Giselle* to Paris we should be paying a tribute to France.' General Bezobrazov shared Benois's opinion, and so did Svetlov.

But Diaghilev made a face and said, 'Shura [*i.e.* Benois] is quite right, of course. But *Giselle* is too well known in Paris, and would not be likely to interest the public. I'm quite prepared to consider it, though. We'll decide at our next meeting.' After that the conversation turned to other topics, including our ever-exciting memories of the summer.

★ ★ ★

Fokine had always wished to compose a ballet based on a Russian fairy tale. The Firebird gave him the opportunity, and he at once began working out a scenario in detail. I obtained several collections of Russian fairy tales; and between us we evolved a story by piecing together the more interesting parts of several versions. This took us about a fortnight; and we were ready for the next meeting at Diaghilev's flat. The scenario was approved; but Diaghilev reported that (as Nouvel had foreseen) Liadov, whom Diaghilev had approached about the music, had said that it would take him a year to write it. Diaghilev had therefore decided, he said, to order the score from a young composer named Igor Stravinsky, whose piece called *Fireworks* he had heard at a concert at the Academy of Music, and whom he considered very talented. 'The composition made a great impression on me,' said Diaghilev. 'It is new and original, with a tonal quality that should surprise the public. I have commissioned him to write the score for the Firebird; and he is extremely enthusiastic about it.' At this an ominous silence fell on the committee, who had heard of Stravinsky, if at all, only as a promising beginner. But Diaghilev was not to be deterred, and asked Fokine to arrange a meeting with Stravinsky as soon as possible in order to discuss the story.

The question of the Firebird being thus disposed of, we passed on to *Schéhérazade*. The theme that had inspired Rimsky's symphonic poem was not really suitable as a ballet plot. Benois tried improvising an altered version; and we all joined in with various suggestions. I remember Bakst's jumping on to a chair, gesticulating, and showing how the Shah's retainers should cut everyone to pieces, '*everyone*: his wives and above all their Negro lovers!' But despite our contributions, the plot as eventually used was the invention of Benois—and not of Bakst. Yet Diaghilev used to attribute it to Bakst—why I do not know; and this led later to a quarrel between him and Benois.

The next item on our agenda was *Giselle*. Diaghilev declared that he was still opposed to our giving it in Paris; and this annoyed Benois. The rest of us remained silent until Svetlov remarked that all the same *Giselle* as an old classic might well enhance the effect of the modern ballets by contrast. I too observed that one advantage of giving *Giselle* would be that it would spare us more time to rehearse the new ballets, which would require much care; and Nouvel pointed out that *Giselle* contained a brilliant solo for the *premier danseur*, in which Nijinsky might exhibit his mastery of classical technique. But all that followed was another silence, during which I watched Diaghilev's face. He had sat listening to what everyone said, playing with his pince-nez, which lay on the open exercise book, and smiling inscrutably. I felt that for some reason he was merely pretending that he did not wish to do *Giselle*, and that secretly he had already made up his mind that he would. However, at this point he abruptly changed the subject, saying that, whether or not we did *Giselle*, we still required at least one ballet more.

★　　★　　★

Whereas Diaghilev entrusted me with negotiating contracts with the rank and file of the dancers, he dealt with the composers and painters and some of the leading 'stars' himself. Calling upon him one morning, I found him drinking coffee in his dressing-gown, busy writing in his black exercise book. I sat down and waited, till after about five minutes, realizing that he was not likely to speak himself, I broke the silence by saying that I had had an idea for the ballet that was still wanted. This was a little ballet produced by Fokine for a charity performance to the music of Schumann's piano suite *Le Carnaval*. Diaghilev looked up from his exercise book and said that he did not particularly care for Schumann, and that though he had not seen Fokine's ballet, he had heard that it was arranged for only a small number of dancers and would therefore be unsuitable for a large stage. However, Benois arrived at this point, and, on hearing of my suggestion, supported me. He thought that if Nijinsky danced the Harlequin, *Le Carnaval* might well be a great success—to which I added that since it had only had one performance, it could pass for a new work. Diaghilev did not argue with us. He merely went on thinking. I could not tell whether we had succeeded in persuading him or whether he was just tired of the subject—when he suddenly made up his mind and wrote down '*Carnaval*' in the black book. Then, looking much happier, he turned to Benois and asked: 'What about *Giselle*, Shura? Do you still insist on *Giselle*?'

'I do indeed,' said Benois. 'I feel sure that it would give our *répertoire* variety and show our dancers at their most brilliant. Besides, I should like to paint you a *décor* for it!' Diaghilev gave a sly smile, and wrote '*Giselle*' in large and ornate characters in his exercise book. I must have guessed aright: that the question of *Giselle* had already been decided in his mind.

Our programme of new ballets was thus complete: *The Firebird* or *L'Oiseau de Feu*, *Schéhérazade*, *Le Carnaval* and *Giselle*. When next the committee met they were so informed, and Diaghilev added that he had another item in reserve: *Les Orientales*, which turned out to be another *divertissement*. The new ballets were, of course, to be added to those we had done the year before, namely *Cléopâtre*, *Les Sylphides* and *Les Danses Polovtsiennes*.

The *décor* of *Schéhérazade*, as I have mentioned already, was to be by Bakst and that of *Giselle* by Benois; and now Diaghilev asked Bakst what setting he would consider appropriate for *Le Carnaval*. Bakst suggested a garden scene, with a wide terrace in front of a house. But Diaghilev did not care for this idea. He said that since *Le Carnaval* was a small ballet, the stage should be correspondingly reduced in size and made more intimate: that a simple back-cloth was all that was wanted. Bakst did not object; but General Bezobrazov feared that such a scene might be rather dull, on which Diaghilev turned to Bakst, saying it was Lyovushka's business to see it was *not* dull! There remained the *décor* for *L'Oiseau de Feu*. This was entrusted, to everyone's satisfaction, to the painter A. Golovine, who worked at the *Mariinsky* and had designed a number of excellent settings.

Our subsequent meetings were concerned with casting. Pavlova had a spring engagement at the London Coliseum; so we could not count on her for our season. All the chief female parts were therefore to be danced by Karsavina—with the exception of Zobeïdé in *Schéhérazade*, which was to be danced by Ida Rubinstein. Fokine and Nijinsky remained the leading men; but we lost Bolm. From Moscow, in addition to Sophie Fedorova, Diaghilev invited the *prima ballerina* K. Geltzer and the male dancer A. Volinine.

From now on Stravinsky began to be present at our committee meetings, and so I met him for the first time. He was rather short, with prominent features and a very serious expression. He took an active part in the discussions, especially those on the production of *L'Oiseau de Feu*. His composition of the score went ahead rapidly and he sometimes played passages over to us. We all listened attentively but, apart from Diaghilev, expressed no opinion. Nouvel did not share Diaghilev's taste for Stravinsky's music, and as for the General, he declared quite frankly that he disliked it and that it was unsuitable for dancing. Diaghilev had certainly been right when he warned us that we should find Stravinsky's music new and unusual.

However, all our business was at length settled; and Diaghilev left for Paris to make final arrangements for the coming season, returning a month later.

★   ★   ★

At our first meeting on Diaghilev's return he told us with pride that this time our season was to take place at the *Opéra*. The initiative had come from the management; and Diaghilev had every reason for satisfaction after the rebuff he had suffered at the time of our first appearance. Our prestige certainly stood high by now. As well as in Paris, we had been invited to give some performances in both Berlin and Brussels, where we were to stop on our way to France.

The time for rehearsals was now approaching. They were to start in

The Diaghilev Ballet

April, and parts were being distributed. The title role of *L'Oiseau de Feu* was to be danced by Karsavina, with Fokine as the Tsarevich; and Nijinsky was to be the black slave in *Schéhérazade*. *A propos* of this, at one of our committee meetings Nouvel said to Diaghilev, 'How odd it is that Nijinsky should always be the *slave* in your ballets—in *Pavillon d'Armide*, in *Cléopâtre* and now again in *Schéhérazade*! I hope, Seryoja, that one of these days you'll emancipate him!' Karsavina and Nijinsky were also given the leading parts in *Le Carnaval* and *Giselle*, while Geltzer and Volinine were to appear in *Les Sylphides* and the *divertissement*.

Fokine began rehearsals with *L'Oiseau de Feu*, since it was clearly the most difficult of the various works; and Stravinsky was then first introduced to the company. Fokine started on a passage near the middle of the score: the great *ensemble* called by Stravinsky 'The Unholy Revels'. From the moment they heard the first bars the company were all too obviously dismayed at the absence of melody in the music and its unlikeness to what they were used to dancing to at the *Mariinsky*. Some of them indeed declared that it did not sound like music at all. Stravinsky was usually present to indicate the *tempo* and rhythms. Now and again he would play over passages himself and, according to some of the dancers, 'demolish the piano'. He was particularly exacting about the rhythms and used to hammer them out with considerable violence, humming loudly and scarcely caring whether he struck the right notes. It was invigorating to watch such a display of temperament, which certainly inspired Fokine in his work. Also the extraordinary music led Fokine to the invention of original steps, which the dancers could not but enjoy and be amused at. This *ensemble* accordingly progressed apace and was soon finished. Other passages in the first part of the ballet, such as the Lullaby and the dance of the Twelve Princesses, were more melodious and did not present the same difficulties. The first *pas de deux* for the Firebird and the Prince was choreographically the most effective. It represented a struggle between them and ended with the Firebird's plea for release and her eventual flight into the wings. When the ballet was danced right through before Diaghilev and his friends, it made a deep impression on them and they were quite carried away.

When *L'Oiseau de Feu* was finished, Fokine proceeded to the composition of *Schéhérazade*. In order to facilitate his work Diaghilev invited Sophie Fedorova to come up from Moscow in advance, to rehearse an important trio with Vera Fokina and E. Poliakova. For this Fokine made them sit in a group on the floor of the stage and use only their arms and heads and the upper halves of their bodies. This was an entirely novel idea, and it rather embarrassed the three dancers, who had never heard of a dance opening in such a way. They were re-assured, however, on being eventually allowed to rise and continue the number in more orthodox fashion. So began the composition of that famous work *Schéhérazade*. Rimsky's tuneful music, of course, made its progress easier than that of *L'Oiseau de Feu* and presented the dancers with a comparatively simple task. Fokine was at that time greatly inspired and highly productive. He composed with extraordinary ease, and without the use of complicated steps contrived to design wonderful combinations of movements, both for solos and for *ensembles*. Every-one was amazed by the wealth of his invention and his inexhaustible energy.

Having completed his new productions and polished up *Le Carnaval*, Fokine again rehearsed our last year's *répertoire*. At this juncture the Paris publishers who produced our programmes wrote urgently to Diaghilev asking him to supply them with material for the spring number of their magazine. As none of the costumes and sets for the other new ballets were yet ready, Diaghilev reluctantly sent them photographs of *Le Carnaval*.

All that now remained was to rehearse *Giselle*. But Fokine unex-pectedly declared that, since the choreography of *Giselle* was not by him, he did not see why he should be asked to rehearse it. Diaghilev pointed out that in that case someone else would have to be called in, since Fokine was his only choreographer. This argument proved conclusive; and the affair was settled accordingly. Diaghilev had meanwhile edited Adam's score, making certain judicious cuts and even adding passages, some from other compositions. Among those deleted in the *Mariinsky* version and now restored was a very attractive fugue in Act Two.

While we were rehearsing, the designers were busy making sketches for the scenery and costumes. Golovine's design for the *décor* of *L'Oiseau de Feu* was entrancing: diaphanous and magical. The committee were also in ecstasies over Bakst's scene for *Schéhérazade* and Benois's romantic settings for *Giselle*. This year our preparatory work in all its branches seemed more peaceful and productive: we had learnt from our experi-ence the year before, and were ready in time. The spring came early; and when we set out the weather was already quite warm.

The Diaghilev Ballet

★   ★   ★

The day after the last performance of the *Mariinsky* season our whole company left St. Petersburg for Berlin. We were to appear at Charlottenburg, which in those days was a suburb full of trees and gardens, without shops. It seemed very quiet, and made us feel as if we had arrived in a small provincial town rather than the capital of Germany. The company were lodged in comfortable little boarding-houses; and our ignorance of the language involved us in some amusing incidents. The contingent from Moscow arrived several days after us. Both Geltzer and Volinine were strangers to us and formed a complete contrast one to the other. For whereas Volinine was quiet and composed, Geltzer was extremely lively and excitable.

Then the performances began; and the Berliners, while on the whole more restrained than the Parisians, showed deep interest. Karsavina and Nijinsky were much appreciated, as was the general excellence of the company. We stayed about a fortnight, during which every seat in the theatre was sold. *Cléopâtre, Les Sylphides, Le Festin,* and above all *Le Carnaval,* were highly successful. This fortnight in Berlin also served, from our point of view, as a prolonged dress rehearsal for Paris.

On arrival in Paris this time we sought lodgings in the centre, near the *Opéra.* We had heard a great deal of this wonderful edifice at Petersburg; and, viewed from without, it was certainly imposing. We could not help, however, being much disappointed with the interior. The stage, though huge, was ill equipped; and even the auditorium seemed rather decayed and badly lit. For our rehearsals the Green Room behind the stage was placed at our disposal. There were also other rehearsal rooms, high up under the roof. It was here that Degas had painted his pictures of ballet girls, of which these rooms reminded us. The whole place had a curiously drowsy air—which made us feel that we had come to awaken and bring back to life the great French ballet of the past.

Conditions of work at the *Opéra* were far from comfortable. The stage was continuously occupied for opera rehearsals; and it was only with difficulty that we obtained the use of it once or twice before our first night—which was by no means often enough. We were not much worried about *Le Carnaval,* the Polovtsian Dances and *Le Festin,* which we had already performed in Berlin. But *Schéhérazade* in particular was new and complicated. It still needed finishing touches; there was all too little time; and the dress rehearsal failed to go smoothly. This upset Fokine and made him nervous. But Diaghilev remained relatively calm, believing in the maxim that a poor dress rehearsal augurs a good first night.

★ ★ ★

Before the opening of our season there was great excitement again in Paris. Apart from the general interest in the ballets, the musical world was anxious to hear the work of the newly discovered genius, Igor Stravinsky, for whom Diaghilev was busy engineering publicity. Our first performance took place on June the 4th. We obtained possession of the stage only after midday, and everything had to be checked at high speed. But our opening nights were always most exciting, with Diaghilev looking particularly earnest and concentrated. As on our first visit the house was filled with a most distinguished gathering, eager and expectant.

The first item this time was *Le Carnaval*, which surprised the audience by the simplicity of its setting. This consisted of a plain green back-cloth with a wide border of stylized dull gold lilies, in front of which, to either side, stood an 1830 sofa. That was all; yet it could not have been more effective. The opening movement of Schumann's suite was used as a short and charming overture, which, excellently orchestrated as it was, at once created the right mood in the spectators. But in *Le Carnaval* setting and music formed no more than a background for the choreography and its execution by the dancers. This, with Nijinsky as Harlequin and Karsavina as Columbine, was brilliant. Nijinsky's *variation*, and especially its close, when after a great *pirouette* Harlequin continues turning and then slowly sits down at the final chord, fairly 'brought the house down'. There is no doubt that the great success of *Le Carnaval* was largely due to Nijinsky.

But the chief item of our programme was *Schéhérazade*. As regards richness of setting nothing could have contrasted more completely with *Le Carnaval*. The *décor* for *Schéhérazade* was all in greenish blues with an orange-coloured stage-cloth; and such was its impact that at every performance, when the curtain rose, there was prolonged applause. *Schéhérazade* is described as a 'choreographic drama'. The main action falls to three characters: the Shah, his favourite wife, Zobeïdé, and the Negro Slave—parts created respectively by Bulgakov, Ida Rubinstein and Nijinsky. Fokine's production was masterly. The individual dances, the *ensembles*, the scenes in mime, seemed each better than the last, and reflected the development of the music with extraordinary fidelity. The 'orgy' in the middle was especially striking. By means of intricate evolutions for the various groups of dancers woven in with a number of individual moves, Fokine contrived to endow this dance with such rich variety that its climax was tremendous. The strongest choreographic moment came when, having combined all the different groups into one, he used a pause in the music suddenly to halt them, and then, while accelerating the pace still more, as it were to unravel this human tangle. The effect was overwhelming: the audience roared its applause, with cries of delight. The ballet concluded with a dramatic scene in mime, beautifully played by Bulgakov and Ida Rubinstein, in which Zobeïdé kills herself with a dagger. The death of the Negro was portrayed by Nijinsky with almost horrifying virtuosity; and a feat by the dancer Orlov also deserves to be recorded. The character he represented was supposed to be killed by the Shah's retainers at the top of the stairs leading to the throne, whereupon he had to hang head downwards, spreadeagled on the steps with open arms, and hold this painful but effective pose till the curtain fell.

In *Schéhérazade* Diaghilev attained an aim once dreamt of by Noverre, when he said, 'If only the painter, the composer and the choreographer could work together in harmony, what wonders would they not show the public!' It was this cooperation that Diaghilev achieved in *Schéhérazade*. It is impossible to describe the reception of this ballet. It took no little time for the audience even to calm down.

This memorable evening ended with the *divertissement Le Festin*, in which Geltzer and Volinine made their first appearance in Paris. It was a joy to watch their perfect classical technique and their extreme lightness and softness of movement. Geltzer insisted on also showing herself in a Russian *boyar* dance. Diaghilev did not really approve of this, but was obliged to give in to her. One of the items of the *divertissement* was the Polovtsian Dances, which had their usual success, with Fokine in the chief male part. The orchestra was conducted by Tchérépnine.

★   ★   ★

The press, after the first performance, was enthusiastic; and the Diaghilev Ballet became once more the talk of Paris. Many of the critics declared that the Russians had surpassed themselves; and

Diaghilev's fears lest the success we had won before would be hard to repeat were thus belied. Valuing the opinion of Paris above all as he did, he was pleased and gratified; and he fully deserved all the praise he received. If there was any adverse criticism of *Schéhérazade* at all in one or two papers, it referred only to the liberty taken with the theme of Rimsky's composition and the omission of Part III of the score; but even these objections did not lessen the critics' admiration of the ballet itself.

Our next first night took place on June the 18th and was devoted to *Giselle*. To lovers of pure classical dancing the performances of Karsavina and Nijinsky were a delight; while the charming settings by Benois and the perfection of the *ensembles* produced an excellent impression. On the whole, however, the ballet failed to win the success hoped for by Benois and the rest of us. Diaghilev was proved right in predicting as he had at St. Petersburg that it was not what the Paris public would wish to see danced by Russians. They in fact found *Giselle* old-fashioned and lacking in excitement. But its comparative failure had no adverse effect on our season as a whole. The theatre continued to be packed as before; and no-one except Diaghilev really minded about *Giselle*. We thought that in a way it served to show up the greater originality and interest of ballets such as *Schéhérazade*. But Diaghilev was annoyed with himself for having been over-persuaded by Benois, and would probably have told him so, had Benois still been with us. But by this time Diaghilev and Benois had quarrelled violently over the scenario of *Schéhérazade* and its unjustifiable attribution to Bakst; and Benois had ceased to appear at the theatre. This was a sad loss to me, since I found him very agreeable and interesting to talk to.

★   ★   ★

After the production of *Giselle* all that remained for us was to show our most important and difficult work, *L'Oiseau de Feu*. The company rehearsed intensively and did their utmost to 'dance themselves into' the unfamiliar choreography, all of us being eager to exhibit the ballet to the best advantage. Diaghilev invited the well-known Parisian conductor Gabriel Pierné to take charge of the orchestra. Stravinsky attended the orchestra rehearsals and endeavoured to explain the music; but energetically though the musicians attacked it, they found it no less bewildering than did the dancers. The first performance was fixed for June the 25th, and once again we found ourselves debarred

from using the stage for rehearsals. For *L'Oiseau de Feu*, however, rehearsals on the stage were absolutely vital; and so were at least two
dress rehearsals, on account of the complicated sets and lighting and,
above all, of the music, which sounded quite different when played by
the orchestra from what it had sounded like when played on a piano.
Diaghilev managed to secure the stage for ordinary rehearsals: but our
one and only dress rehearsal took place only on the day of the first night.
It naturally failed to go very well, and the lighting in particular, which
Diaghilev took charge of himself, could not be properly worked out.
Fokine was again in a fever of anxiety; but Diaghilev comforted him by
promising that in the evening he would operate the electrician's switch-
board himself. This he did in fact, thereby depriving himself of a view
of the first performance from the front.

As *régisseur* my own hands were all too full. The entire company were
employed in this ballet, and it was my business to supervise them.
Moreover, there were a large number of 'supers', who are always an
anxiety. Added to this Karsavina as the Firebird had to be brought on
several times on a wire. This necessitated careful attention to the
machinery, to ensure her appearing at precisely the right moments. But
most trying of all was the participation in the ballet of two real horses.
This was an incongruous idea of Fokine's. He insisted on having them.
As soon as the curtain rose, a horseman dressed all in black on a black
horse crossed the stage from the prompt corner—symbolizing night;
while half-way through the action another, dressed in white on a white
horse, did likewise—symbolizing day. I was surprised, I confess, that
Diaghilev should not have opposed such an idea. Perhaps he thought it
would produce an unexpected effect on the public; and in a sense he
was right. The public were certainly astonished by the horses, and
Fokine was duly delighted. However, to my intense relief these animals
did not last beyond the second performance, after which they were 'cut'
for good. But for those two performances they caused acute discomfort
in the crowded wings, poisoning the stage with the smell of stables.

But to return to the first night of *L'Oiseau de Feu*—this was a notable
event in Paris. The music, as the work of a young and unknown composer, aroused particular curiosity. Fokine's choreography once again
took Paris by surprise, and the fairy-like *décor* by Golovine created an
atmosphere of enchantment. The ballet opens with the appearance of
the Firebird and the Prince in pursuit. Their ensuing *pas de deux*—a
superb example of Fokine's art—takes place on a darkened stage, lit

only by a bright golden spot which follows them as they move. Both Karsavina and Fokine played these parts to perfection. As their scene ends, the stage becomes gradually moonlit, and from somewhere behind appear the twelve Enchanted Princesses, who come forward to perform their charming dance with the golden apples. This passage of the ballet is full of poetry with lovely melodious music, affording an interval of relief between the complicated *pas de deux* that precedes, and the violent *ensemble* that follows it. The latter develops gradually, as it were growing, both musically and choreographically, till it reaches a climax, when in sudden silence the dancers all fall flat on their faces—a dramatic stroke that produced a deep effect on the audience. There then follows the chief solo for the Firebird—the lullaby, full of mystery and magical atmosphere; after which the ballet comes to an end, with the destruction of the wizard Koshchey and a fine apotheosis of the Prince and the First Princess.

Karsavina as the Firebird was incomparable. The movements of her arms, her head and her whole body had something noble and imperious about them. It was undoubtedly an ideal part for her. Fokine, with his fine looks and sincerity, was likewise perfect as the Tsarevich, though his role consisted chiefly of miming and was by no means difficult. 'The Immortal Koshchey' was played by Bulgakov, who looked absolutely terrifying, and being an excellent mimic, interpreted the part with telling effect. Altogether it was not in vain that the whole company had put such hard work into the rehearsals: the *ensembles* were impeccable; and the ovation that the audience gave to all the participants, including Gabriel Pierné the conductor, was tremendous. Next day the press devoted lengthy articles to *L'Oiseau de Feu*, and invariably dwelt on the happy collaboration of Fokine, Stravinsky and Golovine as co-authors of this remarkable creation.

As for Stravinsky, his name was made; and Diaghilev felt justly proud of his discovery. From this moment Stravinsky attached himself to the Diaghilev Ballet, remaining with us for many years.

★   ★   ★

On the first night of *L'Oiseau de Feu* we also produced our second *divertissement*, called *Les Orientales*. This consisted of five numbers, two of which were danced by Nijinsky, the first being an Eastern dance to music by Sinding, and the second his own arrangement of a piece by

Grieg, orchestrated by Stravinsky. Geltzer and Volinine also took part in this *divertissement*.

Once *L'Oiseau de Feu* had been performed, the company, at last free of perpetual rehearsals, were able to relax. Before the end of the Paris season, however, we paid a hurried visit to Brussels, where we gave two performances at the *Théâtre de la Monnaie*. By the terms of our contract with the *Opéra*, moreover, we were bound to take part in three opera performances, in conjunction with the resident French ballet company. The audience at these performances consisted of the ordinary subscribers to seats for the opera season. But though they differed in type from the audiences to which we were accustomed, they greeted our efforts with equal enthusiasm.

The Paris season was due to end on July the 5th. But owing to its outstanding success Diaghilev was asked to prolong it by a few extra performances. He agreed to do so, but thereby faced us with a problem. For Karsavina had counted on being free after July the 5th and had signed a contract to appear at the London Coliseum, which obliged her to leave; and we had no-one to take over her role as the Firebird, since Diaghilev considered Geltzer unsuitable. Fokine, however, suggested our trying a young dancer who had only that year completed her training at the *Mariinsky*, named Lydia Lopokova. He thought her talented and charming and possessed of a good *élévation*; and though Diaghilev at first hesitated, Fokine was so insistent that he eventually agreed.

To learn a part like the Firebird in only a few days was no slight task; and considering Lopokova's extreme youth and inexperience we did not expect her performance to be perfect. She proved nevertheless to have daring, technique and temperament enough to give an excellent account of herself—so much so that she was at once snapped up by an American impresario, and abandoned both us and the *Mariinsky*, to remain for no less than five years in the United States.

★   ★   ★

The *début* of Lopokova was the last incident of our exciting second season in Paris, which had proved no less brilliant and triumphant than the first. The two programmes we had thus shown were, in fact, somewhat similar. But, if anything, the second was the more varied and interesting and so aroused deeper appreciation both in the public and the press. There was a certain correspondence of structure between them: *Giselle* being in some sort the counterpart of *Le Pavillon d'Armide*; *Le Carnaval* that of the romantic *Sylphides*; and the dramatic *Schéhérazade* that of *Cléopâtre*; while the more frenzied parts of *L'Oiseau de Feu* had much in common with the Polovtsian Dances from *Prince Igor*. This correspondence, however, was purely accidental. As I mentioned earlier, both *Giselle* and *Le Carnaval* had been included by Diaghilev in the second programme only with some reluctance, while *L'Oiseau de Feu* owed its existence to Fokine's wish to compose on a genuinely Russian subject. Only Diaghilev's choice of *Schéhérazade* was probably suggested to him by the previous success of *Cléopâtre*. It is interesting to note, moreover, that whereas it was *Cléopâtre* and the Polovtsian Dances that won most success in the first season, in the second it was *Schéhérazade* and *L'Oiseau de Feu*. The correspondence was further marked to some extent by the respective work in the two seasons of the painters Bakst and Benois. On the other hand, the appearance on our horizon of Igor Stravinsky and his original music added extra lustre to our second season. As for the dancers, Pavlova having left us, the first place in the company had been taken by Karsavina, while Nijinsky had, if possible, risen to even greater heights than before. Fokine danced comparatively seldom during the second season; but he was now acknowledged as a superb, and indeed unique, choreographer. Geltzer and Volinine, too, had both won much admiration. But the honour and glory went, above all, to Diaghilev himself. He was talked of and written about everywhere; and no praise seemed too high for what he had achieved.

Once the last performance was over, the company, as such, again ceased to exist. Diaghilev bade us all goodbye; and we returned to our homes in Russia feeling rather sad at the end of our wonderful stay in Paris. Diaghilev was as usual going to Venice for a holiday, and when seeing me for the last time promised that when we met again in St. Petersburg it would be to work together for a longer period. I was delighted, but somewhat puzzled at his use of the word 'longer'. For this summer we had, as it was, spent our entire leave from the *Mariinsky* in first rehearsing and then performing for Diaghilev. However I did not pursue the point, and merely welcomed the prospect of perhaps visiting Paris yet again.

CHAPTER THREE

1911

DIAGHILEV returned to St. Petersburg for the opening of the *Mariinsky* season in the autumn of 1910. He was at once bombarded by his friends and acquaintances with questions about his future plans; but replied that he had not yet made up his mind. However, a fortnight later the committee were summoned to a meeting; and once again we all sat round the oval table, drinking tea and awaiting a pronouncement. Diaghilev always smiled in a peculiar way when about to say something of special significance; and what he said now was: 'Gentlemen. I have decided to form a permanent ballet company and give performances all the year round.'—This was certainly most unexpected, and caused a stir amongst us. But Diaghilev went on: 'As a result of our two seasons in Paris we have built up a considerable *répertoire*, and this will continue to grow. It seems senseless to me to go on assembling a fresh company every year only to perform in Paris for a short season. Our very success proves that abroad there is a demand for ballet, and that we should be all but certain to succeed. After taking everything into consideration, therefore, I propose founding for the first time a large private company of dancers.'

None of us could deny the truth of these observations; but it was clear that great difficulties stood in the way of such a scheme; and these we pointed out. In the first place, where were the dancers for such a company to come from? Up till then Diaghilev had engaged only dancers from the *Mariinsky* and the Moscow *Bolshoy* Theatre during their summer leave; and in those days such a thing as a private ballet school did not exist. The committee considered it most unlikely that the leading dancers would leave the Imperial Theatres, and were equally doubtful whether it would prove possible to arrange continuous seasons abroad. But neither of these objections seemed to worry Diaghilev. As for engagements, he already had offers for at least six months; and as for leading dancers, he felt sure that those from the

Mariinsky would always be able to obtain leave of absence for two or three months in the winter, and during their summer vacation they would also be available, as before. A more difficult problem was the engagement of the ordinary dancers, the *corps de ballet*; this he admitted. But knowing his energy and persistence we were all convinced that, whatever the obstacles, in the end he would get what he wanted.

His first task was clearly to find three people: a *maître de ballet*, a *prima ballerina* and a leading male dancer. For the last Nijinsky was the obvious choice. For by this time Diaghilev and Nijinsky had become close friends; and Nijinsky was present at our meetings. After working with Diaghilev for two seasons, he had come to realize that an enterprise such as Diaghilev had in mind would offer him a brilliant future. He therefore strongly supported the project; and it was clear that he would willingly take part in it. He was faced with this difficulty, however: that having received his training free at the Imperial Theatre School, he was bound by the regulations to serve for five years at the *Mariinsky*, and was as yet a long way from completing this service. But an unexpected incident played into Diaghilev's hands. One night, when dancing in *Giselle*, Nijinsky wore a costume in the style of Carpaccio. This consisted of a much abbreviated tunic and tights, which displayed his figure rather too distinctly; for in order to preserve the character of the costume, he had left off the short trunks he should have worn over his tights. The directors strongly objected to his appearance, and he was ordered to wear the trunks in future. But under the influence of Diaghilev and his friends, who maintained that this would ruin the effect, at the next performance Nijinsky appeared as before; and as ill luck—or luck—would have it, there was present in the audience a member of the Imperial Family, who was duly outraged by this exhibition. A terrible scandal ensued; and Nijinsky was asked to resign for insubordination. But he was thereby set at liberty to join Diaghilev's company whenever he so desired.

Having thus secured Nijinsky, Diaghilev was determined to engage Karsavina as his *prima ballerina*. This was easily arranged, since she was bound to appear at the *Mariinsky* only for a limited number of months, apart from which she was free. There remained, therefore, only the question of a choreographer, which Diaghilev sought to settle by offering Fokine a two-year contract at a very high salary. During the two previous years Fokine had been employed both as a choreographer and as a dancer. But Diaghilev now wished to obviate any rivalry between

PLATE IV

VASLAV NIJINSKY

him and Nijinsky as *premier danseur,* and offered to engage Fokine only as choreographer, to compose new ballets and rehearse those already created. Fokine was at first unwilling to accept this arrangement. He did not see why he should be shelved as a dancer. He had already begun to be restive on this account in Paris, observing as he had that Diaghilev was concentrating publicity on Nijinsky. He now demanded that his name should appear on all programmes and posters with the designation 'Choreographic Director'. Diaghilev agreed, but insisted that he was engaging Fokine only in this capacity. Nevertheless the contract was duly signed; and so Diaghilev obtained his 'three wishes': Karsavina, Nijinsky and Fokine.

His next requirement was a leading dancer for 'character' parts, and to fill this position he approached Bolm, who had so distinguished himself in the Polovtsian Dances. The negotiations took some little time; but such were Diaghilev's persistence and the attraction of a high salary that in the end Bolm resigned from the *Mariinsky* to join us. But the most difficult problem of all was the recruitment of the rest of the company: the dancers of minor parts and the *corps de ballet*. It was clear that these would have to be sought for far and wide, and that, when found, would require considerable training to endow them with the necessary finish. It was for this reason that Diaghilev's next move was to approach the eminent Italian professor of ballet, Enrico Cecchetti, who was at that time a member of the *Mariinsky* company and renowned as a master not only of dancing, but also of mime. Diaghilev's dearest wish was that it should be he with whom Nijinsky and the rest of the new company should study. Cecchetti, to his delight, agreed to join him; and Diaghilev announced the news to the assembled committee in high glee.

★   ★   ★

Every time we met at the flat, Diaghilev seemed to have some pleasant news for us. But nothing was said about new productions till one day somebody—I do not remember who—enquired whether anything had yet been thought of. It then appeared that plans had already been laid in Paris; and we found that Diaghilev had actually ordered two new scores: one from Stravinsky, and the other from Tchérépnine. On his way back from Venice he had visited Stravinsky in Switzerland in order to hear what he had by that time composed, only to find that he had not yet started. However, Stravinsky instead played him a piano concerto

45

he had recently completed; and Diaghilev found this so attractive that he suggested its conversion into a more elaborate work for orchestra, of which the theme, he thought, might be something such as Petrushka, the Russian equivalent of Punch. Thus it was that Stravinsky's *Petrushka* was first conceived. Acting on Diaghilev's advice he amplified his original score with music inspired by a Russian carnival (the revels preceding the Orthodox Lent), including an attractive peasant dance. Diaghilev was very much pleased with the result, and declared at once that Benois must do the sets. Stravinsky agreed; but an obstacle had first to be overcome. As I have related, Diaghilev and Benois had quarrelled over the authorship of *Schéhérazade*; and Benois had told all his friends that he would never again work for Diaghilev. It was now therefore essential to put an end to this estrangement; and Diaghilev did not hesitate a moment. He forthwith took a ticket to Lugano, where Benois then lived; and they immediately made peace. Benois indeed was much attracted by the idea of collaborating with Stravinsky; the theme of the proposed ballet greatly appealed to him; and he and Stravinsky were soon at work elaborating the scenario.

The second ballet that Diaghilev had in mind was one on the myth of Narcissus and Echo. It had been suggested by Bakst during the last season in Paris; and Diaghilev had already commissioned the score from Tchérépnine.

The committee listened attentively to everything that Diaghilev said. Nor was this all: he had other surprises for us. Hitherto all the ideas for productions had come either from members of the committee itself, or from friends of theirs who were actively connected with the ballet. This year, however, a stranger appeared on our horizon, in the person of a Frenchman, Jean Vaudoyer, a writer who had been much impressed by our performances and now put forward the suggestion of a ballet on Weber's *Invitation à la Valse*, with a poem by Théophile Gautier as subject. Diaghilev was greatly taken with this proposal. He saw Nijinsky in the principal part, so composed as to give him ample opportunity of exhibiting his extraordinary *élévation*. Such was the genesis of one of the loveliest of our ballets, *Le Spectre de la Rose*.

The new programme seemed to us excellent. It lacked only one ingredient of its predecessors: a vigorous and exotic *ensemble* item, such as the Polovtsian Dances from *Prince Igor*. To supply this want Diaghilev suggested the sea-bed ballet from Rimsky-Korsakov's opera *Sadkó*, which included such dances; and his choice was approved. He then announced some further news; that Maurice Ravel, the famous French composer, was shortly to arrive in St. Petersburg, bringing with him some of the music for yet another new ballet. Ravel, it appeared, had seen our company two years before, and had shown such interest that Diaghilev had asked him to compose a score. Its subject was another myth, that of Daphnis and Chloe. It had been suggested by Fokine, who, as we all knew, had been much influenced by the classical improvisations of Isadora Duncan, and had long dreamt of creating a Greek ballet. But Ravel, though he had agreed to write the music, had proved exceedingly slow in doing so; and Diaghilev hoped that by inviting him to St. Petersburg he might somehow induce him to hasten its completion. During his stay, which lasted some time, Ravel was royally entertained by Diaghilev and his friends, to whom he played over the passages he had already composed. He also discussed them at length with Fokine. Yet they were still only fragments of the whole that was required; and even by the time that Ravel departed, the score, though then longer, was still unfinished.

However, the programme was now fixed. The *décor* for *Petrushka* was to be by Benois; that for both *Narcisse* and *Daphnis et Chloë* by Bakst; and that for *Sadkó* by another Russian painter, Anisfeldt. The allocation of the chief parts in the new ballets was a foregone conclusion: Karsavina and Nijinsky were to take them all. On the other hand, there was some debate about the Moor's part in *Petrushka*. It was generally agreed that Orlov, the young dancer from the *Mariinsky* whom I mentioned for his part in *Schéhérazade*, should be invited to dance it. He declined, however, to leave the Imperial Theatres; and so Diaghilev decided not to show *Petrushka* before May, when Orlov would be on leave and so available.

★   ★   ★

Now that Diaghilev had become famous abroad, his Russian opponents changed their tone. One result was that the all-powerful Kchessinska became quite friendly, and this was a great help to him in forming his company. But it proved impossible to do this quickly; and Diaghilev grew anxious, since time was short and he wished to return to Paris. Having pretty well exhausted the possibilities of Moscow, he sent General Bezobrazov to Warsaw in search of young and good-looking recruits. As for myself I was on the horns of a dilemma: was I, after eleven years' service, to leave the *Mariinsky*, as Diaghilev insisted? Or was I to leave Diaghilev himself? It was a difficult decision; and I had still not made it when he returned once more from abroad and we all met as usual at his flat.

He was full of news. Everything in Paris was settled. This year we were to dance again at *Châtelet*, and before opening in Paris were to go in April to Monte Carlo, and thence to Rome. What was even more exciting, we were to appear in London, at Covent Garden, at the time of the coronation of King George V. We were all delighted and began discussing these plans with enthusiasm—when Diaghilev opened his large black exercise book. 'Now, gentlemen,' he said smiling, 'let us return to current business. I regret to say that our company is still not complete. Thanks to the labours of General Bezobrazov we have so far assembled seventeen female and nine male dancers; and though the stage at Monte Carlo is comparatively small, we shall require even for it a company of at least forty. I must confess I should have been alarmed, had I not succeeded in finding a further eleven Russian dancers in Paris.' At this we looked at each other in amazement. Eleven Russian dancers in Paris! How was that possible? Diaghilev was obviously delighted at our surprise. Then he explained: he had come across a stranded troupe of character dancers belonging to a certain Molotsov, some of whom were not at all bad and could be greatly improved by Fokine. Fokine smiled sceptically, and said that no doubt they might disport themselves in the Polovtsian Dances. But Diaghilev maintained that they would do, and that, with them and a few more from the *Mariinsky*, all would be well.

'Ah, but will it?' I objected. 'Seeing how unfriendly the *Mariinsky* are to you, will they let you have anyone, do you suppose?'

Diaghilev smiled a little and said slowly, 'Yes—they will—as things stand now.'

'As things stand now?' I thought to myself. If the attitude of the *Mariinsky* to Diaghilev had changed, my own position might be affected. I might be able to go to Monte Carlo as early as March, and stay with him till the end of my leave in September. This cheered me considerably. Nevertheless, I could not assume I should be granted so much leave. So I continued to speculate about my future, while working on contracts and the engagement of new dancers, till one day Diaghilev said I could now apply for leave on behalf both of the artists and of myself, and that he had good reason to believe it would be granted. It was—and hence I was able to work for him without resigning.

Seeing that our dancers came from so many different places, we decided, instead of starting rehearsals in St. Petersburg, all to assemble at Monte Carlo. This did not apply to *Le Spectre de la Rose*, which, since it had only two parts, was rehearsed by Fokine before we left. It is not often that two people fit their parts as Karsavina and Nijinsky did theirs. I happened to come in during one of the final rehearsals of this enchanting ballet, and stopped, quite entranced by their performance and Fokine's composition. Diaghilev loved this ballet too, and prophesied that in it Nijinsky would surpass himself—with which I agreed.

When the time came for Diaghilev to leave for Paris, Svetlov took charge of affairs in his place; and we all soon followed, travelling direct to Monte Carlo.

★ ★ ★

When we arrived at Monte Carlo, Diaghilev was already there, enjoying the sun and the sea after the cold of the Russian winter. He had already arranged about rooms for rehearsals; so we were able to set to work forthwith. Our task was no light one, and we had all too little time for it. For not only were there at least two new ballets to produce, but, since we had so many strangers in the company, all the old ballets had to be rehearsed as well. Diaghilev watched all our proceedings closely—and particularly the classes of *Maestro* Cecchetti. These wonderful lessons, which began from the day of our arrival, were not only of enormous assistance to everyone, but at once imposed a new style and attitude on the dancers not drawn from the Imperial Theatres and were a boon to Fokine by welding the company into a whole.

Towards the end of March, when our opening date was drawing near, the ballerinas Preobrajenska and Karsavina arrived from St. Petersburg. The Monte Carlo theatre, which had been built by Charles Granier, the architect of the *Grand Opéra* in Paris, was then placed at our disposal. The theatre stands on a terrace overlooking the sea. It was both elegant and comfortable, not only in the 'front of the house' but at the back—a rare occurrence, which made our work there very pleasant. Our first night was fixed for April the 6th. It was, as usual, preceded by a *répétition générale*—a performance marked by a tragic accident on the stage, Muoratori, the *régisseur* of the theatre, falling through a trap-door and dying of his injuries. Everyone was naturally most distressed; and Diaghilev, who was deeply superstitious, took this fatality as an evil omen and was much affected by it for some time. Fortunately we were distracted from dwelling on it by having so many last details to attend to.

Diaghilev attached as much importance to this first performance by his own company on April the 6th at Monte Carlo as to that earlier landmark in his career, his very first night of all—in Paris on May the 19th, 1909. This opening at Monte Carlo went very well; and both the management of the Casino and the audience, which included the Prince of Monaco, were delighted. We gave four performances a week, showing *Giselle* with Karsavina and Nijinsky; *Schéhérazade* with Karsavina as Zobeïdé, Preobrajenska in various ballets, and Bolm in the Polovtsian Dances, when his tremendous vigour astonished everyone. Nijinsky, needless to say, was invariably an enormous success—above all, perhaps, in *Le Spectre de la Rose*, the first performance of which took place on April the 19th. The setting of this ballet represented a room with two large windows opening out on to a moonlit garden. A young girl—Karsavina—has just returned from a ball. She sinks into an armchair holding a rose, falls asleep and dreams—of a figure—Nijinsky—who seems to float in through one of the windows. After he has performed some evolutions alone, he rouses her and they dance together—an exquisite *pas de deux*. So unearthly, so romantic was it, this valse, one could scarcely believe it was not indeed a dream. At its end the figure floats out again through the window—a leap managed by Nijinsky with such art as to create a feeling of actual flight. The success of *Le Spectre* was immense; and Diaghilev was delighted, foreseeing that another triumph awaited him in Paris.

Our next interest was to see how *Narcisse* would turn out. Fokine had never been very taken with the idea of it, and would much rather have embarked on *Daphnis et Chloë*. But this could not be done in time, because Ravel had still not completed the score; Fokine indeed suspected Diaghilev of deliberately delaying its production, because for some reason he preferred to try *Narcisse*. Whatever he might suspect, however, Fokine was too much of an artist not to get carried away when once he started composing. Nevertheless on this occasion he seemed at a loss to devise a satisfactory arrangement of Nijinsky's transformation into a flower; and in the end Tchérépnine was obliged to cut a long passage in the music. *Narcisse* was performed for the first time on April the 26th, with Tchérépnine conducting. The attractive scene by Bakst represented a clearing in a wood, with a spring under a tree against a sky flecked with white clouds; it was a summer's day in Greece. The action opened with the appearance of Narcissus pursued by two nymphs.

As always, Nijinsky's appearance was spectacular and his dancing a delight. Karsavina—pensive and poetic as Echo—had little to do except in her *pas de deux* with Nijinsky, when, in character, she repeated his movements with great charm and grace. Fokine's arrangement of the various dances was most attractive; and I was myself very fond of this ballet, with its strange, pleasing melancholy and tuneful music.

I have dwelt on these two works at some little length because they were the first new ones to be danced by Diaghilev's own company. Its *début* at Monte Carlo thus augured well.

★　　★　　★

Our arrival in Rome coincided with the opening of an international art exhibition. Hardly had our train stopped at the station before I was handed a note from Diaghilev, asking me to call on him immediately at his flat. I found him in a bad mood and much preoccupied. He said that very little time remained before our opening in Paris, and that Fokine must be made to finish the remaining new ballets at once. I replied that this was not feasible. He could not devote himself entirely to the new ballets, because of having to rehearse our recruits in the old ones.

'That's nothing to do with *me*!' Diaghilev interrupted angrily. 'Fokine shouldn't have wasted his time rehearsing the old stuff. He should have worked at Monte Carlo on *Petrushka*; and he must find time now, even if he has to keep at it morning, noon and night!' Having learnt by experience that when Diaghilev was in one of his black moods it was useless to argue, I refrained from doing so. But I could not help wondering what had upset him; and I discovered later that Fokine, who had come on to Rome in advance of the rest of us, had already spoken to Diaghilev and had told him that he could not possibly manage all this work in time for the opening in Paris. Later that same day Benois, Stravinsky, Tchérépnine, Fokine and I met in order to work out a programme for our performances in Rome such that it might lighten Fokine's task. He sulked and refused to speak, however; and when in the end Diaghilev suggested that he should work on *Sadkó* and *Petrushka* simultaneously, he was still more annoyed and merely said that he would see me about it. I did my best to calm him down, seeing that he was in no fit state to tackle the arrangement of a ballet like *Petrushka*, of which not only was the music difficult, but parts of the scenario, and particularly the middle scenes, had not yet been properly worked out. Yet when he began composing, as he shortly did, he turned out to be full of ideas; and the rehearsals went quickly ahead. Only when he reached the third scene, where the Moor is left by himself for a time, did his invention fail him. He could not think what to make him do, and lost his temper, throwing the music on the floor and leaving the rehearsal. Next day, however, he appeared looking happier, and said he had thought of some 'business' for the accursed Moor: he would give him a coconut to play with—which would carry him at least through the first part of the scene.

Towards the middle of our stay in Rome, as work on the new ballets went ahead well and it became clear that they would be ready in time, Diaghilev's mood changed for the better—a change that was encouraged by the considerable success of our performances. The *Costanzi* Theatre was invariably packed; and venerable Rome, no less than Paris, seemed to have submitted to a Russian conquest.

★   ★   ★

And now we were once again in Paris, in lodgings near the *Châtelet*. The Theatre was as dusty and dirty as ever, but at least the stage here was always at our disposal and the staff were very friendly. I noticed that Diaghilev was again in a state of agitation and asked him why.

'Do you remember what Napoleon said?' he answered. '"It is not enough to take the Tuileries. The problem is to stay there." And that's what *I* say. This is our third season in Paris, and the most critical.'

'But Napoleon *did* stay in the Tuileries,' I objected. 'Why shouldn't you do the same for Paris?'

'Perhaps,' said he. 'But at the moment we must be very very careful what we do'—and he accordingly decided to give only a very short season—no more than eight performances, showing all four of the new ballets, but only two of the old ones, *Le Carnaval* and *Schéhérazade*.

Our opening date was June the 6th, a Tuesday; and the first programme, which was to be repeated four times, consisted of *Le Carnaval* and three of the new ballets: *Narcisse*, *Sadkó* and *Le Spectre de la Rose*. The name Diaghilev was by now a guarantee of interesting and exciting evenings; and far from displaying indifference, as he had feared, people fell over one another to get into the *Châtelet*. On the first night *Le Carnaval* received a warm welcome; but it was clear at once that *Narcisse*, which followed, was not to the Parisians' taste. Though

Nijinsky scored a personal success, the ballet as a whole was voted dull. *Sadkó*, on the other hand, provided just what they wanted—a rousing display of Russian temperament; and its final *ensemble* produced much the same effect as the dances from *Prince Igor*. But interest was keenest of all in *Le Spectre de la Rose*. So loud was the applause after Nijinsky's leap from the window that the orchestra were unable to finish playing the music. The audience shouted themselves hoarse for an encore; but this was, of course, out of the question, since Nijinsky had already been dancing for fifteen minutes without a pause. Diaghilev was overjoyed: his prophecy had come true: Nijinsky and the *Spectre* had achieved an unequalled triumph. After the performance he was reassured that, like Napoleon, he could remain in the Tuileries.

The second programme consisted of *Petrushka*, *Schéhérazade* and *Le Spectre* again, Diaghilev including the latter on the advice of his friends. Our attention was concentrated on *Petrushka*. Diaghilev invited the young French conductor, Pierre Monteux, to take charge of the orchestra; and he had no less difficulty with the score than Gabriel Pierné had had with that of *L'Oiseau de Feu*. Indeed *Petrushka* was even harder; and Monteux was obliged to split up his orchestra into groups of instruments and study the music separately with each in turn. Fokine, meanwhile, was assiduously rehearsing the *mise en scène* and trying to control the large crowd of 'supers', while Benois was busy with the scenery and costumes, which had just arrived from St. Petersburg. As on our first visit to Paris before the production of *Armide*, the stage was littered with 'props'—on this occasion the paraphernalia of a fair: merry-go-rounds, swings, booths, etc. Everyone lent a hand, while Benois and Diaghilev worked on the lighting and the changes of scene, which had to be managed in the shortest possible time. At this juncture there unfortunately occurred another quarrel between Diaghilev and Benois. On the wall in the third scene of *Petrushka* there was painted a portrait of the magician, the owner of the puppet show; and Diaghilev, not liking the portrait designed by Benois, asked him to alter it. This Benois declined to do, maintaining that it was precisely what was wanted; and so on the day before the *répétition générale*, when Benois was away ill, Diaghilev seized the opportunity to have the portrait repainted by Bakst. Bakst, however, having done the deed, felt somewhat uneasy. He therefore called on Benois and told him that he had 'touched up' the portrait in places where the paint had flaked off. As soon as Benois appeared at the *répétition générale*, however, he saw that the portrait was an entirely new one. He thereupon flung down all the sketches for *Petrushka* that he was carrying under his arm and left the theatre in a rage. A friend of Diaghilev who was present, the painter Serov, was anxious to pacify Benois. He accordingly tried to restore the portrait to its original state, and did so quite successfully—but all to no purpose. Benois refused to attend the first night, and indeed kept away from the theatre altogether.

But to return to the dress rehearsal. There were as usual a good many hitches, due chiefly to the fact that the music as played by the orchestra sounded strange to the dancers, and to the necessity of changing the scenery in complete darkness, with large numbers of people on the stage. To make this latter problem worse, Stravinsky had had four huge drums set in the prompt corner, which went into action throughout these changes of scene. Moreover, Stravinsky and Fokine had repeated disputes over the *tempi* of the music; the dancers complained that with all the apparatus of the fair they had no room on the stage to move; and in the absence of Benois the lighting got out of hand: in a word, there was more than all the usual chaos of a dress rehearsal, from which order had somehow to be evoked. Nevertheless on the first night the reception surpassed our expectations. *Petrushka* made an immense impression, added to the glories of Russian ballet, and was to remain in Diaghilev's *répertoire* till the very end. Karsavina, Nijinsky and Orlov—the three protagonists—could not have been bettered. They enthralled the audience; and the dramatic tension grew with each scene. Nijinsky was inexpressibly moving at the end, in another death scene, but of a very different kind. The ballet ends with the mysterious reappearance of Petrushka on the roof of the booth—an immortal Petrushka, whom the Moor cannot kill—and the precipitate flight of the terrified magician. Petrushka remains alone on the dark stage in the falling snow; the melancholy music dies away; and the curtain slowly, slowly descends. That same evening we gave *Schéhérazade* and *Le Spectre de la Rose*, both of which had become great favourites with the public. If anything, our second programme was even more successful than our first; and the whole season completely belied Diaghilev's apprehensions.

★   ★   ★

Our next goal was London; and our task was to conquer it as we had conquered Paris and Rome. Diaghilev had wished to give a season in

London the year before, but had been unable to secure an engagement on account of the death of King Edward. But this year, with the help of Sir Joseph Beecham, whose son Thomas was to conduct for us, he had negotiated a contract with the management of the Covent Garden Opera House. Our opening performance was to be a gala, in connection with the coronation of King George V.

We were much intrigued at the prospect of seeing London. We had been warned on the Continent that we should find everything in England quite different to what we were accustomed to elsewhere; and, in fact, from the moment we set foot on English soil we began to remark peculiarities. To begin with, something we had certainly never encountered before were the curious two-wheeled vehicles, with the driver seated behind his passengers, known as hansom cabs. We were surprised, again, by the extreme simplicity of the architecture: London houses seemed to us almost excessively plain. We found rooms in the neighbourhood of the British Museum, which was a quiet quarter with an abundance of trees and squares. But here again the gardens of the squares were all locked up, and only the residents had keys to them. What amazed us above all, however, was the Theatre Royal in Covent Garden itself. It stood in the midst of a vegetable market and was closely hemmed in by greengrocers' warehouses and vast mountains of cabbages, potatoes, carrots and all manner of fruit. Being accustomed in Russia to theatres erected in large open spaces, where they might be seen and admired from all sides, we could not understand why the chief theatre in London should be situated in a market of all places, where it was impossible even to obtain a view of the façade. On the other hand, the interior was excellent, both as regards the auditorium and the stage. The stage, to be sure, had one drawback from our standpoint: it was flat instead of being 'raked'; and since our dancers were used to a sloping floor, they found this flatness somewhat disconcerting.

The Coronation Gala was fixed for June the 26th; and we gave a mixed programme of opera and ballet. I remember how the auditorium was decorated: with masses of flowers, and the word INDIA in flowers running along the edge of the balcony. The audience was the acme of elegance: the ladies in magnificent evening gowns with wonderful tiaras and other jewels, and the men in evening clothes or brilliant uniforms. There were a large number of Indian Princes present, and among them we recognized the Aga Khan, whom we knew from Monte

Carlo, where he had been in the habit of attending our rehearsals and had never missed a performance. On this occasion he wore a sumptuous Indian robe and headdress, and looked exceedingly impressive.

To take part in the Coronation Gala was, of course, a great honour for us. But as far as success went, the performance fell somewhat flat. Attention was centred less on the stage than on King George and Queen Mary; and though the company danced as well as ever, the applause was hardly more than polite. Even Nijinsky failed to evoke the usual ecstasy; and the only item that caused much excitement was the exceptionally spirited dance of the Buffoons, led by Rozay, in *Le Pavillon d'Armide*. However, the company understood the reason, and did not mind being thus eclipsed by the spectators.

The real opening of our season took place the next night; and then the success was tremendous, Nijinsky, Karsavina and Bolm coming into their own. It is true that the Polovtsian Dances rather shocked some old ladies by their display of unbridled passion; and later *Schéhérazade* also perturbed the prudish, who objected to the love-making between black slaves and white women. It became clear indeed during this season that the London public preferred our romantic ballets to such works as *Cléopâtre* and *Schéhérazade*; and our greatest successes, accordingly, were *Le Pavillon d'Armide*, *Les Sylphides*, *Le Carnaval* and *Le Spectre de la Rose*. Diaghilev had brought only seven ballets in all to London, and had been very careful in his choice, excluding, for instance, the two ballets by Stravinsky, whose style he supposed too advanced for the English. And the result was that here yet again we conquered the public, whose admiration for the art of Fokine, the perfect *ensemble* and the individual dancers appeared to be boundless. Moreover, the Covent Garden management came forward with the offer of another season in the autumn, which Diaghilev gladly accepted.

★   ★   ★

At the end of July we broke up for our holidays. As the curtain fell on our last performance in London I could not help wondering whether my direction of Diaghilev's company had come to an end. My leave from the *Mariinsky* was all but up, and I must shortly return to my permanent employment. I felt sad at saying goodbye to Diaghilev, but when I reminded him that he would have to find someone to replace me, he said we should discuss this when we met again in St. Petersburg.

Nevertheless, I continued to debate whether to leave the *Mariinsky* or not, and decided against doing so—at least that was my decision till we met again. But the first question Diaghilev asked me when we did meet was whether I wished to stay with him; to which I replied that I did but could not.

'Oh,' said he, 'if that's the case, I shall try and get you a year's leave'—a statement so unexpected that I asked him to repeat it: it seemed incredible that so worrying a problem might be solved so easily. In the meantime I was to go to Warsaw while he himself went to Moscow, each in search of new dancers; for he wished as soon as possible to improve the company by ridding it of the Molotsov troupe, whom he had engaged in Paris *faute de mieux*.

I received my year's leave of absence quite quickly, and called on Diaghilev to tell him it had been granted.

'I've a surprise for you,' said he. 'Madame Kchessinska is to dance with us in London; and as she is at her best in *Le Lac des Cygnes*, I am going to include that in our programme. She could, of course, do *Carnaval* or *Sylphides* and I gather is very keen on *Spectre*. But I shall have to speak to Fokine about it and make sure that he doesn't object.'

'That's all very well,' I said. 'But how can you have the *décor* and costumes for a big ballet like *Le Lac des Cygnes* made in the time?'

Diaghilev had clearly expected this question. 'I've no need to have them made,' he said. 'The management of the Imperial Theatres are selling me their entire Moscow production, designed by Korovine and Golovine! What do you say to that?'

I was delighted; but there was more to come.

'Karsavina cannot rejoin us in the autumn,' he went on. 'She must fulfil her contract with the *Mariinsky*. So I've invited Pavlova to return to us, and she's delighted to do so. I'm thinking of reviving *Giselle* for her benefit, which would make two new ballets, *Lac* and *Giselle*, for London, with two new ballerinas, Kchessinska and Pavlova. But now you must be off to Warsaw. By the time you return I shall have more news to interest you.'

My excursion to Warsaw was well worth while: I found a number of dancers, male and female, both talented and good-looking. And the news I was to be told on my reappearance turned out to be this: that Diaghilev proposed realizing a project he had cherished since the formation of his new company—to exhibit it in St. Petersburg, where he wished the public to see Fokine's ballets and the *décors* of Benois and

The Diaghilev Ballet

Bakst, to hear Stravinsky's music and, above all, to admire Nijinsky, who had by now become a European celebrity. The difficulty was a theatre, and it was a serious one. For none of the Imperial Theatres were available, and the only place to be had was a newly built theatre called the *Narodny Dom* (People's House), which was rather unpopular with the smart public in St. Petersburg. However, Diaghilev's friends thought it better than nothing, and a season in December and January was arranged forthwith. Plans were also begun well ahead for another season in Paris. There was now real hope that *Daphnis et Chloë* would at last be finished; and further items to be included in the programme were another new work, *Le Dieu Bleu*, by the French composer Reynaldo Hahn, and a ballet on the musical poem by Balakirev, *Thamar*.

★　　★　　★

We fully expected, on reaching London in October, to be shrouded in fog, or at least that it would be pouring with rain or blowing half a gale Instead of which the weather, though cool, was calm and sunny, and the people looked perfectly cheerful—a mood which communicated itself to us. The company returned from their holiday well rested; and rehearsals began at once in the Drill Hall in Cheyne Street. On being informed that after our season in London we were to appear in Petersburg, everyone was delighted; and the members of the company who came from Moscow at once enquired whether we were to appear there too. To this Diaghilev gave an evasive answer, and went on to exhort everyone to work hard with *Maestro* Cecchetti. Russian standards were high, he said, and the company must be at its best when appearing in St. Petersburg.

The London public were much excited at the prospect of seeing Pavlova in *Giselle*. During the last few years she had on several occasions appeared in one or other of the leading music-halls, for the most part in solo numbers, and people were anxious to see so great an artist in a proper part. Nor were they disappointed. It was hard to decide in which of the two acts she was more wonderful. In the first she displayed all her immense talent for drama, and in the second her unequalled command of the lyrical. This combination was striking for its rarity; and her success was prodigious. The leading male part was danced by Nijinsky at his best; and thanks to their outstanding performances *Giselle* now became a regular feature in our programmes.

The other 'sensation' of our autumn season in London was the *début* of Kchessinska in *Le Lac des Cygnes*. She was a great exponent of the '*fouetté*'; and her virtuosity created a furore. At the same time she was movingly tender and poetic. Her *pas de deux* with Nijinsky—for which, incidentally, the solo violin was played by Mischa Elman, specially engaged by Diaghilev for the occasion—was truly unforgettable. Diaghilev had reduced *Le Lac des Cygnes* to two acts from its original three, since he considered some of the choreography dull and repetitive; and this entailed an alteration of the scenario. The scene by the lake now constituted the first of these two acts, while the second was set in the palace.

By this time most of us had grown accustomed to our invariable success; but the new arrivals in the company continued to be astonished at it. As during the summer season, so now again we found that what most appealed to English audiences were our romantic ballets. But December was approaching and we began preparing for Petersburg. Diaghilev kept in close touch with his representatives in Russia, and arrangements were duly made for the shipment of our material.

The conclusion of our season in London was truly moving. The public seemed to have taken us to their hearts and bade us farewell with touching warmth. We ourselves took leave of Pavlova and Kchessinska, expecting to see them soon again in Petersburg; and two days later we were in Paris, ready to start on our journey home.

Diaghilev had left London ahead of us, and I reported to him immediately on our arrival in Paris. On seeing him I had quite a shock, he appeared so dejected. Without speaking, he handed me a telegram, which read: '*Narodny Dom* burnt to the ground this morning'. There was nothing I could say. I just stared at him in silence. 'Well,' he sighed, 'it seems I was not destined to show my ballets in Russia now—which is a great pity. For I've a presentiment that after this I shall never be able to show them there at all.'

'That's just your disappointment,' I said. 'You'll surely be able to show them next year if you still wish to.'

But Diaghilev did not answer; and we sat for a time without speaking. Then at last he roused himself and said that apart from anything else the season in St. Petersburg had been meant to provide us with an engagement up to the time of our return to Monte Carlo, and that we must think of some way out of this unforeseen situation. The sad news was then conveyed to the company, whom it greatly distressed.

The Diaghilev Ballet

★   ★   ★

We were thus stranded in Paris in the middle of the winter. I had for some time wished to explore Paris at this time of the year—to study its week-day face, which is the true face of a city; and this sudden lull in our work allowed us some leisure, so that I was able to wander about examining churches and monuments, and to visit exhibitions. Nor was I disappointed. Paris seen in these new circumstances retained all its charm. I saw Diaghilev daily. It took him some little time to get over the Petersburg catastrophe: he kept bróoding over it, and there was always a tone of bitter disappointment in his voice. But his energy, fortunately, was in no wise diminished, and it was never more urgently needed. We had to find employment for the company during January and February, and, thanks to the renown it had by now acquired, he managed to arrange engagements in Berlin, Vienna and Budapest. He also organized some performances at the *Opéra* at the end of December, our first winter appearance in Paris; and though at these we showed none of the new works, but only what had by now become familiar favourites, *Schéhérazade*, *Les Sylphides*, the Polovtsian Dances and *Le Spectre de la Rose*, our success was again considerable. Apart from these ordinary performances, given on December the 24th, the 28th and the 31st, we also took part in a '*soirée de gala*' in honour of French aviation, at which we performed *Le Spectre de la Rose*.

So ended the first year of the Diaghilev Ballet proper, a year that could hardly have been more triumphant, and had been clouded only by the set-back of the Petersburg fire.

CHAPTER FOUR

1912

HAVING seen the New Year in in Paris, we left for Berlin, where on this occasion we were to stay a whole month. We had established our reputation the year before and our reappearance was eagerly awaited. As well as *Cléopâtre*, *Les Sylphides* and *Le Carnaval*, which the Berliners had already seen, we showed some ballets new to them, of which *Schéhérazade*, the Polovtsian Dances and *Le Spectre de la Rose* all made a great impression, whereas *Giselle*, *Le Lac des Cygnes* and *Le Pavillon d'Armide* aroused but little enthusiasm. In general, however, both the public and the press were most eulogistic.

While in Berlin Fokine embarked on the composition of a new ballet. This was Reynaldo Hahn's *Le Dieu Bleu*, the scenario for which had been written by Jean Cocteau. The choreography was inspired chiefly by Siamese dancing, which Fokine had seen when a Siamese company had visited St. Petersburg some years before.

On our way to Vienna we stopped at Dresden, where we gave three performances in a lovely Baroque theatre—and where I was able to gratify my wish to see the famous Raphael Madonna. The company, however, attracted little attention, the Dresden public being too 'provincial' to have heard much yet about Russian ballet-dancing. But Diaghilev had a special reason for this visit to Dresden. He was anxious to further his acquaintance with Jacques Dalcroze, who had a school at Hellerau for 'Eurhythmics', and in whose doctrines Diaghilev was interested. He and Nijinsky paid daily visits to this school. Diaghilev was determined that Nijinsky should imbibe the teaching and apply it to the composition of a ballet. It was now that I learnt, quite by chance, that during the previous spring at Monte Carlo Nijinsky, Bakst and four female dancers had secretly begun rehearsing a ballet to Debussy's *Prélude à l'Après-Midi d'un Faune*. I tried to find out more about it; and was told by the dancers in confidence that the idea of the ballet had

The Diaghilev Ballet

been Diaghilev's own, and that he had been influenced in its conception by Dalcroze, whom he had first met some time before. The reason for the secrecy in which this activity had been shrouded was that, owing to Diaghilev's exclusive interest in Nijinsky, he and Fokine had been getting on less and less well, and that before allowing anyone to know about it Diaghilev wished to make sure that the experiment would succeed. I must confess that I was somewhat disquieted by this discovery, foreseeing what might happen when Fokine learnt of it. But I did not let this perturb me for long, since my leave from the *Mariinsky* would in any case expire in the autumn, when my service with Diaghilev's company would come to an end.

★   ★   ★

Vienna in those days was regarded as one of the great capitals of Europe and an important artistic centre. Diaghilev knew it well and wished the Viennese to see his company and *répertoire* at their best. Not only the Viennese Opera and its orchestra, but even its ballet, were famous throughout Europe; and our programme had to be chosen with particular care. Viennese taste inclined to the traditional and academic. There was no question, therefore, of our showing the Stravinsky ballets. Even *Schéhérazade* was considered risky. However, thanks to its music and the success we had won with it in Paris, there were at least no protests; and the rest of our programme was received with great enthusiasm—Karsavina and Nijinsky conquering Vienna as they had conquered the other capitals of Europe.

While we were in Vienna our ballets were seen by a South American impresario, who immediately offered Diaghilev an engagement for 1913. Diaghilev could not at first decide whether or not to accept, and only did so after protracted negotiations, which obliged him to remain in Vienna, after the rest of us had gone on to Budapest.

Unfortunately, while the company and Diaghilev were thus separated for the first time since its foundation, we encountered a serious *contretemps*. The theatre in which we were to perform, though it possessed a very large auditorium, had only a very small and inconvenient stage. The stage-manager in charge of our scenery declared that it could never be used in so small a space and that we could not give our performances. But all the tickets for the latter had meanwhile been sold; and the management would not hear of cancellation. In Diaghilev's absence responsibility for the administration fell on me. I therefore made a

thorough examination of the stage, and decided that with some adjust-
ment the scenery could be used after all and the performances take
place. But no sooner was this settled than Diaghilev's secretary, a Pole
named Drobetsky, rushed in to say that Nijinsky was ill and could not
dance—an even more serious blow. Nijinsky had never been known to
be ill, and to replace him was practically impossible. But while
Drobetsky, on my instructions, was informing Diaghilev by telephone,
I decided all the same to wait till the next day and see what it brought
forth. Nijinsky, in fact, felt much better the next morning, and by
working all day on the scenery with the *régisseur* of the theatre I
managed to adapt it satisfactorily to the small stage, and overcome the
many technical difficulties involved, so that we were ready for the
performance in the evening—which was a resounding success.

This *régisseur* was a plump middle-aged man with a limp. He wore a
shapeless dressing-gown of indefinite hue and had obviously not shaved
for days; but he possessed a will of iron. Within an hour of the performance he was still sitting on a high stool in the middle of the stage, being
shaved by a barber, while giving last-minute orders to the stage-hands;
and every now and then he would get down off the stool and stump
about with soap-smeared cheeks: a sight to be seen. After the performance, now properly dressed, he limped up to me and placed a large
envelope in my hands, informing me in French that it was a small mark
of gratitude from the management of the theatre for the trouble I had
taken to make the performance possible. When I politely but firmly
declined this tribute, he was quite taken aback. It would have been
interesting to discover what remuneration the management considered
appropriate to my achievement.

Diaghilev was much relieved when he arrived the next day to find
that all was in order. He told me that the contract for South America
had been agreed in principle and that the company were to travel there
next year.

★　　　★　　　★

It was already March by the time we left Budapest for Monte Carlo.
We had a month in which to prepare our new programme. Fokine had
to defer rehearsals of *Le Dieu Bleu* till Karsavina should join us from St.
Petersburg in mid-April. He therefore began by composing *Thamar*.
Diaghilev had several reasons for his choice of *Thamar* for a ballet. In
the first place, the music was already in existence, and Balakirev was a

The Diaghilev Ballet

distinguished composer; in the second he wanted another ballet on a Russian subject; and finally, though he already professed to be tired of Fokine's 'passionate' type of *ensemble*, he knew well enough that the exotic flavour of such works was precisely what most appealed to the public, and that 'Lyovushka' might be depended on to captivate Paris once again with a wonderful *décor*. This time, however, the result fell somewhat short of his expectations—a disappointment due in the main to Fokine. For Fokine was now much disturbed in mind, and this impeded his inspiration. Moreover, the style of his choreography was conditioned by the Caucasian background of *Thamar*, which obliged him to introduce much local colour and traditional Caucasian steps. Choreographically, indeed, the ballet was really a series of variations on one theme and consisted of a single long-drawn dance; and though his handling of the theme was in general masterly, *Thamar* failed to attain the level either of *Schéhérazade* or of the Polovtsian Dances. Nor was Bakst altogether up to his customary form—perhaps because he too was constrained by a necessary adherence to national costume and local colour.

In the meantime Fokine grew more and more depressed and irritable. Not only did he justifiably resent Diaghilev's concentration of all publicity on Nijinsky, but he could not but realize that Diaghilev was no longer attracted by his work. He used often to discuss these developments with me. What puzzled him was Diaghilev's new indifference. Fokine was conscious of having inaugurated a new era in ballet-dancing by his reform of the old classical school. He was convinced that his creative ability was by no means exhausted. Yet Diaghilev, it was clear, thought he had no more to say and was in search of someone to take his place. Moreover, it was clear that his choice had fallen on Nijinsky; whereas neither Fokine, nor I, nor any of us, believed Nijinsky equal to such a task. Our guess was that what Diaghilev saw in Nijinsky was a docile pupil, of whom in time he could make the choreographer he required—hence the experiments on *L'Après-Midi d'un Faune* at Monte Carlo. When in the end Fokine got to know about them, he had a long and heart-searching talk with Diaghilev, after which he decided to quit the company on the expiry of his contract in June. Diaghilev received this decision almost with indifference. But this scarcely surprised me. For I had come by now to realize that he valued his collaborators only as long as, in his view, they had something new to contribute. Once they ceased to fulfil this role he felt no regret in parting with them. And so it was with Fokine.

Our programme for the opening of the Monte Carlo season was to have consisted of *L'Oiseau de Feu, Petrushka* and two acts of *Le Lac des Cygnes*. But since neither Karsavina nor Kchessinska was able to arrive in time, this was altered, and Diaghilev invited Lydia Kyasht, an excellent dancer formerly of the *Mariinsky*, but now permanently established in London, to appear in *L'Oiseau de Feu* and *Le Carnaval*. Kyasht was extremely good-looking and danced delightfully. Though perhaps a little heavy for the rapid leaps of the Firebird, she was perfect as Columbine in *Le Carnaval*. Kchessinska eventually appeared with her accustomed *brio* in *Le Lac des Cygnes*; and Karsavina on her arrival again danced the Doll in *Petrushka*. This, which was new to Monte Carlo and was conducted by Pierre Monteux, met, as in Paris, with warm appreciation.

In the meantime, while Fokine was completing the composition of *Thamar*, Diaghilev was devoting most of his attention to *L'Après-Midi d'un Faune*. A difficulty in this was to cast the part of the chief nymph; and after various attempts to find someone suitable he sent to Moscow for the dancer Nelidova, both for this and for the part of the goddess in *Le Dieu Bleu*.

Now that Fokine had decided to leave the company in June, he grew more and more restless and nervy, till it became almost impossible to work with him. He suspected everyone who stood close to Diaghilev of being his enemy, including even myself. I was obliged by my work to be constantly referring matters to Diaghilev; and my doing so never failed to arouse Fokine's wrath. He even began accusing me of treachery; and a particularly painful incident led to a final quarrel between us. Diaghilev insisted on Nijinsky having a great many rehearsals for *L'Après-Midi*; and however hard I tried to do so, it proved impossible to avoid refusing Fokine the services of the same dancers at the same times. This, however, he chose to regard as a plot against him. He flew into a rage with me; and the quarrel that ensued was the end of our friendship, a close friendship of many years. I was so much upset that I asked Diaghilev to relieve me of my duties; and though he, of course, refused, he agreed to provide me with an assistant, in the person of N. Semenov, the *régisseur* from Moscow; and this relieved me of at least some of my responsibilities.

Although *L'Après-Midi* only lasts for eight minutes, its composition required an inordinate number of exceedingly strenuous rehearsals. Its choreography was not choreography as we understood the term. The dancers merely moved rhythmically to the music and then stopped in attitudes, which they held. Nijinsky's aim was, as it were, to set in motion an archaic Greek bas-relief, and to produce this effect he made the dancers move with bent knees and feet placed flat on the ground heel first (thereby reversing the classical rule). They had also to keep their heads in profile while still making their bodies face the audience, and to hold their arms rigid in various angular positions. All this required a great deal of practice and took up much time. Debussy's impressionistic music did nothing to facilitate such primitive evolutions; and the dancers dreaded the monotony and fatigue of these rehearsals. I seldom attended them, since Diaghilev always watched them himself, and my presence at them was not required.

As soon as Fokine had finished first *Thamar* and then *Le Dieu Bleu*, he returned to *Daphnis et Chloë*. Diaghilev, absorbed as he was in *L'Après-Midi*, showed little interest in *Daphnis*, and it was my impression that he would have abandoned it altogether, but that he did not wish to offend Ravel and that the scenery and costumes were now ready and singers for the accompanying chorus engaged. As it was, he deferred its production to the very end of the Paris season, on the pretext that Fokine was unlikely to complete it sooner; and this in itself militated against its success.

We left Monte Carlo on May the 5th. It was a warm sunny morning; and we were seen off at the station by General Bezobrazov, dressed in a white summer suit and carrying a light cane. As the train moved off he continued waving to us, till we could no longer see his massive figure on the platform; and that was in fact the last we saw of him. For soon after, on falling ill, he failed to recover, but died quite peacefully, still at Monte Carlo—the first member of the Diaghilev committee to depart this life.

★   ★   ★

The season that now opened in Paris was our fourth. During it we were to give sixteen performances, again at the *Châtelet*. It was to start on May the 13th, a date which, considering how intensely superstitious Diaghilev was, appeared, oddly enough, to perturb him not at all. We opened with one new ballet and three of our most popular old ones (*L'Oiseau de Feu*, the Polovtsian Dances and *Le Spectre de la Rose*). The new ballet was *Le Dieu Bleu*, of whose quality Diaghilev was by no means sure. He was doubtful in particular about Reynaldo Hahn's music, which he had been obliged to accept for reasons of policy. The other ingredients were the choreography by Fokine; the scenery and costumes by Bakst; and the scenario by Cocteau. These all had their merits. Yet, as a whole, the ballet was dull and ineffective, and not even the dancing of Nijinsky and Karsavina, Nelidova and Frohman could endow it with much life.

Our second programme included *Thamar*, and for some reason this too was pronounced by Paris to be an indifferent work. To my mind the criticisms levelled at it were quite unjustified. Balakirev's beautiful score was inspired by a poem of Lermontov, and both are highly dramatic. According to legend, Tamara, the Queen of Georgia, used to entice wandering travellers into her castle, where she could first seduce and then murder them, casting their bodies into the River Terek. In the parts of the Queen and the traveller Karsavina and Bolm were extremely effective. So were the *ensemble* dances such as the 'Lezginka'. *Thamar* was always to remain in Diaghilev's *répertoire*, and though it failed, perhaps, to reach the level of *Schéhérazade*, it was always appreciated by connoisseurs.

However that may be, neither *Le Dieu Bleu* nor *Thamar* had any great success. It remained for us to show the public *L'Après-Midi d'un Faune*. From the day of our arrival Diaghilev began preparing opinion for its reception. Friends of his would be brought to all Nijinsky's rehearsals and invited to admire his original choreography, after which they would broadcast news of it all over Paris. The result was that everyone was soon talking about it. Parisians are always eager for what is new and unusual, and were now all agog to see this sensational work, for which an unprecedented success was freely predicted. At the rehearsals attended by Diaghilev's friends Nijinsky never did more than 'walk through' his own part. It was not, consequently, until just before the dress rehearsal, when he first played it in detail, that anyone had a chance to see what it consisted of; and everyone was then astounded at his final pose, when the faun is left with the nymph's scarf, pointing out to Diaghilev that it was highly indecent, and warning him that it would create a scandal. Diaghilev, however, refused to alter it; and at the *répétition générale* Nijinsky repeated it.

This as usual was a notable function attended by all Diaghilev's friends and supporters, as well, of course, as the press. Among the former was the sculptor Rodin, very old and helpless, leaning for support on Diaghilev's arm and deeply appreciative of Nijinsky's performance.

The Diaghilev Ballet

This dress rehearsal was followed by a reception in the *foyer*; and no effort was neglected to nurse opinion and encourage a favourable reaction to *L'Après-Midi*.

The first night was on May the 29th. Our other first nights had been rather dull; but on this occasion the audience were electrified from the start. The ballet was watched with intense interest, and at the end one half of the spectators broke into frantic applause, and the other into equally frantic protests. Diaghilev was visibly put out; for, although forewarned by his friends, he had scarcely expected so violent a reaction. Nor had any of his productions previously met with a hostile reception. He appeared on the stage flushed and agitated—when suddenly we heard shouts of '*Bis, bis!*' from the auditorium, which quite drowned the hissing of the objectors. Diaghilev seized on this demonstration to order a repetition of the performance. This took place in a somewhat calmer atmosphere; and though by the end opinion was still of course divided, the excitement had noticeably abated.

Nijinsky was no less embarrassed than Diaghilev. He had certainly not expected his first composition to provoke any such commotion. Nor, unfortunately, was this all. On the following day half the press tore Diaghilev to pieces, accusing him of immorality and protesting at Nijinsky's final pose; and though Nijinsky was warmly praised by the other half, both for his choreography and his performance, and the whole controversy provided the ballet with much publicity, Diaghilev was far from being pleased with what had happened and felt it his duty somehow to defend himself. His defence was in fact undertaken by Rodin, who wrote a long article in *Le Matin* on the subject; and in subsequent performances to avoid further criticism the offending pose was somewhat modified.

The subject of *L'Après-Midi* is very simple. Some nymphs come to bathe in a spring, unaware that they are being watched by a faun. When he approaches them, they run off in alarm and one of them drops her veil. The faun picks it up, carries it up to his lair on a rock, and reclines on it in amorous delight. The whole action takes place right at the front of the stage, the figures moving not only in a single plane, but also on one level—except for a wild leap by the faun before he regains his lair at the end. The scene, by Bakst, represented a tree-fringed lake; and the nymphs wore pleated Greek tunics of thin gauze, with stylized gilt wigs. In spite of its equivocal reception *L'Après-Midi* became in the end an established success. No-one could deny either its originality or its beauty, though choreographically it was too specialized to form anything but a dead end.

It was in this agitated atmosphere that Fokine completed the composition of *Daphnis et Chloë*. As it became clear that he would not have it ready by the date first fixed for the opening performance, this was postponed, to the annoyance of Ravel, who did not at all relish the idea of having *Daphnis et Chloë* first shown at the tail-end of our season. This ballet, in fact, deserved better treatment than it received—for it had everything to recommend it: a distinguished (if in places somewhat protracted) score; a delightful setting, in three scenes, by Bakst; protagonists of an affecting simplicity in Nijinsky and Karsavina; and choreography devised by Fokine with all his accustomed skill, the *finale* culminating as usual in a highly effective climax. *Daphnis et Chloë* won, indeed, a deserved success. But this would undoubtedly have been much greater if it had first been given earlier in our season, and if Diaghilev from the beginning had devoted greater attention to it.

On leaving Paris at the end of the season, I must confess I felt somewhat depressed. The failure of *Le Dieu Bleu*; Diaghilev's neglect of *Daphnis et Chloë*; the scandal over *L'Après-Midi*; each in its way was perturbing. Our earlier triumphs had spoilt us, moreover; and though this year, as before, the theatre was always packed, I now took that for granted and noticed only that the atmosphere had somehow been poisoned by the *Après-Midi* incident. As for Diaghilev, he was faced with a momentous choice: to let Fokine go and risk the absence of a competent choreographer; or to keep him and renounce his choreographic aspirations for Nijinsky. He decided to let Fokine go, in the firm belief that Nijinsky was capable of higher and more important flights than *L'Après-Midi d'un Faune*.

★   ★   ★

After the storms of this season in Paris, London seemed to us a haven of peace. Diaghilev was able to rest and regain his calm; and the company were no longer exhausted by perpetual rehearsals. Diaghilev decided *not* to show *L'Après-Midi* in London, for fear of compromising his reputation. The new items in our programme were to be *L'Oiseau de Feu*. *Thamar* and *Narcisse*. For Russian music was now becoming popular in London, and all these three ballets were by Russian composers. Till

Plate V

MATHILDE KCHESSINSKA

then, it is true, Diaghilev had refrained from treating London to a score by Stravinsky. Now, however, he thought the time had come to venture *L'Oiseau de Feu*. Our season was to be given at Covent Garden again, and this time, having observed that what most interested spectators in London was less the ballets than the individual performers, Diaghilev decided to employ only the permanent members of his company, who were already known and liked, rather than to invite star dancers from elsewhere.

L'Oiseau de Feu made as deep an impression on London as it had on Paris two years before. Karsavina in particular was immensely admired in what was regarded as perhaps her finest part. Stravinsky's music, moreover, was extremely well received, and *L'Oiseau de Feu* was to remain a favourite ballet in London for years to come. Hardly less popular was *Thamar*. Thomas Beecham, who was conducting for us again, was an admirer of Balakirev and particularly liked it. Finally, even *Narcisse* had more success here than in Paris.

Towards the middle of the London season, his contract having expired, Fokine left the company. His relations with Diaghilev had gone from bad to worse, and I imagine that their parting was cold in the extreme. In the course of his collaboration with our company he had composed no less than fourteen ballets, many of which became famous all over Europe and are still included in the *répertoires* of various organizations. He left us now deeply wounded, and received no consideration whatever from Diaghilev. I should have liked to convey my regret and sympathy to him; but since our quarrel in Monte Carlo we had become completely estranged and had never even spoken. In spite of his difficult nature, the company and I myself liked and respected him. Moreover he was in his prime, and if he could have remained with Diaghilev, he would, I am sure, have created many other beautiful works. But Diaghilev was 'in a hurry to live'. He was looking ahead towards fresh currents in choreography, and rather than rely on Fokine's experience he preferred to guide Nijinsky in his lack of it. I did not, personally, believe in Nijinsky, and was sad to witness (with Fokine's departure) the end of a glorious period in the history of Russian dancing.

As soon as Fokine had left, I asked Diaghilev whom he wished to take charge of rehearsals—to which he unhesitatingly replied that they would now be *my* responsibility. This did not suit my plans at all, since at the end of the London season I intended returning to Petersburg for

good. I therefore protested energetically; but Diaghilev would not hear
of a refusal. Apart from Fokine, he said, I was the only person who
knew the whole *répertoire* and was also thoroughly acquainted with every
member of the company. Besides, we still had *Narcisse* to put on; and
Fokine had not finished rehearsing it again. So I was forced to give in;
and the next day Diaghilev appeared at the Drill Hall in Cheyne
Street and announced to the company that, in view of Fokine's departure, from then on I would take charge of all rehearsals. This I in
fact did, fulfilling the functions of 'rehearsal-master' throughout the
career of the Diaghilev Ballet, with all the choreographers who
succeeded Fokine.

At the end of this, the first rehearsal that I directed, Diaghilev took
me back to his hotel with him, and expatiated on the role of a ballet
régisseur. It was similar, he suggested, to that of the conductor of an
orchestra. Just as the latter conducts the performance of orchestral
works by various composers, so the *régisseur* has to conduct ballets composed by various choreographers. Both must bring to this conducting
all the talent and knowledge they can command. The only difference
between them is that whereas the conductor of an orchestra remains
with his musicians during performances, a ballet *régisseur* has in the end
to leave his dancers to their own devices; and that whereas the conductor has a score before him, the *régisseur* must rely on his memory.
The task of the *régisseur* is therefore harder than that of the conductor.
. . . I was tired after our long rehearsal and listened to all this rather
absent-mindedly. I was bound, however, to agree.

As a matter of fact I began on my new duties quite successfully. With
the help of the company I managed to resuscitate the rest of *Narcisse*; it
was the last item on our London programme; and the other ballets
presented no problem. The season was in fact nearing its end, and
everyone was looking forward to a holiday, when Diaghilev suddenly
announced that we were to go to Deauville for some performances in
August—news which, except to addicts of sea bathing, was scarcely
very welcome.

★   ★   ★

Deauville on the coast of Normandy had recently been opened as a new
fashionable seaside resort. As is usual in such places, it was provided
with a casino, next to which was a theatre. The management were bent
on making the first season particularly glamorous and had spared no

expense in attracting all the celebrities of the theatrical world. We were to give five performances; but as the stage was too small for any of our large productions, we had to confine ourselves to ballets such as *Les Sylphides*, *Le Carnaval* and the Polovtsian Dances, which required a minimum of *décor*. From Diaghilev's point of view, however, the visit to Deauville turned out exceedingly fortunate. It gave him an opportunity of cultivating Gabriel Astruc, recently appointed director of the new *Théâtre des Champs-Élysées* in Paris, which was to open in the spring of 1913. Astruc was determined to engage Diaghilev's ballet for the occasion, and knowing that the management of the *Opéra* were competitors, offered Diaghilev a sum so colossal that Diaghilev himself thought Astruc must be crazy and would be certain to lose on the transaction. However, it was reassuring to have engagements in both Paris and London settled for the following spring; and since he had meanwhile also arranged a winter tour in Germany and Austria, Diaghilev could now take his usual Venetian holiday in peace of mind. The company were to reassemble two months later in Cologne, in preparation for their German tour. Diaghilev and I were to meet again in September in St. Petersburg.

★   ★   ★

I was gradually getting used to the prospect of ceasing to work for Diaghilev; and in September I resumed my duties at the *Mariinsky*. But very soon after his reappearance in St. Petersburg he sent for me as usual and began at once discussing his plans for the coming year. There was first of all the season in Paris to consider. With Fokine out of the company it presented great problems. Diaghilev realized that he could not as yet entirely depend on Nijinsky as a choreographer. Yet it was essential to show some new work at the *Champs-Élysées* in the spring. A new ballet had been ordered from Stravinsky: *Le Sacre du Printemps*; but Diaghilev feared that Nijinsky might not be able to cope with it on his own. In any case, to bolster up the coming season he thought he would return to a mixed programme of ballet and opera and again invite Chaliapine. Astruc welcomed the idea of *Boris* and *Ivan the Terrible*, and Diaghilev wished to add a third opera in which Chaliapine should also sing: Moussorgsky's *Khovanshchina*. In addition to *Le Sacre du Printemps* he had in mind two other ballets: *Jeux* by Debussy, again with choreography by Nijinsky, and *La Tragédie de Salomé* by Florent Schmidt, which one of Fokine's pupils, Romanov, was to be asked to arrange.

73

The Diaghilev Ballet

The interest of Paris in the season was to be concentrated on Stravinsky's music, Nijinsky's choreography and Chaliapine's singing.

Times had changed since the early days of Diaghilev's committee meetings. These took place but very rarely now. General Bezobrazov was no more; Fokine had left us; Bakst and Stravinsky were both abroad. Besides, Diaghilev no longer felt much need for such meetings. He had become accustomed to making up his mind independently. One day, however, when calling on him at his flat, I was introduced to a new personage in Baron D. T. Gunzburg, and was informed that from then on he would take an intimate part in Diaghilev's enterprise. I gathered that the Baron was a man of both substance and leisure, whom Diaghilev had known for years, and that he was much interested in the arts and was prepared to help us both materially and otherwise—such help being precisely what Diaghilev was at the moment in need of. I also gathered that he had been asked to meet me so that both he and Diaghilev might tackle me on the subject of my further employment with the company. I said that I could not possibly join them again without formal permission from the *Mariinsky*; to which Diaghilev replied that he was certain no further leave would be granted. At the same time he was at a loss, he said, to understand why I should not leave the *Mariinsky* and attach myself to him for good. He was ready to make me a very handsome offer, which would compensate me for the loss of a pension from the Imperial Theatres on retirement. He took this to be one of the reasons for my reluctance—and up to a point he was right, since it was, in fact, an important consideration from my point of view. For by then I had come to occupy quite a solid position at the *Mariinsky*; and my Petersburg friends had advised me against resigning. But Diaghilev exerted all his powers of persuasion, insisting that, now Fokine had departed, it was essential to the company's future that I should take charge of it; and in the end my resolve was shaken and I yielded—even, on his insistence, signing a contract, which he placed before me then and there. No sooner had I done so, however, than I began to regret my rashness. I became nearly unhinged by all this argument and my doubts, and flew back to Diaghilev, protesting that I had made a mistake and could not fulfil my part of the bargain. I shall never forget his astonishment and annoyance. I do not remember what either of us said: my one wish was to get away from him. It took me days to recover my equanimity; and by that time Diaghilev had left St. Petersburg and gone abroad.

74

I then resumed my regular routine, my quiet and rather uneventful existence. But before long I began to realize that, compared with my feverish activity of the last few years, it was unbelievably dull; and my doubts vanished away. I called on Svetlov, who was acting as Diaghilev's representative in St. Petersburg, and asked him to send Diaghilev a telegram, saying that if he still wanted me, I would stand by my contract. The reply arrived the next day: 'Agree. Make Grigoriev come at once to Berlin.'

My fate was thus sealed. I sent in my resignation and made all my final arrangements for departure. The day before I left I went for the last time to the *Mariinsky*, and standing quite alone on the stage bade it goodbye. I was never to see it—that beloved stage—again.

★   ★   ★

Meanwhile the company, as arranged, had reassembled in Cologne for its autumn tour, which was to start in Germany. In my absence Diaghilev had entrusted rehearsals to Bolm and general administration to Semenov. But as neither had had much previous experience, various difficulties had arisen: the dancers were discontented, and so was Diaghilev himself. This unsatisfactory state of affairs continued for a month, at the end of which Diaghilev received my telegram; and it was for this reason that he had replied so promptly. Incidentally, during the whole twenty years' existence of the Diaghilev Ballet I was parted from the company only during this one short period—for a single month and no more.

Fokine being no longer with us, the entire management of the company now devolved on me, though Diaghilev was of course always at hand and closely supervised the artistic side of the enterprise. One innovation I found to have been introduced on my return was the abolition in certain cases of coloured tights: whenever till then a dancer had appeared as a negro, he had had to wear black or brown tights; but Diaghilev now gave orders that for such parts the dancers' arms and legs were to be given the required colour by make-up, and though some of them protested, nothing would dissuade him. Another new experiment was the promotion of young and gifted dancers from the *corps de ballet* to solo parts. In the course of its four years' existence some members of the company had made great progress and were now well able to take on important roles; and this led to the emergence of a number of dancers who later became well known.

The Diaghilev Ballet

★   ★   ★

One of the first people I met on my arrival in Berlin was *Maestro* Cecchetti. I was devoted to the old man; and we embraced each other warmly. He greeted me by saying in his peculiar Russian that now the 'Master of the house' was back, order would be restored. The company all gave me a friendly welcome too; and altogether I felt happy to have returned to them, except that I dreaded having to face Diaghilev. To my great relief our meeting was perfectly easy: he behaved exactly as if nothing had happened. After saying that he was glad to see me, and asking after my wife and about our journey, he passed on at once to current business; and the Petersburg incident was never so much as mentioned.

Our performances in Berlin were to be given in the *Kroll* Theatre; and we were informed that the Kaiser would be present on the first night. Diaghilev was somewhat perturbed, since some of the scenery, including the back-cloth for *Cléopâtre* had not arrived; and it was precisely *Cléopâtre* that the Kaiser most wished to see. Fortunately the rest of this *décor* had all turned up; so at my suggestion we slightly altered the lighting, which enabled us to use a plain black cloth behind the colonnade. The theatre on the first night was filled with the Imperial entourage and the *beau monde* of Berlin. The Kaiser highly approved of the performance and sent for Diaghilev, to whom he expressed his satisfaction, especially with *Cléopâtre*, about which he asked a great many questions. The Kaiser's patronage much enhanced the prestige of our season, and we did good business. Diaghilev thought he might now venture to show the Stravinsky ballets. But *Cléopâtre* and the Polovtsian Dances remained the most popular. *L'Après-Midi*, on the other hand, fell completely flat; and this hurt Nijinsky's feelings. However, he was now in the throes of composing *Le Sacre du Printemps*, which was to be his second ballet. He was as helpless as a child and relied entirely on suggestions from Diaghilev and Stravinsky. It was obvious that to bring it off he would again require innumerable rehearsals.

We acquired a new friend in Berlin in the person of Count Harry von Kessler. He and the poet Hugo von Hofmannsthal offered to write a ballet for Nijinsky on the theme of Joseph and Potiphar's wife. The idea appealed to Diaghilev; and they decided all three to ask Richard Strauss to compose the music.

From Berlin we went to Budapest, to give a few performances at the

76

State Theatre; and there Diaghilev again met the South American impresario, Ciacchi by name, who had made us the tentative offer of a tour the year before. This offer was now definite, so Diaghilev told me: the company would be going to South America the next autumn, with Baron Gunzburg in charge. I asked him why he was not going himself. 'Oh, you know I dislike the sea,' he replied, 'and besides, South America doesn't interest me as a country.'

CHAPTER FIVE

⦁ 1913

THE New Year found us in Vienna, where we were to stay a fortnight or so. *Thamar*, in which Paris had found so little of interest when it was first produced, was now proving a favourite whenever we showed it; whereas *L'Après-Midi*, again in Vienna, had no success whatever. One of our most applauded items was no more than a 'turn': a classical *pas de deux* to music by Tchaikovsky, called variously *L'Oiseau d'Or*, *L'Oiseau Bleu* or *La Princesse Enchantée*, in which Nijinsky danced superbly. Whoever was fortunate enough to see him dance this *pas de deux* must surely remember it for ever.

We had rather an unpleasant experience in Vienna. Diaghilev had supposed that by now it would be safe to show *Petrushka* there, since after all Vienna was supposed to be musically advanced. At the first orchestra rehearsal, however, the musicians, despite Stravinsky's presence, pronounced the music 'dirty' (whatever this may have meant) and declared they would not play it: it should receive no hearing, they said, within the sacred walls of the Vienna Opera! What had happened was soon known all over the city, and did us no good. We managed indeed to perform *Petrushka*, but only twice; and on each occasion the players duly tried their hand at sabotage.

In the meantime we devoted every spare moment to the rehearsals of *Le Sacre*. The music once again was inconceivably difficult, full of constantly changing rhythms; and even with Stravinsky's anxious assistance Nijinsky's composition progressed very slowly indeed. Stravinsky, moreover, would not, we found, be able to stay with us much longer. Diaghilev therefore began looking for someone else to help with the choreography; and since this was based largely on 'Eurhythmics', he asked Dalcroze to recommend one of his pupils for the purpose. Dalcroze sent us Marie Rambert; and the particular duties she was charged with were, firstly, to help Nijinsky and the dancers in disentangling the various rhythms of the music, and, secondly, to beat time for the dancers in the more complicated passages of the score for which Nijinsky had already composed their movements.

Owing to the unpleasantness over *Petrushka* and the cool reception of *L'Après-Midi*, Diaghilev was much disappointed with Vienna. The visit had one agreeable result for him, however—a meeting with Strauss, who duly undertook to write the music for the ballet on 'Joseph'.

★ ★ ★

Nijinsky now declared that he could not possibly continue composing *Le Sacre* while at the same time travelling from place to place and dancing. But the alternative for Diaghilev was to refuse further engagements for the time being and retain the company solely for rehearsals—which was very expensive. However, there was nothing else for it; and so, after finishing our season in Vienna, and visiting one or two German towns on the way, we arrived in London six weeks before we were due to start performing. Thomas Beecham very generously put the Aldwych Theatre at our disposal; and here we duly concentrated on the completion of *Le Sacre*.

This ballet had first been thought of by the painter Roerich, who had worked out the scenario with Stravinsky. It was in two scenes, but had no real plot, the action representing merely a series of primitive rites. With one exception there were no individual dances, but only big *ensembles*. Stravinsky's music was indeed quite unsuitable for dancing; but this troubled neither Diaghilev nor Nijinsky, whose aim was to present only a succession of rhythmically moving groups. Yet even with so modest a design they experienced no little difficulty in adapting the action to the music; and Stravinsky had to be telegraphed for more than once. Owing chiefly to Nijinsky's inexperience we were repeatedly 'stuck'; and I often felt sure both that the ballet would never be finished and that Diaghilev regretted ever having embarked on it. Mercifully our free weeks in London allowed us to concentrate our entire attention on it; and *Le Sacre* was in fact more or less ready by the time our performances were due to start again.

This time we were to perform in London only for a fortnight, during which we were to show *Petrushka* and *L'Après-Midi* for the first time in England. It was Diaghilev's calculation that they would serve to familiarize the public with Stravinsky's music and acquaint it with

PLATE VI

TAMARA KARSAVINA

Nijinsky's choreography, and so prepare it for *Le Sacre* and *Jeux*, which he intended including in his summer season. Fortunately both *Petrushka* and *L'Après-Midi* were well received—unlike *Le Dieu Bleu*, which here again failed to make any great impression. So on the whole we were pleased with our short London season; at the end of which the company proceeded to Monte Carlo, while Diaghilev went on a visit to Petersburg and Moscow.

★   ★   ★

Our main concern on arrival at Monte Carlo was to give Nijinsky a chance of putting the finishing touches to *Le Sacre* and starting on the composition of *Jeux*. Even at this stage the rehearsals of the former were far from easy. The company heartily disliked them, calling them arithmetic classes, because owing to the total absence of tune in the music, the dancers had to time their movements by counting the bars. They also saw little point in Nijinsky's composition, which consisted almost entirely of rhythmical stamping without any other movement. It was my delicate duty to settle differences, and keep the peace, between the choreographer and the company; and I did my best to maintain morale by rehearsing some of the old Fokine ballets by way of relief. When on his return Diaghilev enquired about *Le Sacre* and learnt of its enormous unpopularity, he merely remarked that it was an excellent sign. It proved the composition to be strikingly original.

He had contrived while in Petersburg to obtain leave for two important dancers, Liudmila Schollar and Boris Romanov, to join us. The latter, as I have mentioned, was a pupil of Fokine's and was to compose the choreography for *La Tragédie de Salomé*. Diaghilev had also engaged another choreographer, Gorsky, from Moscow, who on his arrival was to work on a new ballet, *The Red Masks*, by Tchérépnine. These arrangements were evidence of forethought in Diaghilev. It appeared that he too was beginning to realize that Nijinsky could not be relied on to produce more than one ballet a year!

Nevertheless Nijinsky was now due to tackle *Jeux*. He had not done so before because we had been awaiting the arrival of Karsavina and Schollar, who were to partner him in it. The ballet was to be based on the game of lawn tennis; and though, with only three dancers, it seemed simple and was quite short, Nijinsky was again baffled by Debussy's score. He was also exhausted by the rehearsals of *Le Sacre*, and seemed devoid of energy; while Diaghilev, for his part, was entirely occupied with arrangements for Paris. *Jeux*, accordingly, made little progress. But despite these back-stage preoccupations, our Monte Carlo season followed its usual satisfactory course.

★   ★   ★

The *Théâtre des Champs-Élysées*, where we were to perform on this occasion, had only recently finished building. Its architecture was modern in style, and it was provided inside with all the latest adjuncts. We arrived a week before the opening of our season, and not without difficulty found lodgings in the surrounding well-to-do quarter.

This was to be Diaghilev's fifth season in Paris. Yet it was the first during which he had to rely all but entirely on his own company, since our only 'guests' were Sophie Fedorova and Liudmila Schollar. The singers for the operas, on the other hand, were all of course from the Imperial Theatres. But as they were unable to reach Paris before May the 18th, our season was to start, three days earlier, with ballet performances. It had been announced that we should give *Jeux*, as a new work, on the first night. But *Jeux* was still unfinished when we arrived in Paris. Diaghilev, on realizing this, was extremely put out, and appearing at a rehearsal, insisted that it should be completed without more ado. Unfortunately it was one of Nijinsky's bad days. He stood in the middle of the practice-room with his mind an obvious blank. I felt that the situation was desperate, and suggested a 'run-through' of what had been composed, in the hope of stimulating his invention. This luckily produced the desired effect; and the choreography of *Jeux* was duly completed.

The opening of the *Théâtre des Champs-Élysées* was a great occasion, which attracted a distinguished audience anxious to see both the new building and the new Debussy-Nijinsky ballet. *Jeux* had no story to speak of. Two girls, playing tennis, lose a ball and run about the stage in search of it. They are joined by a young man; on which they forget the ball and start playing and dancing with him till another ball, thrown to them from the wings, interrupts them and they run off. *Jeux* had some quite good choreographic ideas in it. If he had had more time in which to work on it, Nijinsky might well have made something of it; but as it was, it was helpless and immature. The public were puzzled by the angularity of the dancers' gestures; they were inclined both to laugh at this departure from the classical canon and to pity the per-

82

formers for having to execute such ugly movements. The scenery, by
Bakst, passed all but unremarked, and nothing was really enjoyed but
Debussy's music, conducted by Pierre Monteux. Diaghilev, who had
hoped for a better reception, was much disappointed. But he could not
afford to dwell on this reverse, having his hands more than full with the
coming opera performances and the production of *Le Sacre*.

On May the 22nd *Boris Godounov* was performed in superb scenery and
costumes brought from St. Petersburg. The *mise en scène* by Sanine, the
régisseur of the *Mariinsky*, could not have been more effective; and as for
Chaliapine, his genius was then at its height.

A week later, on May the 29th, we came at last to the first night of
Le Sacre du Printemps. Since none of our 'stars'—Karsavina, Nijinsky and
Bolm—were taking part in this ballet, which, as I have remarked, consisted almost entirely of *ensembles*, Diaghilev made up the evening's programme with *Les Sylphides*, *Le Spectre* and the Polovtsian Dances, hoping
by thus showing each of them in one or more favourite roles to ensure
the success of the performance as a whole. For he clearly had misgivings
about the reception of Stravinsky's music and warned us that there
might be a demonstration against it. He entreated the dancers, if so, to
keep calm and carry on, and asked Monteux on no account to let the
orchestra cease playing. 'Whatever happens,' he said, 'the ballet must
be performed to the end.'

His fears were well founded. We began with *Les Sylphides*. Then, after
the first interval the curtain rose on *Le Sacre*, and not many minutes
passed before a section of the audience began shouting its indignation;
on which the rest retaliated with loud appeals for order. The hubbub
soon became deafening; but the dancers went on, and so did the
orchestra, though scarcely a note of the music could be heard. The
shouting continued even during the change of scene, for which music
was provided; and now actual fighting broke out among some of the
spectators; yet even this did not deter Monteux from persisting with
the performance. Diaghilev, who was with us on the stage, was extremely agitated; and so was Stravinsky. The dancers, on the other
hand, were quite unmoved and even amused by this unprecedented
commotion. As for Nijinsky, he stood silent in the wings. Although he
realized that the demonstration was directed rather against the music
than against his choreography, it upset him that for the second time
a work of his should be so rowdily received. Diaghilev tried every
device he could think of to calm the audience, keeping the lights up

in the auditorium as long as possible so that the police, who had been called in, could pick out and eject some of the worst offenders. But no sooner were the lights lowered again for the second scene than pandemonium burst out afresh, and then continued till the ballet came to an end.

The dancers, rather naturally, were reluctant to take their curtain calls; and I purposely prolonged the next interval so as to give the excitement the more time to subside. When the curtain next rose, on *Le Spectre*, quiet was in fact restored; and this ever-delightful ballet evoked the usual enthusiastic response.

We were in a way surprised that *Le Sacre* should have met with such a hostile reception—and that, whatever might be thought of the music, the choreography should not have attracted more notice. For this, despite its limitations, was a serious attempt at the creation of something new, and was at least highly dynamic and original. Diaghilev himself regarded it as an important work; but now realized that the time had not yet come for a due appreciation of either Stravinsky's score or Nijinsky's choreographic conception. As for the execution of *Le Sacre* by the dancers, it was beyond praise. The countless rehearsals had in fact borne fruit; and the company had triumphantly overcome all the difficulties of the score. Maria Piltz, who danced the one solo part, of the sacrificial victim, was truly excellent, and her performance was much admired by everyone, including Diaghilev.

But rather than repine at the fate of *Le Sacre*, we had now to give all our attention to our next production, fixed for June the 5th, when Moussorgsky's opera *Khovanshchina* was to be sung for the first time in Paris. Moussorgsky died before orchestrating this composition, which was accordingly completed by Rimsky-Korsakov. Diaghilev, however, did not entirely approve of Rimsky's work on it, and for this production invited Stravinsky and Ravel to recast some passages. Chaliapine was to sing the chief male part; and the chorus, which included some of the finest basses in Russia, was to be reinforced by a number of French singers. Émile Cooper was to conduct, and the production was again in the hands of Sanine; the dances—Persian in character—had been composed by Bolm, and the *décor* designed by the painter Fedorovsky. *Khovanshchina*, as the product of so much combined talent, could scarcely fail to achieve an outstanding success; nor did it; and the encouragement this afforded us overlaid the distress of our experience with *Le Sacre*.

There now remained only one further first night, that of *La Tragédie de Salomé*, which was to take place on June the 12th. As I have mentioned, the music for this was by Florent Schmidt and the choreography by Fokine's pupil Romanov. The *décor* was by Soudeikine; and the title-role was danced by Karsavina. But this ballet was a failure, the chief reasons, to my mind, being a confused scenario and uninteresting scenery; for neither the music nor the choreography was by any means inferior. Thus none of the three new ballets of our fifth season in Paris was approved of either by the public or by the press. We appeared indeed to have reached an *impasse* and to have lost our way. When Diaghilev parted from Fokine and embarked on a new course in choreography, he hoped that the Paris public would acclaim it. But the precise opposite occurred; and after the fiasco of *Le Sacre* Diaghilev realized he had fallen out of step with current taste and must again alter direction.

The season ended on June the 17th, after which, not without relief, we exchanged the frenzies of Paris for the peace and quiet of London.

★   ★   ★

This summer we were to appear at the Theatre Royal, Drury Lane. The season was again sponsored by Sir Joseph Beecham. Neither Chaliapine nor any Russian opera had ever before been heard in London; and rumours of our triumphs in Paris had provoked the most eager expectations. In Fokine's absence Diaghilev wisely laid greater emphasis on the operas than on the ballets; for it was now clear that had he failed to do so also in Paris, we might well have met with disaster. Both *Boris* and *Khovanshchina*, with Chaliapine, conducted in turn by Cooper and Thomas Beecham, were resounding successes; and as the ballet performances alternated with the operas, and the London public had a predilection for the works of Fokine, they too were invariably well received. It is true that with the exception of *L'Après-Midi*, which was admired, Nijinsky's ballets were regarded chiefly as curiosities. Nevertheless we played to full houses; and Karsavina, Nijinsky and Bolm, as well as various other members of the company, were all as ardently applauded as ever. What was more, Sir Joseph Beecham offered to back yet another season of opera and ballet in the summer of 1914. Nor was he deterred by the huge estimate of expenditure with which Diaghilev presented him.

The Diaghilev Ballet

★   ★   ★

While we were still in Paris Diaghilev had told me that we were to leave for South America in August. This news had a mixed reception by the company. Whereas some of the dancers were excited by the prospect of a long sea voyage, others were alarmed and asked Diaghilev to release them from their contracts. He and I discussed this problem privately, and came to the conclusion that we might as well agree. In this connection he told me that we had a prospective recruit, in the person of a young Austrian or Hungarian girl, who was eager to join us. When I asked if she could dance, he replied, 'Yes—a little.' Not approving of amateurs I was rather against accepting her; but for some unknown reason Diaghilev said that in this case he could not refuse. So a day or two later this girl appeared at rehearsal. Her name was Mademoiselle de Pulska.

In the end about twelve of the company remained behind, in addition to *Maestro* Cecchetti and of course Diaghilev himself. Moreover, Pierre Monteux was replaced by a new conductor, René Baton. Foreseeing that I should be faced with many teasing responsibilities, what most perturbed me was the absence of Diaghilev himself. However, as he had told me when first discussing it, he was to be represented by Baron Gunzburg. Just as we were drawing up a final list of all those who were to go, Mademoiselle de Pulska applied to be included. She would pay for her own passage, she said; and Diaghilev consented.

★   ★   ★

Our London season ended on July the 25th, and on August the 15th, after a short holiday, at the end of which Diaghilev came to say goodbye to us in London, we sailed from Southampton in the liner *Avon*. Nijinsky and Baron Gunzburg both accompanied us; but Karsavina was to follow by a later ship. The voyage was thoroughly enjoyable: the sea smooth as a pond, a clear sky, wonderful sunsets and moonlit nights. After our arduous months in Paris and London we revelled in this interval of absolute idleness.

We had been at sea about a fortnight when there occurred a most astonishing turn of events. Nijinsky, as I mentioned, was on the boat with us. Till then we had scarcely seen him apart from Diaghilev. He had never been known to talk to anyone in the company, and was anyhow unusually taciturn and retiring. Now, however, he was often to be seen in animated conversation with Mademoiselle de Pulska; and though this rather intrigued me, I did not regard it as a matter of any importance. What was my surprise, therefore, when Baron Gunzburg suddenly announced that they were to be married! To start with, we merely took this as a joke: it sounded too improbable to be serious. But the Baron assured us that it was true: the engagement was shortly to be made public and Diaghilev informed. I was absolutely astounded; but Diaghilev's former valet, Vasili Zuykov, who had by then been promoted to be Nijinsky's dresser, confirmed the Baron's statement when I cross-questioned him. He even alleged that the Baron favoured the match; and this I found the less difficult to credit in that I had before heard rumours, which I had disregarded, that it was the Baron's intention to detach Nijinsky from Diaghilev in order to form a company of his own. In any case, this news was deeply disturbing. For it was very clear that Nijinsky's marriage must have far-reaching consequences for Diaghilev's whole enterprise. Since the departure of Fokine, Nijinsky had become not only our chief dancer but our chief choreographer; and though Diaghilev had been disappointed with his latest efforts, he had certainly intended their collaboration to continue. It was already understood, for instance, that he would compose *La Légende de Joseph* (as the Strauss ballet was to be called) as soon as we returned from our tour of South America.

But with Nijinsky married, the whole situation would clearly be altered. Having no mind of his own, Nijinsky would certainly fall entirely under the influence of his wife; and I could not imagine that this would suit Diaghilev for a moment. However, two days later the whole company (who were still in the dark) were invited by the Baron to dinner; and at this, to everyone's stupefaction, the engagement was announced. Moreover, the wedding took place almost as soon as was possible—only two days after our arrival in Buenos Aires.

*   *   *

The appearance of Buenos Aires rather surprised us. Large though it was, it seemed to have only one wide street, the tree-lined *Avenida de Mayo*, leading from the Parliament to the President's Palace. The rest of the streets were all very narrow, and the houses that bounded them were small and styleless. There was also a singular absence of trees and green spaces, which gave the city an air of dullness. The streets were crowded, but only with men; there were few if any women to be seen at all. We were to discover later that women in Buenos Aires went about not on foot but in carriages. The ladies of our ballet consequently attracted much attention, walking as they did all over the city. The management of the theatre, however, soon warned them to be careful where they went, and to be even more careful in making acquaintances. For casual acquaintanceships had been known, they said, to lead to the disappearance of the ladies who made them!

The *Colón* Theatre, where we were to appear, was a handsome structure, exactly like any large European theatre. Its public was to some extent made up of regular subscribers to its opera seasons. These had two of our performances specially reserved for them; and we gave four others to the general public. We opened on September the 11th with *Le Pavillon d'Armide*, *Schéhérazade*, *Le Spectre de la Rose* and the Polovtsian Dances. The theatre was full, with a fashionable-looking crowd, the men all in tail-coats and white ties and the ladies—for here at last there were some on view—good-looking and well-dressed. To begin with, our success was no more than moderate, ballet being new to Buenos Aires; but it increased with each performance. It was during this season that my wife, Liubov Tchernicheva, began to make her name. Several of our leading dancers such as Nelidova, Astafieva, Piltz and Bronislava Nijinska (sister to Nijinsky) had not come out with us. Their parts, therefore, had to be taken over by other dancers; and before we left Diaghilev had suggested that some of them should be danced by my wife. She had only recently finished her training at the Imperial School, but had evident talent and remarkable looks. She performed the parts now given to her very well and began to be singled out for her graceful and accomplished dancing.

We remained in Buenos Aires for a month, during which our popularity visibly increased. From there we went to Montevideo, but only, to our regret, for two performances; for it struck us as an attractive place with a public much more appreciative of ballet than that of Buenos Aires. From Montevideo we took ship to Rio de Janeiro; and like all the world were overcome by the beauty of its harbour and the tropical vegetation. The theatre, we found, had only just been completed. It stood in the midst of an open space; but its architecture was that of a Paris department store. Our performances began on October the 17th. Here again ballet was an art unknown to the public and failed to arouse any great interest, our audiences assembling chiefly out of curiosity.

They were again well dressed, but not very large. In fact the theatre at some of our performances was rather empty—which positively offended us.

Our South American tour came to an end at Rio, and on the whole we had all enjoyed it. About half-way through our season in Rio, however, another peculiar incident occurred. It began with my being told one day by Baron Gunzburg that Nijinsky, so he had announced, did not intend appearing that night. The Baron, I noticed, seemed greatly agitated, and pointed out that by failing to appear Nijinsky would be breaking his contract with Diaghilev. His refusal also put *me* in a very difficult position. For *Le Carnaval* had been announced for the performance that night, and Nijinsky had no understudy for the part of the Harlequin. However, I at once arranged for the dancer Gavrilov to rehearse the part, and myself went to see Nijinsky and try to persuade him to perform after all. But despite all my entreaties, to which I added warnings that Diaghilev never forgave dancers who missed performances without good reason, Nijinsky and his wife both insisted that he would not on any account come to the theatre that night. Gavrilov accordingly appeared in his place.

According to the rules of the company and the terms of our contracts, the non-appearance of any dancer at a performance, unless he could produce a doctor's certificate of illness, was the gravest offence he could commit and one that led to dismissal. But in this case there was no pretence that Nijinsky was indisposed. On the contrary, he was perfectly well and appeared as usual the following day. I gathered from Gunzburg that he had informed Diaghilev of the incident in a lengthy telegram.

★   ★   ★

Our tour was nearing its end; the Nijinsky incident was forgotten; and all of us could think of little else than the voyage home and the Christmas holidays. At the last moment, however, to our acute annoyance, we learnt that for some reason the departure of our boat was to be delayed for ten days. Neither the Baron nor the Nijinskys were to sail with us; so I was to be in sole charge of the company. We again had a very agreeable crossing: the same calm sea and every day some fresh excitement. One day off Pernambuco we sighted some small whales and a school of porpoises. Now and again a swarm of flying fish with lace-like fins or some dolphins would follow the ship. All this made the voyage fascinating. Pacing, as I would, up and down the deck for hours, I could not help speculating about the future. I wondered in particular what Diaghilev's attitude would be to the situation created by Nijinsky's marriage. It seemed to me that Nijinsky and the Ballet were all but inseparable. It was round Nijinsky that our now considerable *répertoire* had been largely built up; and the fact that Diaghilev had always concentrated publicity on him had resulted in his being identified with our Ballet in the public mind. Moreover, there was the new movement in choreography inaugurated by Diaghilev's collaboration with Nijinsky, about which so much had been said and written. I could not, in short, conceive how Nijinsky could be replaced; and yet, in the course of my five years' association with Diaghilev I had begun to understand the complexity of his character. He was not a man to depend on other people, however necessary to him they might appear to be; and now that Nijinsky was married I could not see how their collaboration could continue. Yet such was my faith in Diaghilev's immense resource that I felt sure he would find a solution to this problem. . . . But now we were nearing the Spanish coast. A cold wind from the north began to blow; and in a few days we landed at Cherbourg— where I was handed a telegram from Diaghilev, welcoming our return.

★   ★   ★

When we arrived in Petersburg, deep in winter snow, we were so sunburnt after our voyage through the tropics that people in the streets turned round to look at us. Hardly had I unpacked before I received a note from Diaghilev asking me to call on him the following day. I had imagined Diaghilev to be in Moscow, where I had expected him to remain for a time. However, I called at the flat as instructed; and the door was opened by Zuykov, who asked me to wait. Diaghilev, he said, now lived at the Hôtel de l'Europe, where he had an Italian valet looking after him. I enquired how he was. But all Zuykov would say was, 'You'll see for yourself'. I did not have long to wait; and when Diaghilev came in he seemed pleased to see me. Then, after a few enquiries about the tour, he handed me a telegram, saying, 'Look at what came yesterday'. The telegram was from Nijinsky. It asked when rehearsals were to start and when he was to begin work on a new ballet, and requested Diaghilev to see that during rehearsals the company should not be employed on anything else. When I had read the telegram Diaghilev put it on the table and covered it with the palm of his hand.

This was what he always did with any communication that annoyed him. Then, looking at me sideways with his ironical smile, he said, 'I should like you, as my *régisseur*, to sign the telegram I propose sending in reply to this'. He then took up a telegraph form from the table, and screwing his monocle into his eye and biting his tongue (as he would when worked up), he wrote his answer. It read: 'In reply to your telegram to Monsieur Diaghilev I wish to inform you of the following, Monsieur Diaghilev considers that by missing a performance at Rio and refusing to dance in the ballet *Carnaval* you broke your contract. He will not therefore require your further services. Serge Grigoriev, *Régisseur* of the Diaghilev Company.'

I now understood why Diaghilev had summoned me so urgently. By causing the answer to Nijinsky's telegram to go from me, he wished to show that their former friendship now counted for nothing and that their relationship had become purely formal. When I had read it he took the telegram from me again, and turning to Zuykov, who was in the room, said to him, 'This is what it means in Russian' (for the telegram was in French), and translated it for his benefit. After a short pause he then handed it back to me and said it must go off at once. When showing me out and helping me on with my overcoat, Zuykov remarked, 'Your telegram won't improve Madame Nijinsky's sleep I dare say!' I turned and saw he was silently laughing.

The interview had lasted only a few minutes; and I was so much taken by surprise that I could hardly collect my thoughts. My immediate impulse was, naturally enough, to blame Diaghilev for treating Nijinsky so harshly. For, after all, Nijinsky had spent years in his company and had perhaps done more than anyone else to win it fame. I remembered how he had treated Fokine eighteen months before; and his treatment of Nijinsky was, at least, no better. Unfortunately, to influence Diaghilev in what he did and persuade him to reverse his decision was entirely beyond me. And so the fatal telegram was despatched. But I continued to brood over the episode. I could not help thinking that the violence of Diaghilev's reaction was due in part to the failure of Nijinsky's last two ballets. Diaghilev, I thought, must already have decided that Nijinsky did not have it in him to become a great choreographer. From the artistic standpoint, therefore, their parting was the less painful. Yet the replacement of Nijinsky would, I still thought, be immensely difficult. However, for the moment, it was useless to speculate on how this difficulty might be overcome.

CHAPTER SIX

1914

THE dismissal of Nijinsky was the last important event of 1913 in the history of the Diaghilev Ballet, and marked the end of its second choreographic period. Had the Rio incident not produced this result that period might well have been prolonged; for although Diaghilev was beginning to realize that with Nijinsky he had taken a wrong direction, *L'Après-Midi* was an encouraging exception among Nijinsky's compositions, and whatever talent he possessed Diaghilev would probably have persevered in developing. As it was, however, Diaghilev again found himself minus a choreographer; and it was imperative that further new ballets should be composed.

I was still racking my brains for a solution when Diaghilev, to my astonishment, asked what I should say to Fokine. I was so much taken aback that I merely looked vacant and could only ask what he meant. 'I mean to come back to us,' said Diaghilev.

'But you're on the worst possible terms with him,' I said. 'He thinks very poorly of both of us.'

'What does that matter?' said Diaghilev. 'Fokine's an excellent dancer and a no less excellent choreographer. Why not try? Let's ring him up and see what he says'—on which he went to the telephone and, wiping the receiver with his handkerchief as was his habit, obtained the number and said that Sergey Pavlovich Diaghilev wished to speak to Mikhail Mikhailovich Fokine. There was then a to me ominous pause before a conversation started. It lasted no less than five hours. I could not hear what Fokine said, but it was evident enough that Diaghilev was having no easy time with him: that Fokine was venting his wrath and bitterness at the way he had been treated. He began by flatly refusing to have anything more to do with the Ballet. But Diaghilev was not deterred. He let him say all he wished, biding his time, and then protested at Fokine's accusations, defended his own standpoint and embarked on persuasion as only he knew how. The result was that despite all Fokine's stubbornness (and he was of a far from tractable nature), after five hours of interrupted talk Diaghilev wore him down and obtained his promise to call the next day. As he replaced the receiver Diaghilev heaved a sigh of relief. 'Well, that's settled, I think,' he said. 'He was a tough nut to crack, though, all the same!'

It *was* settled—but on conditions. After their meeting had taken place, Diaghilev told me that Fokine was definitely returning to us, but that he had demanded the dismissal of four or five members of the present company, I being one and Nijinsky's sister another. 'That's quite absurd, of course,' said Diaghilev, 'and I've absolutely refused. On the other hand, you two must make peace,'—and so we eventually did. Our reconciliation, such as it was, took place at Diaghilev's flat: we shook hands without a word. So Fokine returned to the company not only as choreographic director but as *premier danseur*. He had fallen in with all Diaghilev's proposals but one. Diaghilev was obliged to agree that while Fokine was in the company none of Nijinsky's ballets should be given. On the other hand, Diaghilev reserved the right to employ outside choreographers, after consultation, should the need arise.

★   ★   ★

I could not, personally, have been better pleased at Fokine's return. I had always felt that the original success of our *répertoire* had been due, above all, to his compositions and that as long as he remained with us we should keep on the right path. Moreover, I was much relieved at our having at least patched up our personal quarrel.

Owing to the various internal troubles that had disturbed the existence of the company, Diaghilev now again began convening his committee and consulting its members, many of whom were by chance in St. Petersburg. We greatly missed dear old General Bezobrazov; but in his place we had Baron Gunzburg, who was invariably present; and in place of Nijinsky, to everyone's delight, we once more had Fokine. No-one had really approved of the Nijinsky period in choreography. It had seemed to be leading us nowhere, whereas Fokine's return gave us fresh hope of success.

Diaghilev's first care was to decide on the spring programme of ballet and opera. This year we were expected to give a large number of performances in London; but whereas the operas were all, so to speak, ready, new ballets had still to be prepared. Our chief new item was to be *La Légende de Joseph*, for which Strauss's music had by now been completed. It had originally been intended, of course, that Nijinsky should both compose the choreography and dance the part of Joseph; and now that Fokine was taking his place, he wished also to do both. Diaghilev rightly decided, however, that he did not look young enough and that someone else would have to be found. Fokine had two other ballets in mind: *Papillons*, to Schumann's suite of that name, and *Midas*, to music by Steinberg; but both were rather short. Moreover, Tchérépnine had not yet finished the score for *The Red Masks*, the ballet it had been intended that A. Gorsky should compose as a 'guest' choreographer; so that that could not be included. The committee all tried their hardest to think of a fourth work to complete the list. Diaghilev, as ever, was eager for a new composition by Stravinsky; but after the fiasco of *Le Sacre* Stravinsky was averse from writing another ballet. On the other hand, he had an unfinished score for an opera on Hans Andersen's tale of the Nightingale and the Emperor of China; and Diaghilev suggested that he should finish it in time for presentation, under the title *Le Rossignol*, in Paris. It might then also figure as one of the four new operas he had promised to show in London, others of which were to be Borodin's *Prince Igor* (from which the Polovtsian Dances were taken) and *Une Nuit de Mai* by Rimsky-Korsakov. This, however, got us no further with the missing fourth ballet.

Diaghilev and his friends would often bemoan the inability of opera singers, with the exception of a few such as Chialapine, to act; and Benois had more than once remarked how pleasant it would be if the singers could remain hidden and their parts be mimed for them by a cast of actors. Now, therefore, in our predicament over the subject for a new ballet, he suggested quite seriously our trying this with another opera of Rimsky-Korsakov's, *Le Coq d'Or*, letting the characters be presented on the stage by dancers, while the singers were concealed in the orchestra pit. Diaghilev was immediately fired with this idea, and declared it must be tried. To begin with, it was proposed that only a few scenes should be so treated, but in the end it was decided to perform the whole work in this way. Fokine was also much taken with the suggestion and began at once inventing action to illustrate the story in conformity with the music. Diaghilev was thus able to add to his programme what amounted at the same time to another opera and another ballet. With so many new productions on hand he also realized that he must employ

94

not only Bakst and Benois but other designers of *décor* too. He accordingly approached the Russians, Natalia Goncharova, Roerich, Korovine and Doboujinsky, and the Spaniard, José-Maria Sert. The programme for Paris and London thus promised exceptional interest.

★ ★ ★

As regards the Ballet, these winter months of 1913 had much in common with those of 1908, when Diaghilev was preparing his first season. His energy was enormous and appeared to infect us all. It is true that Nijinsky was not with us as he had been then; but, strangely enough, Diaghilev seemed like someone who has shed a load and can at last breathe freely. It was in this exhilarating mood that he left for Moscow, where he had much to busy him in connection with the staging of the operas. It happened that for personal reasons I too had to visit Moscow, and when I had completed my business I called on Diaghilev at his hotel. In the passage outside his room I passed a young man in a long overcoat, wearing a hat pulled low over his face, which I nevertheless noticed was strikingly handsome. I found Diaghilev in high good spirits. Everything was in excellent shape, he said. Having done all he wished, he was ready to leave; and 'Do you know?' he said. 'I have at last found a dancer for the part of Joseph!' I congratulated him and enquired who it was.

'Oh, he's not up to much as a dancer yet,' said Diaghilev. 'I saw him in a character number at the *Bolshoy* Theatre, where he takes part in the *ensembles*. But we had a long talk together, and he made a good impression on me. He was intending to give up ballet and become an actor; but I've persuaded him not to, and to join us instead. If he shows any inclination to hard work, I think he may achieve something. At any rate, his appearance is exactly right for Joseph. But now I come to think of it you must have passed him in the passage. For he left me only a minute before you came in.'

'Yes, I *did* meet a young man, with a good-looking face,' I laughed.

'Of course he's rather provincial,' said Diaghilev. 'But we'll soon put an end to that. His name is Massine, and I've signed a long-term contract with him. He's to join us in a fortnight's time, when Fokine can start work with him at once.'

Such was my first sight of Léonide Massine, our future choreographer and *premier danseur*.

The Diaghilev Ballet

$\star$ $\star$ $\star$

In February, when our holiday was over, we reassembled, by arrangement, in Prague. Diaghilev, who had gone to Paris, was kept there longer than he had expected, and Fokine had also been delayed in St. Petersburg; so that it fell to me to begin rehearsals without them. It was now that the company first learnt of all the changes that had taken place: of Nijinsky's departure and Fokine's return. The latter came as a most pleasant surprise to everyone.

We set out on our second German tour from Prague; and it was in marked contrast to its predecessor. We were now well known and much admired in Germany. Nor did Nijinsky's absence affect our success; for Fokine took over most of his parts and danced them extremely well. He also began composing *La Légende de Joseph*, over which, and in particular over Massine's progress with his part, Diaghilev kept a close watch. After the first rehearsal he asked Fokine what he thought of Massine. 'A talented young man,' said Fokine, 'but a poor dancer. I'm afraid I shall have to simplify his part.' Diaghilev did not mind this at all. Indeed he preferred Massine to do simple movements well rather than difficult movements badly. Moreover, there were still four months before we opened in Paris; and Massine fully recognized that, apart from working intensively with Cecchetti, it would be useful for him to dance in the big *ensembles*. However, as he had joined the company rather late I was unable to place him in many of them; and he started in *Petrushka*, where he played the tiny part of the watchman on guard at the fair—a performance that constituted his *début*.

$\star$ $\star$ $\star$

Our tour in Germany went very well. Wherever we appeared we had full houses. Fokine meanwhile continued the composition of *Joseph*. But Strauss's music was difficult; nor did the scenario, which had not been thoroughly worked out by the authors, always fit it. Hence, on our arrival in Berlin, Strauss, Kessler, Diaghilev and Fokine went over it together and did their best to reconcile these discrepancies. The casting of Potiphar's wife was also a problem: our dancers were all too young for the part. Karsavina, it is true, was somewhat older, but was scarcely tall enough; for the authors saw the character as tall and stately. In the end Diaghilev invited the opera singer Maria Kuznetsova to play it,

96

since she was at the same time a good actress. Diaghilev set great store by *Joseph*. It was the first ballet ever to be written by the celebrated Richard Strauss; and it was hoped that he would conduct it in person on a tour of Europe, Diaghilev being prepared to pay him a very large fee for doing so. Kessler, as a friend of both Strauss and Diaghilev, was to help in the organization of this tour, even though he was disappointed that Nijinsky, of whom he was an ardent admirer, was not to dance the title role.

During our tour of Germany we learnt that Nijinsky was appearing in London at the Palace Theatre in some of our ballets, such as *Le Carnaval* and *Les Sylphides*, to which he had no right. But before Diaghilev could do anything to restrain him, Nijinsky's enterprise came to a sudden end, having existed for precisely a fortnight. He was never again to appear on the stage except under Diaghilev's auspices.

★   ★   ★

At this juncture Diaghilev was obliged to return to Russia on business. Before he left, Fokine warned him that with the best will in the world he would be unable to finish all the ballets in time. On this occasion Diaghilev saw reason, and suggested that Romanov should undertake the choreography of *Le Rossignol*. Fokine readily agreed to this, since he did not relish the idea of composing to music by Stravinsky.

Now that Nijinsky was no longer with us, Diaghilev felt that we were perhaps weak in male dancers, and, while in Russia, accordingly invited Vladimirov, the classical *premier danseur* of the *Mariinsky*, to join the company. He also re-engaged Bulgakov, whom I have mentioned before. Being an exceptionally talented mime, Bulgakov was to be entrusted with the leading part of Tsar Dodon in *Le Coq d'Or*. Incidentally, this visit of Diaghilev to Russia was destined to be his last.

★   ★   ★

When we at length arrived back in Monte Carlo, only three weeks remained before the opening of our next season in Paris. By this time *Joseph* was all but finished, and Fokine was starting the rehearsals of *Le Coq d'Or*. At the same time he was composing *Papillons* and rehearsing other ballets, among them *Daphnis et Chloë*. Fokine was especially attached to *Daphnis*, and eventually, while we were still at Monte Carlo,

97

The Diaghilev Ballet

danced the title role with Karsavina as Chloë—when some critics preferred him to Nijinsky in the part.

Papillons, which we gave as a novelty during our Monte Carlo season, was a slight but charming work, to an orchestration by Tchérépnine of Schumann's music. Fokine himself danced the only male part, of Pierrot, and the ballerina was again Karsavina. The scenery was by Doboujinsky and the costumes by Bakst. *Papillons* was usually much applauded and remained for a long time a stand-by in our *répertoire*, Diaghilev later endowing it with an enchanting Schumann overture. We also showed *La Tragédie de Salomé* at Monte Carlo. But here again it had so little success it was almost immediately dropped.

Diaghilev rejoined us towards the end of this season. He had been rather anxious lest the absence of Nijinsky should affect the attitude of the management of the Casino adversely. But not only were his fears groundless; the management actually preferred the dramatic ballets that were Fokine's speciality, and were comparatively indifferent to the personnel of the company. We left Monte Carlo, as usual, with regret. But none of us imagined that many years would elapse before we should see it again.

★   ★   ★

As regards Paris, Diaghilev, curiously enough, seemed more anxious about obliterating the bad impression created the year before by his excursions into a new choreography than about the absence of Nijinsky from the company. Our season this year was at the *Opéra*, and our programme included *La Légende de Joseph*, *Le Rossignol* and a new version of *Schéhérazade*, for which the entire score of Rimsky-Korsakov was used, with the aim of silencing those critics who had condemned the former cuts. We showed this new version on our first night, together with *Papillons* and *Joseph*. Unfortunately the latter failed to fulfil our expectations. Strauss's music, though interesting in itself, was not really suited to dancing; both the black and gold scene by Sert and the costumes by Bakst failed in some way to create the proper atmosphere; and Fokine had been hampered in his composition by the vagueness of the scenario, which resulted in an unconvincing plot. Massine was much liked, not so much for his performance as for his attractive looks; but Kuznetsova failed to make any great impression. However, in spite of all these shortcomings, this first night was a brilliant and memorable occasion. 'All Paris' was there; and interest in Diaghilev's Ballet was clearly as lively as ever.

Our next *première* was *Le Coq d'Or*; and this at once became the chief feature of the season. The public had been bored with Diaghilev's recent experiments and were eager for something that would recall the glories of his first creations; and *Le Coq d'Or* did precisely that. In the first place, the experiment, the idea of which had given rise to the production, of using a double cast (of singers who merely sang and dancers who merely moved) was entirely justified by the result. In the end, incidentally, the singers were not concealed in the orchestra pit, but ranged in tiers on either side of the stage all dressed, men or women, precisely alike, in a kind of ancient Russian uniform. Apart from its choreography, which was in Fokine's most charming and spontaneous vein, the *décor* by Goncharova, inspired by Russian peasant art, was a revelation of brilliant colour and primitive fantasy; while the score, full of enchanting Russian and Oriental themes, was beautifully orchestrated; and its performance, under the direction of Monteux, by a large orchestra and magnificent Russian singers and chorus, quite carried the audience away. The scenes—an ingenious mixture of dancing and mime—between Karsavina as the Queen of Shemakhan and Bulgakov as Tsar Dodon were particularly delightful. *Le Coq d'Or* showed once again what triumph could result from a due combination of the various arts that are the ingredients of ballet.

The chief appeal of *Le Rossignol*, which was our next production, was to lovers of the modern school of music. The general public remained puzzled by the lack of melody in the score. Moreover, neither the *décor*, in three scenes, designed by Benois in soft colours, nor the choreography by Romanov, which was similarly mild, in any way suited the stridencies of the composer. Stravinsky's new work provoked no scandal or incident. But neither did it make any great impression.

Fokine by this time was exhausted. Not only had he composed three ballets; he had also danced at nearly every performance. It was not surprising, therefore, that in the composition of the last new ballet on our list—*Midas*—his inspiration failed him, particularly since neither the subject itself, nor Steinberg's music, attracted him. Doboujinsky's designs for the *décor*—after Mantegna—were also somewhat uninspired; in short, *Midas* was still-born. It was only, in fact, shown about three times towards the end of this season in Paris, at the first of which it was sandwiched in between *Petrushka* and *Cléopâtre*. Incidentally that performance of *Cléopâtre* remains in my memory for the extraordinarily brilliant dancing of Vladimirov, in Nijinsky's old part of the Negro slave.

The Diaghilev Ballet

Three of our new productions of this year, *Joseph*, *Le Rossignol* and *Midas*, had thus misfired in varying degrees; only *Le Coq d'Or* had been an unqualified triumph. Nevertheless Diaghilev felt that he had attained his aim. The absence of Nijinsky appeared to have made little difference to the public's appreciation of the Ballet as a whole; and the unfortunate experiments of the year before appeared to have been forgotten.

★   ★   ★

Having finished in Paris we once again crossed the Channel, for the season at Drury Lane which Sir Joseph Beecham had arranged with Diaghilev the year before. We actually arrived after the first opera had been given—*Boris Godounov* on May the 30th—in time to take part on June the 7th in *Prince Igor*. Chaliapine was, of course, singing the chief part in both these operas as well as in *Ivan the Terrible*; and the combination of the Polovtsian Dances with his amazing performance in *Prince Igor* produced a tremendous impression on the London audience.

On the following evening we gave a ballet programme, showing *Daphnis* for the first time in London. This was extremely well received, the last scene, in which the Moscow chorus took part, being considered especially impressive. Later we also showed the new version of *Schéhérazade* and *Papillons*, which was much to the taste of English audiences. *Thamar*, conducted by Thomas Beecham, was always, as before, a sure success; but the triumph of the season, as in Paris, was *Le Coq d'Or*.

Diaghilev's policy was to mix the more popular with the less popular ballets, so that the public could extol what most appealed to them and disregard what pleased them less. In this way he managed to make use of both *Midas* and *Le Rossignol*, neither of which was really very good.

Our last new work to be shown in London was *La Légende de Joseph*. Diaghilev was particularly eager for its success and spared no effort to advertise it. Richard Strauss was to conduct it in person; and great publicity was given to Sert and Fokine and the new young dancer, Léonide Massine. Our London audiences were therefore well prepared for something remarkable; and Diaghilev in fact succeeded in exciting more enthusiasm for *Joseph* than it had provoked in Paris. As for the operas, there remained only *Une Nuit de Mai*. Being lyrical rather than dramatic, it made somewhat less impression than the others; and this despite the exquisite singing in the leading part of the famous tenor Smirnov.

On the first night of *La Légende de Joseph* in London Diaghilev received

100

a telegram from Count Harry von Kessler. After sending his wishes for the ballet's success and his regrets at being unable to be present, the Count expressed his fear lest our projected autumn season in Germany might not, after all, take place. 'The dear Count must be ill,' said Diaghilev, when telling us about this telegram. 'Why should my tour, so beautifully planned, fail to take place, I should like to know?' But Kessler knew all too well what he was talking about. He stood near to Court circles in Berlin; and his telegram was in fact a warning to Diaghilev. Scarcely a fortnight was to pass before war broke out, and put an end to a whole era of the Diaghilev Ballet.

From the middle of July rumours of war were persistent. But we failed, in company with half the world, to take them seriously. Our season finished on July the 25th in triumph: the ovation seemed endless: old Sir Joseph Beecham was led on to the stage and made a speech, in which he thanked the public for its support and promised another season with Diaghilev the next year, no less wonderful than the one then ended. Our 1914 season in London had indeed been wonderful. As regards the ballet it had been above all a triumph for Fokine, no less than fifteen of whose works—in which the public delighted—were now in our *répertoire*. Karsavina, moreover, was then at the height of her power and had received in Vladimirov a worthy partner. But the promises of Sir Joseph Beecham were, alas, to be nullified, and many years were to pass before the Diaghilev Ballet was able once more to appear in London.

The next day Diaghilev said goodbye to the company, who were dispersing for a holiday. We were all to reassemble on October the 1st in Berlin.

★   ★   ★

Two days after my arrival in St. Petersburg, Russia declared war on Germany. For reasons of health I was rejected for military service; so I went to my home in the small provincial town of Tikhvin. For a long time I received no word from Diaghilev. I did not even know where he was. Month after month passed and 1914 came to an end. I began to think of returning to the *Mariinsky*; but decided, if I could, first to get into touch again with Diaghilev. I did not in fact have long to wait for a reply to the letter I wrote him. It told me he was about to start work again and was arranging a tour in North America. He hoped, he said, that I would be able to help him. As far as it went, this news was cheering. But all I could do, after receiving it, was to be patient and await developments.

CHAPTER SEVEN
1915

I WAS again in St. Petersburg for New Year 1915. No-one thought the war would be a long one: everyone believed the Allies would soon win; and life went on almost as usual. I kept on receiving telegrams from Diaghilev asking me to see to various matters on his behalf; and to judge by these, the affairs of the Ballet seemed to be shaping well. At length, at the beginning of May, I received a telegram summoning me to Switzerland for an important discussion. I found on enquiry that I must travel via Finland, Sweden, Norway, England and France, but was assured that though slow—it would take a fortnight—the journey should be quite comfortable. I therefore telegraphed to Diaghilev that I was coming; and found that the Travel Bureau had been right: I reached Switzerland safely and in comparative comfort.

Diaghilev greeted me as one returned from another world and was full of questions about my adventures. Then he told me that he had already signed a contract for North America. I asked whether he intended to go there himself. 'Unfortunately, yes,' he said. 'They insist on my doing so.' I was glad to hear this, despite his reluctance, being persuaded that his presence would much improve the prospects of success. It then appeared that his purpose in sending for me was to ask me to help in collecting a company in Russia. To start with, he wished to discover whether Karsavina and Fokine would rejoin him. He had so far failed to get an answer from either. I was also to engage as many dancers, male and female, as possible; while he, on his side, would do what he could to recruit others abroad. He told me, to my great surprise, that one of his most urgent tasks was to obtain the release of Nijinsky, who had been interned in Austria. For it appeared that the American tour was being backed by the banker Otto Kahn, who had made it a condition in the contract that Nijinsky should rejoin us. Diaghilev had already pulled some strings, so he said, and some of his friends had good hopes that, owing to the intervention of the King of Spain, Nijinsky

would soon be set at liberty. I could not help reflecting, while listening
to what Diaghilev was telling me, on all that had happened two years
before.

★   ★   ★

Diaghilev was now living in the Villa Belle Rive at Lausanne. Bakst,
Stravinsky, the painter Larionov, Massine and several of Diaghilev's
Paris friends were living there too. It was here that I first met Ernest
Ansermet, who was then the conductor of the Geneva Symphony
Orchestra, and whose handsome bearded face reminded me of a
Byzantine Christ. He and Stravinsky, whose music he much admired,
were great friends; and Diaghilev wished him to go with us to America.
These people now formed Diaghilev's entourage, with whom he discussed artistic problems and the planning of future productions, more
or less as he had been wont to do with his 'committee' in the past.
Maestro Cecchetti was there as well, giving lessons to Massine. It was
now Diaghilev's hope to develop Massine and make a choreographer of
him; but after his experience with Nijinsky he was wary. Instead of
wasting his own energy before he had proof of Massine's ability, he
charged Larionov with the task of instructing him in choreographic
theory, and made Massine begin modestly, with the composition, in the
manner of Fokine, of some simple dances on music from Rimsky-
Korsakov's opera *The Snowmaiden*. Nevertheless he could not resist
working on some of his own pet ideas in composition. He was still much
attracted by the principles of 'Eurhythmics'; which he and his friends
had it in mind to apply in a new ballet, to be called *Liturgie*. The chief
character in this ballet was to be the Virgin, impersonated by Tchernicheva; and instead of to music, it was to be danced to the sound of
rhythmical stamping, with choreography by Massine of the type employed by Nijinsky in *Le Sacre*, and costumes designed by Goncharova.
It sounded an interesting idea; but by the time I returned to Switzerland from Russia it had been abandoned—owing, I fancy, to a lessening
of Diaghilev's attraction to mere rhythm.

★   ★   ★

I spent only a week in Lausanne before starting on my return journey.
As I had to pass through London I took a message from Diaghilev to
Thomas Beecham, which I duly delivered, and also engaged a new
dancer: Stanislas Idzikovsky. As soon as I reached St. Petersburg I

The Diaghilev Ballet

called on Karsavina; but found that she could not go to America with us, since she was having a baby. I was thus faced with the task of finding a ballerina to replace her; and I accordingly approached a young and exquisite new dancer, somewhat reminiscent of Pavlova, who was then coming to the fore at the *Mariinsky*, Olga Spesivtseva by name. After a good deal of persuasion on my part she at first agreed to join our company; but when it came to signing a contract she suddenly changed her mind. She had been dissuaded by a friend of hers, the writer and critic Volinsky. He apparently influenced her by arguing that she was essentially a classical dancer, to whom Diaghilev's *répertoire* would not offer the right opportunities.

Spesivtseva's refusal rather nonplussed me. There was no-one else at the *Mariinsky* capable of taking Karsavina's place. So off I went to Moscow, although its dancers in those days were by no means particularly good. I found, however, that the leading ballerina, Makletsova, would be willing to join us, and sent Diaghilev a telegram to that effect. 'Continue looking for someone better,' came his reply. 'But failing that engage Makletsova.' I obeyed this instruction, but without success, and so duly despatched Makletsova to Switzerland.

★   ★   ★

My next endeavour was to engage Fokine. But this too failed, since he would not leave Russia in war-time. I found indeed that people were alarmed at the idea of the lengthy journey to France and the still lengthier journey to America, and required much persuasion to undertake them. Meanwhile Diaghilev kept urging me to send him dancers with all speed; and this I did, in groups of six or eight. Since most men dancers had by this time been called up there were very few of them about. Still, I succeeded finally in securing practically all the girls we needed and about half the men; and in December I myself left for Switzerland with the last contingent—this being my third experience of the devious route involved.

★   ★   ★

Whilst I was away in Russia Diaghilev had also been searching for dancers—all over Europe; with the result that when I returned to Lausanne I found a considerable company assembled. Only Nijinsky was still missing; but Diaghilev felt sure he would soon be released and would reach America in time for our tour.

104

Diaghilev did not seem to mind my failure to secure Fokine as much as I had expected. He even said now that ever since the last season in London he had felt that he and Fokine were moving in different directions. Fokine's choreography was superb of its kind. But the time had come when it should make way for something new. 'In fifty years' time,' said Diaghilev, 'it will probably be rediscovered; then it will be thought amusing, and finally be regarded as classical. But now what's wanted is something quite different: a movement of liberation in choreography; some fresh form of achievement, with new music.'

★   ★   ★

The dances Massine had composed on the *Snowmaiden* music, and his abandoned rehearsals for *Liturgie*, had by now convinced Diaghilev that he had the makings of a choreographer in him. That was one reason why Fokine's absence troubled him so little. Another was that on the American tour Fokine would be replaced as a dancer by Nijinsky. Moreover, the leading male parts in the various ballets were in fact distributed between Bolm, Massine, Idzikovsky and other young dancers. On the other hand, Karsavina's absence was a source of anxiety to Diaghilev, since good though Makletsova was as a dancer, he did not care for her. Great was his pleasure, therefore, on suddenly receiving a telegram from Otto Kahn, informing him that Lydia Lopokova was in New York and ready to rejoin the company. Ever since leaving us after her *début* in *L'Oiseau de Feu* Lopokova had remained in the United States; and her unexpected reappearance just suited Diaghilev. Karsavina's absence was thus made good by Lopokova and Makletsova between them. The only problem that remained was how to cast the parts of Zobeïde (in *Schéhérazade*) and Cleopatra, since Ida Rubinstein was not available. A solution, proposed by Bakst, was found by giving them to a French singer, tall and of striking appearance: Mademoiselle Flora Revalles. Diaghilev rather doubted the wisdom of so employing a singer, but engaged her since no-one else as suitable could be found.

★   ★   ★

Having thus completed his new company, Diaghilev wished to give it a trial before its departure for the United States. He also wished to see a performance of Massine's first essay in choreography—the *Snowmaiden*

PLATE VII

IGOR STRAVINSKY

ENRICO CECCHETTI

BORIS KOCHNO

BORIS ROMANOV

dances—which was now entitled *Le Soleil de Nuit*. He therefore arranged to give two charity matinées for the Red Cross, one in Geneva and one in Paris. The first, in Geneva, took place on December the 20th, with the participation of Stravinsky and the famous soprano Félia Litvine. It marked the *début* of Idzikovsky as Harlequin and Makletsova as Columbine in *Le Carnaval*; and Makletsova also danced the *pas de deux*, *L'Oiseau Bleu*, with Bolm; but the main interest of this *matinée russe* lay in Massine's *Le Soleil de Nuit*. At the sound of the first bars of the overture to *Le Carnaval* I was filled with a great joy, for I felt that the Diaghilev Ballet had been resurrected.

Le Soleil de Nuit, in which Massine had been helped by Larionov, was highly effective. The choreography virtually consisted of one long dance, for which Massine had succeeded in inventing a great many interesting and varied steps and patterns. The effectiveness of the ballet was further enhanced both by Larionov's bright and original Russian costumes exposed against a background of dark blue and gold, and by Rimsky's brilliant score.

★   ★   ★

Diaghilev's success in launching a new company without any of his three former 'stars', Karsavina, Fokine and Nijinsky, and in discovering a new 'generation' of dancers, all of whom were to become famous, was a remarkable feat. The chief women of this 'generation' were Lopokova, Tchernicheva, Sokolova and Nemchinova, the last a girl I had engaged in Moscow; and the chief men: Massine, Idzikovsky, Gavrilov, Zverev, Kremnev and Woidzikowsky (Woidzikowsky being a particularly talented young dancer, whom Diaghilev had discovered in Warsaw). All were evidently highly gifted and gave great promise for the future. Moreover, Massine's *début* as a choreographer was extremely encouraging.

★   ★   ★

As we now realized, Diaghilev's aim was always to have at his command someone who could interpret the fruits of his own imagination. He was overflowing with new ideas and impatient to see them realized. With Nijinsky he had failed; but with Massine it was otherwise. Massine, so Diaghilev used to say, would understand at a mere hint; and after his *début* at Geneva with *Le Soleil de Nuit* Diaghilev was assured that he no longer had any need of either Fokine or Nijinsky.

The Diaghilev Ballet

★ ★ ★

From Geneva we went to Paris, where on December the 29th we gave our second charity matinée at the *Opéra*. Once again the theatre was packed with an elegant audience, and the receipts were sensational. We gave the same programme as in Geneva except that *Le Carnaval* was replaced by *Schéhérazade*; and the orchestra was conducted by Ansermet, who was to go with us to America. *Le Soleil de Nuit* was again a great success; and I remember Diaghilev saying to Svetlov, who stood with us in the wings, 'You see: given the talent, one can make a choreographer in no time!'

These two performances redeemed 1915 from being a barren year in the annals of the Diaghilev Ballet. Having given the second, we left Paris for Bordeaux and set sail for the New World on January the 1st.

CHAPTER EIGHT
1916

IT was very cold and windy on the voyage, with rough seas. Everyone was seasick except Diaghilev, who did not seem to mind the motion of the ship at all, but never left his cabin for fear of catching cold. I was often summoned thither both to discuss business and to keep him company, since he hated being alone. His immediate entourage consisted of Ansermet, his secretary Drobetsky and our new administrator, Randolfo Barocchi. I had made the latter's acquaintance in Paris, when Diaghilev engaged him to manage the business of the American tour. He was an Italian by birth, but had spent many years in America and spoke English fluently. He was a most amusing talker and had an inexhaustible fund of theatrical anecdotes, which relieved the tedium of our eleven days at sea.

We had, of course, been excited at the prospect of seeing America; and were certainly impressed on arrival by the New York skyscrapers and the tremendous crowds and traffic in the streets. But in the neighbourhood of our theatre—the Century—the streets were quiet and the houses small and much like those of Europe. Nor, at a first superficial view, did the American way of life seem very different from the European, either.

★ ★ ★

One of the first people we met in New York was Lydia Lopokova. She had not changed at all since leaving us in Paris five years before and was just as charming and gay and full of laughter as ever. She appeared delighted to be back in our company, and Diaghilev made her very welcome. Makletsova, on the other hand, resented her presence. They danced many of the same parts, and Makletsova at once scented a rival. Complications soon arose. Makletsova was the stronger technically; but Lopokova had enormous charm and a remarkable *élévation*; and both

The Diaghilev Ballet

Diaghilev and the public greatly preferred her. The crisis was not long in coming; and in Boston, to which we went after New York, Makletsova 'walked out' on us.

We found on arrival that Nijinsky was not, after all, to arrive until the spring and that we should consequently be without him both while in New York and during our tour. We were not, however, much perturbed by the prospect of his absence, since the only ballet that had never before been done without him was *L'Après-Midi d'un Faune*. Diaghilev now gave the part of the Faun to Massine and that of the First Nymph to Tchernicheva.

We opened in New York on January the 17th, five days after our arrival. The programme consisted of *L'Oiseau de Feu, La Princesse Enchantée, Le Soleil de Nuit* and *Schéhérazade*. The American public had scarcely seen any Russian ballet before; and it provoked great interest. The absence of Nijinsky appeared to make no difference, and we danced to full houses. The press was exceedingly favourable, singling out Lopokova, Bolm and Massine for particular praise. We spent a fortnight in New York, and then set out on our tour.

American tours, we found, were quite different from European. We had to dance in a different place every evening and often travel by night in sleeping-cars. A large orchestra and a crowd of stagehands, carpenters, electricians, dressers and even 'supers' travelled with us, which in some respects made arrangements easier. We visited sixteen towns in this fashion and then returned to New York—this time to the Metropolitan Opera House.

★   ★   ★

Our second season in New York opened on April the 3rd; and again we had to start minus Nijinsky, who had still not arrived. He did arrive, however, four days later, when we were all struck by his vagueness and unfriendliness. I heard that his meeting with Diaghilev was cold and formal. He merely enquired when and in what ballets he was to dance. Diaghilev asked me to give him as many rehearsals as possible and also an orchestra rehearsal—which in view of working conditions in the United States was no easy matter. Nijinsky's first appearance was in *Petrushka* and *Le Spectre* on April the 12th. His late arrival was unfortunate for his reputation. For the public had seen his parts taken by other dancers; and not being particularly knowledgeable, liked those dancers in them just as much. Moreover, after a two years' interval he was out of practice and his dancing was by no means what it had been, though it improved as time went on. His relations with Diaghilev and the company, on the other hand, went from bad to worse. He was suspicious of everyone and hostile, and it soon became clear that we could not continue with him indefinitely on such terms.

★   ★   ★

The war showed no signs of coming to an end; and Diaghilev became anxious about the future of his company, since it was now all but impossible to obtain continuous engagements in Europe. He therefore tackled Otto Kahn about another tour in the United States in the autumn and winter; but Kahn again stipulated that Nijinsky should be included in the company. Nijinsky's recent behaviour made this extremely unwelcome. Yet Diaghilev sent Barocchi to talk to him. From this it transpired that Nijinsky would agree only if Diaghilev would give him complete control of the company! This was embarrassing for Diaghilev. On the one hand, it was impossible for him to accept such a condition and remain in New York as a 'sleeping partner'; on the other, he could not refuse Kahn's offer on account of the company. He therefore proposed that, when the time came, he should place his whole organization at Kahn's disposal, while himself retiring from its management; and that the Metropolitan should sign a contract direct with Nijinsky as head of the company. Kahn agreed to this arrangement; and it was in due course carried out.

Diaghilev was not really sorry at the prospect of being thus quit of the company for a time, because he realized that the perpetual travelling entailed by an American tour would in any case have prevented him from working during the next winter on any new productions. On the other hand, by remaining in Europe with Massine and a few other dancers, he would be able to plan a whole new *répertoire* in peace. When telling me of this arrangement, about which he evidently felt quite happy, he added that there was someone else whom Nijinsky did not wish to retain with the company—namely myself. This did not altogether surprise me. Nor was I dismayed at the prospect of remaining with Diaghilev in exile. I was, however, worried at what might happen to the company in my absence. Diaghilev acquainted Otto Kahn with my fears; but Nijinsky insisted on his decision to banish me.

The Diaghilev Ballet

★   ★   ★

Our season in New York ended on April the 29th. However, about a fortnight earlier Diaghilev received an invitation for the company to visit Madrid and dance at the *Teatro Real*. It appeared that King Alfonso wished to see our ballet. We had not visited Spain before; and Diaghilev was delighted at the idea of doing so, besides feeling under an obligation to the King for his help over the release of Nijinsky from internment. Altogether this suited our plans exactly, since it provided the company with a summer engagement.

Just before leaving New York we heard that Lydia Lopokova had married Barocchi.

★   ★   ★

We left America on May the 6th in the *Dante Alighieri*. The cargo consisted of ammunition, horses and the Russian Ballet. Fortunately the weather was calm and the sea smooth as a lake. Diaghilev asked the captain what danger there might be from submarines, and was told that there was little as long as we were on the high seas, but that the risk would increase as we neared the coast of Spain. However, we made Cadiz without any alarm, our only misadventures occurring after our arrival. When our belongings were being landed, a case packed with all our orchestral parts was dropped into the water and carried away by the tide. It was rescued, thanks to the agility of Diaghilev's secretary Chausovsky. But no sooner had this case been retrieved, than another, containing the scenery for *Thamar*, fell into the harbour too; and by the time it was fished out the sea water had soaked all the canvas and ruined it beyond repair.

Two members of the company had remained behind in New York: Nijinsky and Mademoiselle Revalles. When, therefore, we gave *Schéhérazade* in Madrid their parts had to be reallotted; and Diaghilev decreed that thenceforward the part of Zobeïdé should be played by Tchernicheva.

We gave our first performance in Madrid on May the 26th. The occasion was highly festive: King Alfonso was present and so were most of the Spanish aristocracy. Lopokova enchanted everyone by her extraordinary lightness in *Le Carnaval* and *Les Sylphides*; Tchernicheva was a thrillingly dramatic Zobeïdé; and Massine's *Soleil de Nuit* was much applauded. Diaghilev was sent for by the King; and both he and the Queen warmly congratulated him. The King thereafter came to every one of our performances; and all the leading dancers were presented to

PLATE VIII

STANISLAS IDZIKOVSKY   ADOLF BOLM
LÉON WOIDZIKOWSKY   ALEXANDRE GAVRILOV

him. We were delighted with our season in Madrid, the only slight cloud on our pleasure being the late hour—10 P.M.—at which the performances began. Fortunately we did not have to give one every day.

★ ★ ★

After our last night in Madrid Diaghilev gave the company two months' holiday; whereupon I seized the opportunity of returning to Russia to collect my small son, whom we had left there. Diaghilev was opposed to my venturing on this journey, fearing that I might after all be called up for military service. Nevertheless I went, and stayed about a month. As Diaghilev had foreseen, I experienced some difficulty in obtaining permission to leave the country again; for despite my having been permanently exempted, the authorities at first insisted on my remaining; and it was not until Diaghilev made a personal application to the Minister for War that I was allowed to depart.

When I arrived back in San Sebastian I found that much had happened during my two months' absence. Firstly, Massine had produced a small new ballet to music by Gabriel Fauré, *Las Meninas*, for which Sert had designed costumes after Velazquez and scenery had been devised by the French painter Socrate. Diaghilev was in ecstasy at the beauty of Spain; and this was the first result of his enthusiasm. In the second place, Larionov and Goncharova had joined him at San Sebastian; and Larionov, who was learned in Russian folk-lore, had been helping Massine to arrange another ballet on the Russian fairy tale 'Kikimora' to music by Liadov, with scenery and costumes by Goncharova and himself. Lastly, in addition to these two new works, Diaghilev wished to revive the dances from *Sadkó*. But since they had had only four performances as long before as 1911, Fokine's choreography had been almost entirely forgotten; and Diaghilev, therefore, asked Bolm to arrange a new version. These three new items had had preliminary showings at San Sebastian and Bilbao. *Las Meninas* was a great success; and King Alfonso, who came to see the ballet even there, liked it particularly and sent bouquets to Lopokova and Tchernicheva.

★ ★ ★

The date of the opening of the American tour was now approaching; and Diaghilev was particularly exercised over whom he should send in my place as *régisseur*. He eventually chose Nicolas Kremnev, who had earlier acted as my assistant in Switzerland. The administration was to be in the hands of Barocchi and Drobetsky. None of them, however, seemed likely to get on well with the others; and the idea of their working at Nijinsky's orders filled me with forebodings. Diaghilev was fully aware of all this, but said he was powerless to do anything about it, since he and I were debarred from taking part in the tour. So off the company finally went without us, embarking at Bordeaux on September the 8th in the *Lafayette*.

About six women of the company, among them Tchernicheva, and an equal number of men, including Massine and Idzikovsky, remained behind; and Diaghilev decided that we should all spend the winter in Rome.

★   ★   ★

It was about a fortnight later that we first received news from New York. It was to the effect that two more dancers had joined the company, namely Spesivtseva (whom I had failed to engage the year before) and Frohman, who had been with us in our earlier days. I felt sorry that Spesivtseva, whom I greatly admired, should start her career with the company while it was in Nijinsky's control. We also learnt that Nijinsky was composing a ballet on Strauss's *Till Eulenspiegel*; and we gathered that trouble was already brewing between various factions in the company. That this was so was confirmed not long after in a lengthy telegram from Barocchi, which informed us that disputes had arisen over both the distribution of the leading parts and the composition of the programmes, and asked for Diaghilev's advice. After this telegrams arrived daily; and we found ourselves in the anomalous position of having to direct a company in New York from no nearer than Rome. This flow of enquiries culminated in a telegram from Nijinsky asking me to come to New York immediately. But I decided that things had gone too far by now for my doing so to serve any useful purpose. Diaghilev entirely agreed, and we duly replied, 'Grigoriev declines the honour of rejoining the company while under your management'. On October the 23rd *Till Eulenspiegel* had its first performance, but was a failure. This ballet, incidentally, was unique in the history of those danced by Diaghilev's company in never being seen by either him or myself.

At the end of their engagement in New York the company went on tour, and the spate of telegrams died down. However, we received letters instead, and they described an incredible state of chaos. This was such as seriously to affect business. Receipts gradually declined; and their decline involved us too. Diaghilev ceased receiving all remittances from the United States; and if he had not obtained an advance, the small group who had remained with him in Europe would soon have been reduced to a very sad plight. In the end the management of the Metropolitan Opera House appointed a Mr. John Brown to restore the affairs of the company to some kind of order. Nevertheless not only did this season saddle our accounts with a large deficit; it also compromised our reputation so gravely that the Diaghilev Ballet was never able to appear in America again.

★ ★ ★

While these unfortunate events were occurring in the United States, our life in Rome was proving not only pleasant but also productive. Diaghilev discovered music for several new ballets, and Massine began composing them. *Maestro* and Madame Cecchetti arrived from Turin, bringing with them an attractive new dancer named Ladetta; and as Diaghilev also engaged other dancers, our little company gradually grew larger. The mornings were occupied by Cecchetti's classes, and from three till six o'clock in the afternoons Massine rehearsed. He began on a ballet to piano music by Scarlatti, which Diaghilev commissioned Tommasini to orchestrate. It was based on a play of Goldoni's, *Le Donne di Buon' Umore*, and was accordingly to be called *Les Femmes de Bonne Humeur*. Diaghilev had also unearthed some old Italian works on choreography, which contained much material that proved of use to Massine in his compositions. Throughout his career with the Diaghilev Ballet, indeed, Massine always guarded these books most jealously, and would never allow anyone else to look at them.

Diaghilev was present at all rehearsals, and took an active part in them, making suggestions and criticizing passages he disapproved of. As, for once, we were in no hurry, Massine had ample time in which to perfect every step, pose and gesture, and succeeded in thus achieving an unusually perfect finish. *Les Femmes de Bonne Humeur* was completed during December, and was extremely ingenious and original.

At Christmas Diaghilev and Massine went on business to Milan, leaving the company in my care. Having quite a lot of spare time at my disposal, I revelled in sight-seeing. The more I saw of Rome the more attached to it I became. Indeed, whenever I revisited it in after years I was always to feel as if I were coming home.

CHAPTER NINE

1917

IT was clear to Diaghilev that after the failure of the tour with Nijinsky there was no hope of his obtaining another engagement in the United States. Hence his visit to Milan. For in Milan one could usually count on coming across some South American impresarios with whom it might be possible to do business; and he in fact returned with a contract for a season in South America in the autumn of 1917.

Diaghilev having made Rome his headquarters, some of his friends began to forgather there too, just as they had forgathered before in Switzerland. In addition to Bakst, Larionov, Goncharova and Stravinsky, who were now usually in his company, a new friend in the person of the Spanish painter Pablo Picasso appeared on the scene; and the French poet Jean Cocteau began paying us frequent visits. They both took a keen interest in Diaghilev's work and contributed new ideas. Diaghilev was noticeably influenced by modern tendencies in the arts and began considering how they might be applied in ballets. He would often talk to me at this time about the Fokine and Nijinsky periods, and without minimizing the talents of those choreographers (and keeping the works of both in his programmes) made it clear that he no longer wished to collaborate with either, since he considered their approach old-fashioned. Massine, on the other hand, he thought capable of becoming the very incarnation of all that was modern in art and of putting Diaghilev's own ideas into practice; and while we were in Rome he lost no opportunity of instilling these into him.

The Massine period of choreographic history thus began in Rome. Whereas in *Le Soleil de Nuit* he had still been affected by Fokine's influence, in the ballets he composed in Rome he took a completely new direction; and they already exhibited what was to be the distinctive Massine style. They ceased to have anything in common, not only with Fokine's ballets, with their simple, clear and beautiful design, but also with

117

the older classical ballets, and became complicated, mannered and dry.

After completing *Les Femmes de Bonne Humeur*, Massine started composing the Kikimora ballet with music by Liadov, which it was decided to entitle *Les Contes Russes*. In this he relied a great deal on help from both Diaghilev and Larionov; and the result of their collaboration was a delightful work, distinctively Russian, in three scenes connected by interludes and ending in a tremendously vigorous *ensemble*. His third Roman creation was *Parade*. This was an example of modern art *par excellence*. The scenario was by Cocteau, the *décor* by Picasso, and the music by Eric Satie, all three of them extremely 'advanced'. When shown in Paris in the following spring *Parade* was to create a 'sensation'.

★   ★   ★

The company's American tour under Nijinsky came to an end in the middle of March; after which they returned to Europe. Diaghilev sent me to meet them in Spain and convey them thence to Rome. They numbered about fifty; and in those war-time days it was by no means easy to arrange transport for so many people at a time. It was only, indeed, by exerting a great deal of energy and ingenuity that I contrived to surmount all the difficulties of the journey. In the meantime Diaghilev had announced our first performance for April the 9th, and hearing no news of our movements (since I had omitted to send him a telegram), began to be alarmed lest we should fail to arrive in time. However, arrive we did; and his reunion with the company was positively touching. They were full of tales of what had happened in America; and to our dismay we found at their first rehearsal that they were woefully out of training and in need of the Cecchetti discipline to pull them into shape.

On the very day of their return a telegram arrived from Nijinsky in which he offered Diaghilev his services, saying that since Spain was a neutral country he would be able to go there. 'Yes,' said Diaghilev, not without some satisfaction. 'No doubt, after the *débâcle* in America he would be very glad to join us! Well, he can—after Paris. The King would like to see a released prisoner, I expect!'

★   ★   ★

Diaghilev's friends urged him to show the new ballet, *Les Femmes de Bonne Humeur*, in Italy before leaving, particularly since he called it his

'Italian ballet', on account of its scenario and music. Moreover, the scenery and costumes, by Bakst, were ready. In the first sketch for the setting, which represented a *piazza*, the houses on either side were drawn leaning inwards towards the centre of the stage. Diaghilev, seeing that this puzzled me, asked me whether I liked the drawing; to which I replied that I did not, and could not understand why everything in it was crooked. It appeared from Diaghilev's answer that Bakst had aimed at producing the effect of a convex mirror. This, however, seemed pointless to me; and Diaghilev also later changed his mind and ordered Bakst to produce a new design, this time with buildings normally upright. The costumes, on the other hand, were most attractive.

So Diaghilev arranged with the *Costanzi* Theatre for us to give four performances—which proved most successful. We gave *Les Femmes de Bonne Humeur* on April the 12th; and the public were delighted with it. Massine's choreography was considered most original and beautifully wedded to the Scarlatti music. As for its execution, never had any ballet given by our company been so perfectly danced, partly perhaps because no ballet had ever been so thoroughly rehearsed. It was hard to say who of the cast was best: they all seemed equally accomplished. Lopokova, Tchernicheva, *Maestro* and Madame Cecchetti, Massine, Idzikovsky and Woidzikowsky were all brilliant. It was altogether an exceptional performance and showed the ballet to have been one of the best Massine ever composed. On the same night Diaghilev included in the programme the piece, *Fireworks*, that had first attracted his attention to Stravinsky in St. Petersburg. For this he devised a setting, ordered from the Cubist painter Ballo. It consisted of various geometrical structures, such as cubes and cones, made of some transparent material that allowed of their being lit from within in accordance with a complicated lighting plot, which Diaghilev devised and worked himself. He maintained that it interpreted the music; and this Cubist fantasy proved much to the taste of his advanced artistic friends.

From Rome we went to Naples, where we gave several performances at the lovely *San Carlo* Theatre; and from there, stopping for one night at Florence on the way, we went to Paris.

★   ★   ★

Although the war had by this time been in progress for almost three years, until now we had seen but little of its effects. Our arrangements

The Diaghilev Ballet

had, of course, been entirely upset by it. But even in Russia during my visits since 1914, St. Petersburg, and still more Tikhvin, being so remote from the front, life had seemed to go on very much as before. I had done little more than set foot in England and France on my journeys from Switzerland to Russia and back; although Italy was belligerent, there had been but slight evidence of the fact in Rome; and the rest of our time had been spent in the United States and Spain, both of which were neutral. Now, however, in Paris the Western front was comparatively near. Nevertheless life here too seemed surprisingly normal. A good many of its inhabitants had left the city and, all men of military age being in the army, it had little of its habitual gaiety. Yet its fascination was as great as ever. After sunset, owing to the 'black-out', which of course precluded all street and other outside lighting, I was reminded of the 'white nights' of St. Petersburg, and used often to stroll in the Tuileries gardens, or stand in the Place de la Concorde, watching the day fade. I had plenty of time for such wanderings, since we did not appear every evening, and indeed gave only eight performances in all, again at the *Châtelet*.

It was three years since we had last been in Paris, and many changes had meanwhile taken place in our company, not only in its composition, but also in its ideas. The last important dancer of the older generation to perform with us, Adolf Bolm, had remained behind in the United States, and the young dancers who now took the leading roles were for the most part new to Paris. As for ideas, Diaghilev, under the influence of his new friends, had greatly changed his outlook, and was now ardent in his advocacy of the latest developments in art.

We were to give our first performance on May the 11th with *L'Oiseau de Feu* in the programme, and a day or two before it Diaghilev announced that he had decided to make an alteration in the final tableau of that ballet to accord with the spirit of the times. Instead of being presented with a crown and sceptre, as he had been hitherto, the Tsarevich would in future receive a cap of Liberty and a red flag. This was by way of homage to the first, the 'Liberal', Russian Revolution of February 1917. For at that time, though he professed himself a Monarchist, Diaghilev favoured the recent change of régime and wished to pay it a tribute. His idea was that the red flag would symbolize a victory of the forces of light over those of darkness, represented by Koshchey. We all thought this gesture of Diaghilev's decidedly out of place; but he was obstinate and would not heed us. When, however, the reaction of the public to it was unmistakably cold, and he even received several abusive letters on the subject, he realized that he had been ill-advised and soon restored the scene to its original form. In any case the incident was forgotten as soon as Paris saw *Les Femmes de Bonne Humeur* and *Les Contes Russes*, both of which enchanted it.

Our first performance was given for charity, and the audience were for the most part obviously in sympathy with the new trend in our *répertoire*. The press shared this attitude, and so prepared the ground for a favourable reception of the most advanced of our three new ballets, *Parade*, which was performed for the first time on May the 18th.

Parade had for its subject a circus, and consisted of a series of circus turns treated choreographically: namely a pair of acrobats, a Chinese conjuror, an American female child impersonator and a performing horse. The latter was danced by two men, whose quite complicated steps were stamped out to rhythms which took the place of music—to the delight and vast amusement of the audience. There were also two managers who wore by way of costume large cubist constructions made of cardboard, representing skyscrapers with staircases and balconies yet with the semblance of a human outline. The dancers detested these costumes, which were a torture to move about in; and between each of the turns they too had to do a lot of stamping, which was intended to suggest conversations between them. This was a relic of the fascination exercised over Diaghilev by 'pure rhythm' divorced from music. Those taking part in *Parade* were all admirable in their various turns. The American girl was danced by Maria Shabelska, the male acrobat by Zverev and the conjuror by Massine himself. In fine, *Parade* was witty and entertaining and caused the spectators much amusement. At the same time they took it seriously as a work of art, and realized that in its own fashion it represented a synthesis of several modern aesthetic principles.

It was for *Parade* that Diaghilev first ordered a special act drop, as he was to order others for most later ballets. This one, which also represented some of the performers and paraphernalia of a circus, was designed, like the *décor*, by Picasso, who not only supervised its painting but finished it off himself. Of the costumes, his design for that worn by Massine as the conjuror became particularly familiar to audiences, since it was reproduced on all the subsequent programmes of the Ballet, of which it became a kind of emblem.

In our last two programmes we gave *Las Meninas*; but in comparison with our other new and more exciting works it fell rather flat. Nevertheless, this season in Paris entirely revived our reputation, which the war and our long absence had considerably obscured.

★   ★   ★

From Paris we returned to Spain—a country we had grown extremely fond of. It was unlike any others we knew, reminding us if anything of Russia. We were thrilled by Spanish dancing and bullfights, and found that the Spaniards shared our Russian love of spectacle. Our affection was returned. We had become truly popular in Madrid; our reappearance was warmly welcomed; the theatre was always packed; and once again King Alfonso never missed a performance. To our surprise, of the new ballets the one that met with least appreciation was *Les Femmes de Bonne Humeur*. The Spaniards much preferred dramatic ballets such as *Cléopâtre*, *Schéhérazade* and *Thamar*. In the last Liubov Tchernicheva now played Queen Tamara, and her interpretation of the final scene electrified our audiences. The Madrid public also admired *Sadkó* and *Les Contes Russes*. *Las Meninas*, on the other hand, despite its Spanish theme, was appreciated by few but the Royal Family.

When the season was nearing its end, the King asked to see *Parade*, which he had heard much of and was interested in because the *décor* was by a Spaniard. Diaghilev had not included it in our programme for Spain, for which he judged it too 'advanced', and, sure enough, the public did not care for it. The King, on the other hand, was delighted with it, and particularly with the horse, whose appearance convulsed him.

★   ★   ★

At the opening of our season in Madrid we were rejoined by Nijinsky. He behaved quite amiably at first; and we hoped that his relations with Diaghilev would improve. Our hopes, however, were soon disappointed. For Nijinsky found his position to be very different from what he had expected. He had imagined that in the absence of Fokine he would be indispensable to Diaghilev as a choreographer, and that it had been for this reason that Diaghilev had been so anxious to obtain his release from internment in Austria. The experience of the American tour over which, however unsuccessfully, he had exercised complete control, had fostered illusions in him and his wife. They had lost touch with us, and failed to realize that Diaghilev had ceased to depend for success on names such as Nijinsky, Karsavina and Fokine, and had now at his command a number of excellent new dancers, round whom a new *répertoire* had been built up. Massine in particular had developed into a remarkable choreographer, and though he might not possess Nijinsky's almost incomparable genius as a dancer, so hard had he worked and such progress had he made, that he was well on the way to becoming an exceedingly good one.

That this was so was gradually borne in on the Nijinskys during our season in Madrid. They realized with dismay that, in spite of his celebrity, Nijinsky's success was far from being exclusive, and that Massine, however he might compare with him as a dancer, had surpassed him as a choreographer. They accordingly grew more and more discontented; their relations with Diaghilev took a turn for the worse; and Nijinsky followed the company to Barcelona, whither we next went, in an exceedingly nervous state.

★   ★   ★

Apart from our interest in Barcelona as the capital of Catalonia, with its strange medieval cathedral, half ruined and half unfinished, we were amazed by the unceasing life and traffic of its streets. Its main street, the *Ramblas*, was never still: the cafés remained open day and night, and it was for ever thronged with a mass of people, to whom rows of hawkers cried their wares—sweets, flowers and lottery tickets—at the tops of their voices. In the midst of this perpetual hubbub stood the excellent opera house, the *Liceo*, where we were to give six performances before setting out for South America.

The Barcelona public were theatre-minded and eager to see the Russian Ballet, of which they had heard much. Nijinsky's name was even better known here than in Madrid, and so we were sold out in advance for all performances. In Diaghilev's publicity, however, he laid more stress on the artistic merits of the company as a whole than on any individual performer; and this deeply displeased the Nijinskys, who at once concluded that it was Diaghilev's intention to minimize Nijinsky's importance. They grew more and more hostile until one morning, after the second or third of our performances, as Diaghilev was crossing the entrance hall of his hotel, at which they were staying too, he noticed their luggage piled up near the door. When he enquired what this portended, he was told that Monsieur and Madame Nijinsky were catching the night train for Madrid. He was naturally astounded, particularly since Nijinsky was billed to appear that night. He therefore telephoned to his local lawyer and asked for advice; on which they both called on the governor of the city. The governor, without hesitation, declared that by Spanish law once an artist was billed to appear, whatever his differences with the management, he was bound to do so. Moreover, he forthwith sent two policemen to the hotel, who informed Nijinsky that he was forbidden to leave Barcelona.

This incident very naturally produced a most painful impression on Nijinsky, and upset his nerves still more. Madame Nijinsky blamed Diaghilev for this result. But it must surely be allowed, in fairness to Diaghilev, that Nijinsky's unaccountable behaviour had placed him in an intolerable position. From then onwards the Nijinskys and Diaghilev ceased to be on speaking terms, and Nijinsky was persuaded by Barocchi to accompany us to South America only because Diaghilev was not going himself.

★   ★   ★

Diaghilev, as I have indicated, disliked the sea, particularly in war-time. Moreover, he considered his presence in South America unnecessary, and accordingly confided the management of the company to me and the administration to Barocchi. When I looked into the contract, however, I discovered that one of its conditions was that both Karsavina and Nijinsky were to be included in the company and that Bakst, Stravinsky and Diaghilev himself were to accompany it. I pointed this out to Diaghilev; but he told me that in subsequent conversations with the impresario it had been agreed to rescind this condition except as regards Nijinsky. Another passage in the contract laid it down that we were to travel on a British ship. But Diaghilev insisted that for safety we should take a neutral one instead. This, however, involved an alteration in our itinerary. For whereas the British ship in question had been going straight to Rio, where we were to open our tour, the Spanish ship that he now wished us to travel on was bound for Buenos Aires. There ensued a prolonged exchange of telegrams with South America, which resulted in our missing the British ship and being left with only three days before the departure of the other. No decision was actually come to indeed till July the 3rd, the day before the latter was due to sail. The hurry this involved was appalling. Nevertheless by that same evening the company, except for Nijinsky, who was to follow on a Dutch liner, and all our material were safely on board the *Reina Victoria-Eugenia*. We were seen off at the quay by Diaghilev and Massine, who stayed behind to prepare new productions.

★   ★   ★

On landing at Montevideo, I and my wife went to the hotel we had stayed at in 1913 and were given the same room as before. The hotel had a restaurant celebrated for its cooking; and Barocchi and I were to meet our impresario, Monsieur Mocchi, for luncheon there, having been informed that he wished to have a talk with us. Despite the delicious food I seldom enjoyed a luncheon less. Mocchi made no attempt to conceal the fact that he was much annoyed with us and declared at once that Diaghilev had broken his contract. Not only had he shipped us to Montevideo instead of to Rio, but he had also neither come with us himself nor sent out Bakst and Stravinsky. In these circumstances, he said, we were useless to him and might as well return to Europe forthwith.

Barocchi and I were somewhat taken aback by this onslaught. However, though we could not help feeling that up to a point his irritation was justified, we saw that his threats were largely bluff; since, having paid our transport expenses, he would clearly be loth to throw the money away. So after sitting silent for a moment, to allow his anger somewhat to subside, we explained that Diaghilev's motive in sending us to Montevideo had been to spare his company the risk of being torpedoed in a British ship. This was followed by another silence, which was broken only when Mocchi at length proposed that we should alter the contract. This put us on our guard at once. However, what he suggested turned out to be quite reasonable. He explained that we could not go on to Buenos Aires, because the theatre there was not available, and must therefore proceed to Rio as arranged. But to compensate him for the unforeseen expense of conveying us there, he would be satisfied if we would give three extra performances without being paid for them. As we realized that Diaghilev had been to blame for this confusion, we agreed to this proposal, only stipulating that Nijinsky should not take part in these performances. We did this because we had arranged with Nijinsky for a fixed number of appearances, so that if any were added we should have to pay him considerable extra sums for them, which would unbalance our budget. Mocchi saw the force of this

The Diaghilev Ballet

contention, and in the end our difference was amicably settled, and a fresh contract signed, on this basis.

Nijinsky was late in arriving at Montevideo, doing so only after two of our regular performances (that is to say those we had originally contracted to give) had already taken place with outstanding success. Shortly afterwards Mocchi informed us that the ship on which we were to go to Rio had been delayed, and asked us to seize the opportunity of giving our three extra performances at once. On learning that they were to be given, Nijinsky expressed a wish to take part in them. We therefore had to explain that he could only do so unpaid, since they were additional to the number agreed in his contract. The Nijinskys, however, refused to believe this and suspected a plot. Moreover, they now turned against me, accusing me of some hidden stratagem, though up till then our relations had been quite friendly. However, such was the success of our Montevideo performances that we were able to square our accounts with Mocchi, who ever after was more than amicable.

We embarked for Rio on the British liner *Amazon*. She was armed, and apart from our company carried very few passengers. An understandable feeling of anxiety prevailed; and sure enough, on our first day out as I was standing on deck, thinking of the lovely bay at Rio that I was soon to see again, there was a sudden flurry and someone shouted 'A submarine!' Madame Nijinsky happened to be standing next to me. She seized my arm and said in a nervous voice, 'Are we going to be sunk?' I said we might or might not be; and then the ship swung violently off course: the engine throbbed and the whole hull shook, as she moved away as fast as possible. Her guns were then trained on some point in the sea, and everyone crowded to that side. All I could make out, however, was a mass of foam on the water. Then, after about an hour, which seemed like an age, we changed course again and were told that the danger had passed; and the following day we reached Rio in safety.

We were to appear again in the large theatre that was so like a department store. But this time we did much better business, since the public had grown more interested in ballet. There were no further incidents with Nijinsky at Rio; but I noticed that he was more than usually quiet and absent-minded, as if for ever brooding: he never smiled and his eyes had a frightened look. He would never speak to either Barocchi or myself, and all arrangements had to be made through his wife.

From Rio we went to the industrial centre of São Paulo, which was

new to us. I and Barocchi went by car and arrived ahead of the company who went by train. They arrived only at about ten in the
evening, and were heralded by Kremnev, who burst into our hotel pale
as a ghost. It appeared that the truck containing all our scenery and
costumes had caught fire from a spark in a tunnel and been burnt out. I
was completely stunned by this announcement and could only gape at
Kremnev without speaking; this would mean the end of our tour, I saw,
with no season in Buenos Aires: disaster! However, Kremnev was soon
followed by Chausovsky, from whom, though he was equally agitated, I
gathered that the tragedy was slighter than had at first been feared;
what we had actually lost was all the scenery for *Le Spectre de la Rose*
and *Cléopâtre* and odd pieces from other ballets, but, fortunately, no
costumes. The *Spectre* scenery, moreover, was simple and could easily be
copied. For *Cléopâtre*, however, I had to use my ingenuity. It happened
that we had with us a set, never used, for a ballet we had thought of
doing called *La Péri*, also by Bakst; and this I eventually contrived to
adapt for *Cléopâtre*. We created no particular stir in São Paulo. But our
performances went well and the theatre was regularly filled. We could
now depend on our reputation.

After São Paulo we were due to appear in Buenos Aires. The difficulty was to get there. There was then no railway between the two, and
ships were few and infrequent. In face of this our impresario decided to
charter a small German ship that had been requisitioned by the
Brazilians and rechristened the *Cujava*. She had not been used for some
time, but was quickly, if rather sketchily, overhauled and proved quite
cosy and capable of holding us all quite comfortably. We sailed from
Santos, and at first all went well. On about the third day out, however,
I woke up to realize that the engines had stopped. I went up on deck
and there met Barocchi, who told me there had been a breakdown and
that they were trying to repair it. On going below I found that the
engines had been taken entirely down, and that some broken parts were
being mended. We said nothing to the company, who, as there was a
thick fog, probably attributed the stoppage to that; and ten hours later
the Captain announced that the damage had been made good; whereupon we cautiously resumed our voyage and reached Montevideo,
where we were to tranship, without further mishap. We learnt later
that our poor cosy little *Cujava*, after having been properly repaired,
had been caught and sunk by an enemy submarine on her way to Chile.

At Buenos Aires, where we were again to dance at the *Colón*, Mocchi

ceased to act as our impresario and we passed into the hands of a
Portuguese called Da Rosa. Our season opened on September the 11th
and proved one of the most trying I ever managed. To begin with, here,
as in Rio, the public had changed. During the war a large number of
Europeans had emigrated to the Argentine and had influenced the
Argentines in their attitude to the arts. The effect was, it is true, to
make them somewhat more discriminating and capable of taking a more
intelligent interest in our spectacles than before. But it was now considered naïve and uncultured to applaud, so that all applause was
virtually left to the professional *claques* that appeared to infest every
theatre in South America.

Then from the moment of our arrival in Buenos Aires I found it more
and more difficult to cope with Nijinsky. He was more silent and
irritable than ever; and every day something occurred to show with
what animosity he regarded myself and Barocchi. Also he would suddenly inform me that he could not remember a part he was to dance—
for instance that of Narcissus, or he would refuse to be lowered through
the trap-door at the transformation of Narcissus into a flower, but
would lie on the stage saying he was frightened in case I should give the
wrong signal, so that he would fall through and be killed. I never knew
what might not happen next. One day we were giving *L'Après-Midi* as
the second item on the programme, and when the stage was set I sent
for him. He arrived in a highly wrought-up state, and began pacing up
and down near the curtain, staring at the floor. The music was about to
begin, and I asked him to take up his position on the rostrum that
represented the Faun's rock. But he took no notice, even when I asked
him a second time. I then decided to wait, in the hope that he would
recover; but this, too, proved useless. By that time we were ten minutes
late and the audience was becoming impatient. I was completely nonplussed, till I suddenly had an idea. I ordered everyone off the stage,
leaving him alone on it, still pacing up and down, and then brought up
the curtain. The shock was so unexpected that he rushed into the wings;
whereupon, after lowering the curtain again, I went up to him and
sternly ordered him in a loud voice to take up his position. This time he
obeyed; the ballet started; and he performed his part as usual. After
this incident it was obvious that Nijinsky was seriously ill. A day or two
later, moreover, I noticed that he was being followed about by a man
and realized that this person had been engaged to protect him from
imaginary attacks on our part.

In the meantime serious misunderstandings had arisen with our new impresario Da Rosa. According to our contract he was bound after our eighth performance both to pay us for the week and to hand us our tickets for the return journey to Europe. When the moment came for him to do so, however, he said that he would settle with us at the end of the whole season. We had been warned that Da Rosa was not to be trusted. So now we consulted a lawyer, who informed us that, unless we were paid and received the tickets on that same day, before our ninth performance, we must refuse to give it; otherwise we should forfeit the money. We accordingly warned the management of the theatre, who did not, however, I think, believe us, and told the company to assemble in a neighbouring café and await instructions. At 8.30 P.M. the management, finding that none of the dancers were in the theatre, telephoned to Barocchi; and he and I then met Da Rosa, who begged us to give the performance, promising to pay us the following day. Remembering the lawyer's advice, however, we firmly refused. In the meantime the audience—mostly subscribers—began arriving at the theatre, where they had to be informed that the performance had been cancelled. This naturally produced a bad impression; but what suffered chiefly was Da Rosa's reputation. I went to the café and sent the company home to their hotels; and next day we were duly paid and given the tickets.

These business unpleasantnesses and the trouble over Nijinsky consumed too much of my time and energies, which should have been entirely devoted to the smooth running of the ballets. I therefore asked Barocchi to make himself solely responsible for dealing with Nijinsky; and from that time he did so, always remarking after seeing him, 'Poor Nijinsky! He's finished for good!' I too had the impression that this was so, and watching him from the wings whenever he appeared, tried to impress on my memory for the future a picture of his incomparable dancing, in which even now he seemed able to lose himself and find solace for his distress. I was loth to believe that I might never see such dancing again, and that his meteor-like career was drawing to a close— far away from Europe, before a public comparatively unappreciative of his genius. But, alas, my fears were all too well justified. The last time Nijinsky ever danced was at Buenos Aires on September the 26th, 1917, in two ballets that seemed symbolical of his tragic end—*Le Spectre de la Rose*, in which he sprang out of the window never to return, and *Petrushka*, in which he was slain, for ever, by the cruel Moor.

Despite all these worries, which fell upon Barocchi and me as from a

cornucopia, our season in Buenos Aires was most successful. As time
went on, the company enormously improved and the *ensembles* became
quite excellent. Lopokova and Tchernicheva were extremely popular
and so was Gavrilov, who alternated in the same parts with Nijinsky—
to compete with whom was a feat in itself. As for myself, I was kept
perpetually busy with rehearsals and the patching-up of scenery dam-
aged in the fire, and my responsibilities began to weigh upon me so
heavily that I longed for the day of our return to Europe. But when this
at length arrived and we found ourselves once more on board a ship, I
was met with a final unpleasant surprise. An hour before we were due to
sail I was informed that the shipping company had declined to load our
materials, since their transport to Europe had not been paid for. Da Rosa
had thus contrived to swindle us after all. We were accordingly forced
to meet this charge out of our own pockets and were faced with the
anxious task of ensuring at the eleventh hour that all our possessions
were safely on board.

Some of our friends came to see us off at the port, and among them
Nijinsky, who was to follow by another ship. He looked melancholy and
pensive: what was he thinking of, I wondered: that the company with
whom he had gained his world-wide celebrity were parting with him—
for good? I felt for him deeply, knowing as I did how ill he was in mind,
and being convinced that I was never to see him dance again.

In years to come people interested in the history of Nijinsky used
often to ask me the same question: 'Is it true,' they said, 'that Nijinsky's
madness was due to Diaghilev?' To this I always made the following
reply: 'From August 1913, when Nijinsky left Europe with us on our
first South American tour, he had nothing more to do with Diaghilev
personally; and at that time he was still perfectly sane. He did not even
meet Diaghilev again till April 1916, almost three years later, in New
York, and then for only one month, at the end of which Diaghilev
returned to Europe while Nijinsky remained in the United States. In
the following year they again met for no more than a month, in Spain;
immediately before Nijinsky sailed for South America, leaving Diaghilev behind. It was in South America that Nijinsky first showed signs
of losing his reason; and by the time Diaghilev saw him again he was
irremediably mad. Since, therefore, during the four years from the
summer of 1913 to that of 1917 Diaghilev and Nijinsky were thrown
together again by Nijinsky's re-engagement with the company for no
more than two months in all, to suggest that Diaghilev can have been

responsible for Nijinsky's madness is patently absurd. My own opinion
for what it is worth is that Nijinsky had the potentiality of madness in
him always, and that sooner or later this would in any case somehow
have shown itself.'

★   ★   ★

By the time we arrived back in Barcelona we had been away four
months. On the very day of our return Diaghilev summoned the entire
company, and after greeting them told us that owing to the long con-
tinuance of the war he was finding it more and more difficult to secure
engagements. He was far from despairing, and was confident that the
Ballet would again see better times; but all he had been able to arrange
so far were some dates at Barcelona itself, Madrid and Lisbon—after
them there was at present nothing to follow. He also told us that during
our absence Massine had planned some new ballets, which were to go
into rehearsal at once.

One of these new ballets had been conceived as the result of a conversation I had had with Diaghilev about the *Mariinsky*, before we set
out on our South American tour. An item in their *répertoire* that I looked
back on with delight was the ballet called *Puppenfee*, with choreography
by the brothers Legat; and I had suggested to Diaghilev that we might
revive it. Diaghilev had agreed and said he would consider it; and I
now found that while we were away he had pondered the idea, and not
only devised an entirely new scenario on the same theme, of dolls that
come to life, but had even chosen the music. In various libraries in
Paris and Rome he had discovered a number of little known compositions by Rossini, and after choosing those he thought suitable had
invited the Italian composer Respighi to orchestrate them. He had even
fixed on a title: the ballet was to be called *La Boutique Fantasque*; and we
began rehearsing it on the day after our arrival in Barcelona.

But to return to the previous day, after speaking to the company
Diaghilev detained Barocchi and myself and questioned us about the
tour, the burning of the scenery and Nijinsky's state of health. He was
greatly distressed by our account of the last. He had never, he said,
expected this to happen so soon. He also questioned Zuykov, who had
again accompanied us as Nijinsky's dresser and was able to give him
more detailed information.

On this occasion we stayed for a long time in Barcelona and danced a
large number of ballets, including *L'Oiseau de Feu* and *Petrushka*. We also

The Diaghilev Ballet

gave a single performance of *Parade*, to show the Spaniards Picasso's *décor*, since Picasso was by then beginning to be celebrated. We then went first to Madrid, where the King was eager to see us again and, as usual, was always in the audience, and finally, for the first time, to Lisbon.

The theatre in Lisbon at which we were to appear was enormous and resembled a circus. It was indeed called the *Coliseu des Recreias*. Diaghilev greatly disliked it and resented having to exhibit his company there. But nothing else was available, what had formerly been the Royal Theatre being closed.

On the day after our arrival Diaghilev and I were on our way to the *Coliseu*, which was not far from our hotel, when, just as we were about to go in, we heard some firing. Then some people appeared, running and being chased by mounted police; on which others took cover quickly in doorways. They informed us at the theatre that a revolution had broken out, and advised us to return as quickly as possible to the hotel and stay there. We duly reached the hotel to the accompaniment of further shooting, and were there counselled by the management to take the mattresses from our beds and protect ourselves with them as best we could from being cut by flying splinters of glass. A shell had just burst in the lounge and wounded several people, and there was no knowing what more might happen next. For the following week, while the fighting among the Portuguese continued, we led a most strange and uncomfortable life. We had to sleep without ever undressing, either on the floor of our rooms or on the stairs; we had very little to eat, since the hotel had only meagre reserves; and we were excruciatingly bored. This enforced inactivity was a torture to Diaghilev, and since it was at this juncture that news arrived of the Communist coup in Russia, he began cursing the revolutionaries of every country. Diaghilev was deeply disturbed by the October Revolution, foreseeing its terrible consequences for Russia. For however aloof he might keep himself from politics in general, whatever affected his own country he took truly to heart.

As regards Portugal, however, order in Lisbon was restored as suddenly as it had been disrupted: the victorious general appointed himself president; and life at once became, to all appearances, perfectly normal. This stirring episode indeed had somewhat unfortunate results for us. For not only was the opening of our season delayed for a fortnight, but its success, when at length it started, was no more than moderate. Apart from anything else, on our third night there was a failure of the city's electricity supply, so that the theatre was plunged into total darkness and we were obliged to stop the show. Diaghilev contrived in the end, however, to give two performances at the ex-Royal Theatre of *San Carlos*, reopened for the occasion; and there we were at least able to exhibit ourselves to better advantage.

CHAPTER TEN

1918

AT the beginning of January 1918, although Diaghilev was in touch with agents in various countries, we had not a single firm engagement in view. Our impresario in Madrid was trying to arrange another tour for us in Spain, but his negotiations required much time and had been further held up by the revolution in Portugal. By the terms of his contracts with the members of the company Diaghilev had the right to devote one month in the year to rehearsals at half-pay; and this he now decided to exercise, asking me to remain with them in Lisbon, while he, Barocchi and Massine went off to Madrid in search of fresh engagements.

I felt uncertain what ballets I had best rehearse, but since *Daphnis et Chloë* had not been done since 1914 and was all but forgotten, I decided to tackle that. However, the dancers soon came to feel that these rehearsals amounted to no more than a means of filling in time; they saw little immediate prospect of actually dancing *Daphnis*, and found it hard to display much interest. January passed without our receiving a word from Diaghilev. We grew despondent; rumours began to circulate that our enterprise was doomed; and minor theatrical agents appeared on the scene, tempting the dancers with offers of other employment. At last, in the middle of February, Diaghilev reappeared, and his presence was enough somewhat to reassure us, even though, so far from bringing any news of a definite engagement, he announced that the Spanish tour was not likely to start for another two months, during which he would be unable to pay us. He then returned to Madrid. This long enforced holiday was, of course, most unwelcome to the company. But there was nothing for it but to remain in Lisbon and while away the time—a process assisted by the Portuguese, who shortly afterwards indulged in another smaller and even swifter revolution.

It was not in the event more than a month before we at last received

some hopeful news; and this was soon followed by detailed instructions
from Diaghilev, to the effect that we were to leave Lisbon for Spain on
March the 28th. We reopened on Easter Sunday, March the 31st, at
Valladolid.

★   ★   ★

Our tour took us for the most part to smaller places in the Spanish
provinces, where we met with many amusing adventures. We were
always enthusiastically received by the public, who greatly appreciated
our dancing and were particularly taken with ballets such as *Schéhérazade*
and *Prince Igor*. Unfortunately, however, although we filled the theatres,
our takings were inadequate, since in the small towns it was impossible
to charge high prices. Diaghilev was unable to cover his expenditure and
could pay the dancers only subsistence salaries, with a promise to make
up the difference on the advent of better times. We all accepted this quite
cheerfully, finding life in Spain most interesting and the people delightful.

Massine spent much of his time in the study of Spanish steps. He
would go to small workmen's taverns to watch the dancing and miming,
the latter being singularly expressive, despite its simplicity. Diaghilev
indeed made it a point that the whole company should watch and
assimilate the national dances; and we were immensely impressed, for
instance, by the wonderful *jotas* we saw at Saragossa and the wide
variety of steps and miming *ensembles*, inspired by bullfighting, that we
saw at Bilbao.

★   ★   ★

Impressed as he was with the charm of Spanish dancing, it is hardly
surprising that Diaghilev should have begun thinking of a Spanish
ballet for our *répertoire*. But this, he insisted, must be based on authentic
Spanish steps and rhythms, and so differ from most of what passed
elsewhere for Spanish dancing, which had but little in common with
the genuine thing. At that time, however, there existed no such creature
as a Spanish choreographer. Massine, therefore, must steep himself in the
study of Spanish dancing and seize the very essence of its character.
Massine adopted this idea with enthusiasm, and with his accustomed
zest and talent was quick to achieve most promising results. Diaghilev
thereupon ordered a score from the Spanish composer Manuel de Falla
and designs for scenery and costumes from Pablo Picasso. As for dancers, he was persuaded that, to obtain real authenticity, the principal

The Diaghilev Ballet

parts should be taken by Spaniards. He therefore began a search for suitable artists, and pitched first on Felix Fernández, a most remarkable young dancer from Seville: As soon as we arrived in Madrid, he invited the whole company to the theatre, to see Fernández in his *répertoire*; and we were all quite carried away: I had never indeed seen anything to equal his performance. Next, having secured Fernández, Diaghilev began looking for a girl to partner him; and found one who would have done so admirably in Zelita Astolfi. She was then performing at a small popular theatre in Madrid itself, and Diaghilev went to watch her night after night, finally offering to engage her. Unhappily, however, neither she nor her parents, who were simple people, could bear the prospect of her leaving Spain and joining us. So, to Diaghilev's great disappointment, she turned us down.

Our season in Madrid was as pleasant as ever. The King, who as usual attended every performance, now took to having long talks with Diaghilev in his box, and came to be known as the Ballet's godfather.

★　　★　　★

Preoccupied though he thus was with the creation of the new ballet, Diaghilev was also much exercised over what was to become of the company when our tour should come to an end in Barcelona. The market for our wares was then severely restricted. After the Nijinsky fiasco of the previous year we could not hope for any engagement in the United States; and though we received a tentative offer from South America, Diaghilev did not think it firm enough to accept. It was therefore in Europe that we must seek our fortune; and, since England was at least not the scene of actual hostilities, Diaghilev thought a season in London might be a possibility. He did not, of course, expect one of prewar scale. All he aimed at was taking a medium-sized theatre, where he could establish the company and there await the end of the war. It was with this in mind that he approached the London theatre agent, Eric Wolheim, who, however, replied that at the moment a theatre such as Diaghilev had described was unobtainable. At the same time he asked whether Diaghilev would consider presenting the Ballet as a turn in the programme of a music-hall, the Coliseum. Many of the English music-hall stars being in the forces, the Coliseum management, he said, were hard put to it to fill their programmes, and despite the fact that the Ballet would be very expensive, he thought they might well offer Diaghilev an engagement.

Diaghilev was at first inclined to reject such a proposal. After our triumphs at Drury Lane in 1914 to appear at a music-hall seemed to him too sad a decline. Yet so bad was the financial position of his enterprise, it meant either accepting or disbanding the company. The choice was a hard one; and he hesitated long; but under pressure from all of us he eventually accepted in principle, and opened negotiations with the Coliseum management.

★   ★   ★

Barcelona was, as ever, seething with life; and we revelled in listening to Spanish singers and guitarists and in watching wildly exciting dancers performing on floors no larger than tables—all to be found in quite humble cafés. The public, moreover, had by now acquired a taste for Russian music and our ballets; and the theatre was packed full at every performance we gave. Lopokova, Tchernicheva, Massine, Idzikovsky and Gavrilov soon became their especial favourites and were invariably greeted with tremendous applause.

But we were conscious that with Barcelona our Spanish tour would end, and pinned all our hopes on the engagement in London. Yet the season finished with nothing settled; and the question of our future began to alarm us. Diaghilev decided to return to Madrid, from which it would be easier than from Barcelona to keep in touch with London and, for that matter, with other countries. Before he left he told the assembled company that because of the war he was still unable to offer them anything definite. He had hopes, he said, of the season in London. But as this was still uncertain, they would be at liberty, if they chose, to accept other work as soon as their contracts with him expired, as they would within a month. Meanwhile, if he were to secure a definite engagement, he would at once renew their contracts and pay up all arrears of salary.

★   ★   ★

There now ensued for us a most trying time. Barcelona became hot and airless; our small savings dwindled to nothing; and this precluded us from moving elsewhere. All we could do was to wait in patience. But week after week passed and there was still no news. We began to think that our days with Diaghilev were over and that we should all be obliged to fend for ourselves. And then, one morning—and what a beautiful morning, fine and cool, it was!—I was handed a telegram, which read: 'London contract signed. Arriving day after tomorrow—Diaghilev'—on which our drooping spirits at once revived.

In the meantime, it is true, a few members of the company had been tempted to desert us by one or other of the theatrical agents who had begun haunting us once again. Our situation being so desperate, I had been powerless to dissuade them; and most of them had gone off to South America. One of our most talented young dancers, Léon Woidzikowsky, I had indeed induced to hold out; and I do not think this can have been a source of regret to him, since in a very short time he became one of our *premier danseurs*.

Diaghilev duly arrived; our contracts were all renewed; and we were ready to start for England, when a fresh and quite unforeseen obstacle arose: the French government declined to grant us transit *visas*. Clémenceau, it appeared, was so disgusted with Russia for retiring from the war after the Communist Revolution that he was determined no Russian should set foot on French soil. It was only through the intervention of our godfather King Alfonso, who instructed his Ambassador in Paris to put in a word for us, that this decision was rescinded. We were delayed for three weeks; but in the end the *visas* were granted.

★　　★　　★

Diaghilev now went to London ahead of us, leaving me to arrange transport for the company and our belongings. With the existing shortage of both coaches and trucks this was no simple matter; and it was yet another three weeks before space could be found for us. However, we finally set off on August the 4th, duly arriving in Paris one early morning. But here another unpleasant surprise awaited us. The trucks containing our luggage had been detached from our train *en route* and could not, we learnt, arrive for another few days. Despite our having only transit *visas*, accordingly, we were obliged to remain in Paris and wait for it. Paris was much changed, we found. It looked empty and sad; and the people seemed despondent, as well they might be under the bombardment of 'Big Bertha'. We were glad to depart as soon as our luggage arrived.

★　　★　　★

London was also 'blacked out' at night, and its life was hardly less affected by the war. Nevertheless its atmosphere was very different from that of Paris. Far from being empty, it was all too full; and we had considerable difficulty in finding anywhere to live.

We were to open at the Coliseum on September the 5th—which gave us roughly a month in which to make our preparations. This interval had been allowed for in the arrangements made between Diaghilev and Mr. Oswald Stoll, the manager. For not only had we to renew some of our scenery; we had also to fill the gaps in our company caused by the defections we had suffered during our time of uncertainty in Barcelona.

To engage foreigners in his company was a new departure for Diaghilev. But circumstances now obliged him to do so. However, the recruits in question were rapidly assimilated. They were immediately subjected to a strict training in Russian methods not only of dancing, but also of walking on the stage, wearing their costumes and making-up. Some of the English girls who now joined us were given Russian surnames such as Istomina, Grantzieva and Muravieva; and, what with living as they did among Russians, with our incessant rehearsals, with the example of the leading dancers, and, not least, with the daily lessons of *Maestro* Cecchetti, not only were these newcomers considerably 'Russianized', but they also underwent a whole artistic education.

★   ★   ★

The Coliseum, like all music-halls in those days, gave two performances daily, with a change of programme every week. This meant that we were to give twelve performances weekly of our 'turn', which was to be placed about the middle of the bill. But Diaghilev disliked the idea of showing only one ballet twelve times a week, and insisted that three or four different ballets should be performed alternately. This, he argued, would be less monotonous, not only for us but also for the public.

Remembering how popular it had proved in London before the war, we chose *Cléopâtre* for our first matinée. To replace the old setting, which had perished in the fire, we had a new one designed by Robert Delaunay; and new costumes were also provided for Tchernicheva as Cleopatra and for Massine, who now for the first time played Amoun. At our first evening performance we gave *Les Femmes de Bonne Humeur*.

Diaghilev considered, rightly, that any success we might enjoy would depend largely on what impression we created at the start. He was therefore very nervous before these performances. He was uncertain, in particular, how *Les Femmes de Bonne Humeur* would be received in London.

PLATE IX

SERGE GRIGORIEV

London had so far seen none of Massine's creations; and the ballet represented a new choreographic trend. It had been well received in Paris: that was true. But, on the other hand, it had not been liked in Spain. He need not, however, have worried. *Les Femmes de Bonne Humeur* was a success of the first order. Just as Karsavina's finest part was the Firebird, so Lopokova was never more entrancing than as Mariuccia. She herself, Massine, Idzikovsky and Woidzikowsky were all of them new to London audiences. Nor, before the war, had Tchernicheva danced any such leading parts as Costanza. They were all at once accepted as wonderful dancers; and Diaghilev could pride himself on having virtually 'made' every one of them. Our press was excellent; and no-one seemed to mind coming to see us in a music-hall. The place was packed for every performance.

★   ★   ★

From this moment onwards we began living the orderly and peaceful existence for which we had been longing throughout the turmoils and anxieties of the preceding years. Every Monday and Thursday we put on two new ballets, to see which large and eager audiences assembled. Next after *Les Femmes de Bonne Humeur* we showed *Le Soleil de Nuit*, which was lengthened by a solo arranged by Massine on other music from *The Snowmaiden* and danced with tremendous zest by Lopokova. At Christmas we gave a considerably expanded version of *Les Contes Russes*, with the *finale* altered and much improved by Massine. The chief figure in this ballet was now the Swan Princess, danced by Tchernicheva in a beautiful Russian costume and headdress designed by Larionov: a part to which she was exactly suited by her looks. This new version of *Les Contes Russes* was especially popular; and we were asked by the management to give it as often as possible.

Meanwhile, in November, the war had at last come to an end; the Allies had won; and London had been transported with joy and relief. The year that was now ending was the tenth of the Diaghilev Ballet, and might, for us too, have been marked with celebrations—of our jubilee. Diaghilev, however, had a horror of anniversaries. Neither this, nor our thousandth performance, which took place a week after the Armistice, on November the 18th, would he consent to mark with any special festivity.

CHAPTER ELEVEN

1919

Diaghilev seemed very happy in London, and he hoped that, owing to our continued success, we might be able to remain there for some time to come. He watched every performance as usual, but rarely attended rehearsals. For these took place in the mornings, and he disliked early rising: it suited him rather to lie in bed talking on the telephone, reading the newspapers, planning new productions and interviewing us, his colleagues. He would often summon me to his hotel, since for the moment I was less occupied than usual with rehearsals. For Massine took up much of the company's time with his preparation of *La Boutique Fantasque*, the composition of which he had begun in Spain. On these occasions Diaghilev would usually give me some instructions about the company, or just talk, or indulge in reminiscences of the past—on days, that is to say, when he was in a genial mood. But when he was annoyed by some unpleasant incident he would profit by my presence to vent his irritation. Then I would be addressed merely as 'Grigoriev', instead of his usual 'Sergey Leonidovich'—and my sole desire in such an event was to escape with all speed.

The pleasantness of our life in London during this visit was marred only once, by a most distressing incident. Felix Fernández, whom we had brought over from Spain with us, was both a wonderful dancer and a delightful young man, much liked by everyone. He was always, it is true, somewhat silent and absent-minded; but no-one had guessed he was on the verge of a nervous collapse. What was our dismay, therefore, on hearing one day that he had been arrested! He had been discovered dancing before the altar of a London church, after smashing some of its windows. He was declared insane; and we afterwards heard that, like Nijinsky, he was incurable.

★   ★   ★

In the middle of March, after we had been about six months at the Coliseum, Stoll suddenly gave us a fortnight's notice. This was utterly unexpected: we had been praying for our engagement in London to be prolonged as much as possible. Diaghilev was dumbfounded, and for some days was at a loss what to do. But, very fortunately for us, just at this moment a revue failed at the Alhambra, another of Stoll's theatres. It thus fell empty; and Diaghilev immediately offered to put on his Ballet there in the pre-war manner. Stoll agreed, and a contract was signed forthwith; but in order to give London a respite from ballet, it was decided to defer our opening for a month, during which we were to pay a visit to Manchester. Our last performance at the Coliseum took place on March the 29th—the ballet was *Les Sylphides.*

★   ★   ★

After a fortnight in Manchester we returned to London to prepare for our season at the Alhambra. Most of our *répertoire* had already been shown at the Coliseum; but Stoll insisted that at the Alhambra we should give four new ballets. As *Parade* had not yet been seen in London, it, we decided, would do for one; and for two of the others Diaghilev proposed *La Boutique Fantasque* and Massine's Spanish ballet, which was to be called *Le Tricorne.* For the fourth it was thought, more vaguely, that we might do another Spanish ballet, hardly yet started, *Les Jardins d'Aranjuez.*

We were to open the season with *Petrushka* and *L'Oiseau de Feu,* neither of which had been done at the Coliseum; and to strengthen the cast Diaghilev re-engaged Lydia Kyasht, who was well known and very popular in London. Another new dancer, Vronskaya by name, was also billed as a member of the company, not only on posters but even in our programmes. Yet for some reason or other, unknown to me, she never in fact put in an appearance. The ballerina whom above all Diaghilev wished to have with us again, however, was Karsavina. He always cherished a special affection for Karsavina, associating her as he did with the glory of his early days. But Karsavina was in Russia; and though he wrote to her, he at first received no answer. The Civil War was still in progress and all communications were interrupted; but one day to his delight he heard she was on her way and would be able, after all, to take part in our season.

143

The Diaghilev Ballet

*   *   *

Our first performance at the Alhambra took place on April the 30th.
The programme consisted of *Les Femmes de Bonne Humeur*, *Petrushka* and
Les Sylphides. 'All London' was there, and it was a most festive occasion:
we had a tremendous reception, with innumerable bouquets and curtain
calls, reminding us of the enthusiasm of the nights before the war.
Diaghilev had feared that our long season at the Coliseum might detract
from the interest of our appearance at the Alhambra. But his fears were
unfounded: the theatre was always full; the public were enthusiastic;
and interest in the Ballet seemed to be growing from day to day.

The first notable event of the season was the return of Karsavina.
But, strangely enough, this provoked less interest than her admirers had
expected. As with Nijinsky, when he rejoined us in 1913, so with
Karsavina now: in her case, as in his, the season had already started; and
this seemed to blunt the impact of her appearance. Moreover, on her
arrival from Russia Karsavina was out of training; and Diaghilev
would have done better to give her due time for practice and rehearsal.
Apart from anything else, also, she had now to face a new and exacting
public, to whom she was less familiar than any of the other dancers.
However, Karsavina soon regained her perfection and re-established her
renown as firmly as ever.

*   *   *

The next landmark in this season was the first performance of *La
Boutique Fantasque*. As I mentioned before, the score was a collection of
odd pieces by Rossini, the orchestration of which by Respighi had
turned out most effective. It had originally been intended that the
décor should be designed by Bakst. But Diaghilev later dropped this
proposal and ordered it instead from André Derain—at which Bakst
was naturally offended, so that this led to a quarrel between him and
Diaghilev. When I first saw Derain's designs for this ballet I was taken
aback by their complete unsuitability. The scenery consisted of two
most attractive cloths—one a back-cloth and the other an act-drop. But
the back-cloth was to be seen only through two large open windows and
a doorway minus a door; and though the whole setting was charming
and decorative in itself, not only did it utterly fail to suggest a shop that
had to be closed at night; its whole style was at war with the scenario,
which was realistic. Diaghilev was irritated by my comments on these

designs and dwelt on their aesthetic merits, which I did not deny. He also countered my criticism that they were unsuitable by remarking that this *boutique* was, after all, *fantasque*, and could not be expected to exhibit any realism. Yet as soon as we began rehearsing in this setting, the incongruities I had foreseen became all too evident. The ballet is divided into three *tableaux*; and at the end of the first the shopkeeper has to lock up for the night. But how could he do so with two vast windows and a doorless doorway? I was just waiting for this moment and watching Diaghilev's face! We had in fact to adopt a compromise, by providing curtains for these openings, which the shopkeeper drew before his departure. But this was never satisfactory, at least to my mind. For not only were these curtains unconvincing as regards the action; as long as they were visible, they ruined the design.

However, the incongruity of this *décor* by Derain in no way detracted from the success of the ballet. What with Rossini's enchanting and then little-known music and Massine's witty, variegated and vigorous choreography, *La Boutique Fantasque* evoked exceptional enthusiasm, and at once became one of the public's particular favourites. The dancers were all excellent and well suited to their parts. Above all, Lopokova and Massine in their *can-can* fairly 'brought the house down' at every performance. Of the three *tableaux* the most admired was perhaps the second. It culminated in a most brilliant, animated *finale*, which was invariably drowned in overwhelming applause.

★   ★   ★

Until she appeared at the Coliseum Lydia Lopokova had never danced in London. But now, after the production of *Les Femmes de Bonne Humeur* and *La Boutique Fantasque*, she became an especial favourite with the London public and received most laudatory notices in the newspapers. She was indeed exceptionally light, with a wonderful *élévation*. Such were her charm and temperament, also, that although her performance was sometimes slightly slap-dash, she rivalled both Karsavina and Kyasht in her appeal. In her interpretation she combined complete unself-consciousness with a certain eccentricity; and both these qualities met with Diaghilev's approval. Yet—despite her attainment of so enviable a position—she suddenly left us and for a time abandoned the stage. On July the 9th I received a short note from her. It read: 'Dear Sergey Leonidovich, Since Diaghilev is away I am writing to you. For

PLATE X

LYDIA LOPOKOVA

reasons of health I shall be unable, from today, to appear with the ballet—Lydia Lopokova.'

This letter was less clear than brief. For she had danced the night before and had seemed in her usual form. I at once rushed round to her hotel to see her—only to be told that she had left London that morning. I gathered subsequently that her sudden departure was not due to ill-health, but had quite another, private, cause. But with her usual impetuosity she had decided to throw up everything, and so vanished from our sight for quite a considerable time.

Diaghilev was in Paris; so I had to take it on myself to replace Lopokova. I consulted Massine; and we decided to give her part in *La Boutique* to Nemchinova—whom I had brought from Moscow four years before, when she was still a pupil. Nemchinova had meanwhile developed into a very able dancer; and from that distressful day, when she took over the *can-can*, not only did she succeed quite satisfactorily in stepping into Lopokova's shoes, but was able to rank as a new ballerina.

On his return from Paris Diaghilev was no less astounded by Lopokova's sudden departure than we had been. This was the second time she had deserted us. Nevertheless I was convinced, and rightly, that she would return.

★ ★ ★

The outstanding success of *La Boutique Fantasque* greatly encouraged Massine in the composition of his Spanish ballet *Le Tricorne*. Both he and Diaghilev mourned the loss of poor Felix, and Diaghilev still regretted that the chief parts in the ballet should not be danced by Spaniards. As things were, the Miller was to be danced by Massine himself and the Miller's wife by Karsavina. At the dress rehearsal it was clear that *Le Tricorne* would also be a success. The scenery by Picasso, in whites and greys and pale pinks and blues, was truly exquisite; the costumes were no less so, both in shape and colour; and the appearance of the dancers in their costumes against the set was singularly satisfying. The period of the story being the eighteenth century, Picasso had given Massine knee-breeches. But the most important of all the dances was the Miller's *Farruca*, for which dancers in Spain usually wear long, very tight trousers. Diaghilev therefore insisted that Massine should wear such trousers, maintaining that otherwise the true character of this dance would be obscured. Picasso, however, equally insisted on the knee-breeches; and it was only with some reluctance that he agreed to a compromise, whereby Massine should wear long trousers during the first half of the action and then change into knee-breeches for the rest. Diaghilev was delighted with the *décor* as a whole. He thought, however, that the Miller's house was a trifle dull, and to enliven it asked Picasso to paint a vine growing against its wall. This Picasso did with his own hand; and it was certainly an improvement. Diaghilev was equally pleased with de Falla's score and with Massine's choreography. Our long sojourn in Spain had been turned to good use; and Massine had mastered both the general style and the characteristic steps of Spanish dancing. The only weakness of *Le Tricorne*, if there was one, lay in the plot, by Sierra, which was lacking in clarity. But this seemed to matter little in face of the superb performances not only of Massine and Karsavina, but also of the young dancer Woidzikowsky, who was likewise a master of Spanish steps and played the part of the decrepit but libidinous governor. The *corps de ballet* had little to do in *Le Tricorne* except in the '*Sevillana*', most cleverly arranged by Massine, with which it closed.

Le Tricorne was performed for the first time on July the 22nd, when it took the audience by storm. To Diaghilev's regret de Falla was in the end unable to conduct, having been obliged to return to Spain on urgent family business. A much admired adjunct of the ballet was its act drop by Picasso. This represented a group of Spaniards watching a bullfight from a box, and was painted almost entirely by Picasso himself.

★ ★ ★

Our season at the Alhambra ended on July the 30th. We were sorry it could not continue longer; but London was emptying for the holiday season. Diaghilev hoped that Stoll would now make him a further offer. But since we had by this time been with him for the best part of a year he, perhaps not unnaturally, failed to do so. However, a rival manager, Sir Alfred Butt, came forward instead; and Diaghilev gladly accepted his proposal for an autumn season at the Empire Theatre. Both the Alhambra and the Empire have now been pulled down to make way for cinemas; but in 1919 they were charming theatres usually housing musical shows. We were therefore delighted at the prospect of dancing at the Empire after our holidays, for which we now scattered in all directions. Diaghilev went off to his beloved Venice, which, on account of the war, he had not visited for four whole years.

PLATE XI

LÉONIDE MASSINE

The Diaghilev Ballet

★ ★ ★

Towards the end of our season at the Alhambra some changes took place in the composition of our company. Diaghilev required a permanent replacement for Lopokova, since Nemchinova was insufficiently experienced to take over all the parts she had been dancing; and the need for such a reinforcement was all the greater in that Karsavina could not for personal reasons remain with us indefinitely. It was for these reasons that he engaged a dancer from Warsaw named Halina Szolc. But her *début* in *La Boutique* was so unsatisfactory that her engagement was terminated after only three performances. It was at this time also that, despite my efforts to retain him, we lost Gavrilov—the remarkable dancer who had once shared certain parts with Nijinsky and had afterwards taken them entirely over. On the other hand, we now acquired two new men from Moscow in Novikov and Svoboda. Neither of them, however, remained with us for long.

We began at the Empire on September the 29th. Since the *répertoire* was virtually the same in both, this season may be reckoned as a continuation of that at the Alhambra. The only new ballet we showed was *Parade*, which was regarded by the London public as amusing but no more. *Les Jardins d'Aranjuez* was also announced. But it was not in fact given, since Massine never finished it.

While we were at the Empire our patron the King of Spain paid a visit to London; and at his request we gave performances of his favourite ballets *Schéhérazade* and *Les Sylphides*, and also of *Le Tricorne*, which was, of course, new to him and of which he highly approved. Other royal spectators were King George V and the Shah of Persia. The latter came on an official visit to London; and, at a gala performance in his honour, we gave *La Boutique, Cléopâtre* and *Les Sylphides*.

The London public disliked long intervals. But these were necessitated by our elaborate changes of scenery, costumes and make-up. In order to render them less tedious, however, Diaghilev instituted, first at the Alhambra and later at the Empire, the performance during each of them of some orchestral piece. These pieces were conducted by Ansermet and Adrian Boult and appeared to be much enjoyed.

★ ★ ★

When signing his contract with the management of the Empire, Diaghilev resolved that this season should, for the present, be our last in

London. He feared lest, otherwise, the public should tire of us, and aimed at our leaving England at the end of December. He accordingly now began making frequent trips to Paris, which, since the end of the war, had been gradually returning to normal. Its artistic life was being resumed, and a renewal of our regular seasons there now at last seemed possible. His ambition, of course, was to return to the *Opéra*; and this he was fortunate in being able to realize. The *Opéra* management offered him forty performances—half in January and February and the rest in the spring.

We accordingly left the Empire on December the 20th and opened at the *Opéra* on Christmas Eve. *La Boutique Fantasque*, which we then gave as a novelty, failed, however, to provoke as much enthusiasm as we had expected. The applause was much louder for the Polovtsian Dances—an old favourite in Paris. This, incidentally, was the five-hundredth performance of this ballet. It was distinguished also by the temporary return to us of Koralli as the Polovtsian girl.

CHAPTER TWELVE
1920

THE year 1920 opened for us with a set-back. The orchestra of the Opéra chose to go on strike and put us out of work for three weeks —which was awkward financially. Rehearsals, however, went on as usual; and as Diaghilev considered *La Boutique* and *Le Tricorne* insufficient for Paris in the way of novelties, we soon began work on another ballet, for which the music had meanwhile been put in hand. This was a symphonic suite by Stravinsky, drawn from the score of his opera *Le Rossignol*. It was almost six years since Stravinsky had done anything for Diaghilev. Ever since 1916 they had been less friendly than before; and Stravinsky had ceased composing for ballet, till, at this time, they both felt the wish for a reunion. Whether it was Diaghilev who suggested this remodelling of the opera, or Stravinsky, I do not know. But in any case, as soon as the new score was completed, Massine set to work in haste on composing the choreography, so that the ballet might be included in our present season. Now also, at Diaghilev's suggestion and under his guidance, Stravinsky began the re-working of some music by Pergolesi that was to result in the score of another ballet, *Pulcinella*.

In the meantime, thanks to its music, its *décor* and its magnificent execution, *Le Tricorne* had made a deep impression on Paris audiences. And when *Le Chant du Rossignol* was in due course presented, it too turned out to be exactly what Paris liked. Apart from the music, which to those who had not heard the opera was entirely new, the ballet had an exquisite *décor* in white and turquoise by Henri Matisse, and choreography of a pleasing and interesting variety. The real Nightingale was danced by Karsavina, the mechanical Nightingale by Idzikovsky, Death by Sokolova and the Emperor by—myself. Once shown, we gave this ballet at every performance up to the end of the season.

★   ★   ★

Owing to the strike of the orchestra, this season in Paris finished later than it should have; and since Karsavina was unable to remain with us beyond the date at which it had been scheduled to close, she was replaced thereafter by Nemchinova in *La Boutique*, by Sokolova in *Le Tricorne* and by Tchernicheva in *Le Rossignol*; all three of these replacements winning Diaghilev's approval. Another 'star' of the company was, as I have mentioned, Koralli. As well as in the Polovtsian Dances she appeared during this season in *Thamar*, but left us again as soon as it was over.

While we were still in Paris Stravinsky completed the score of *Pulcinella*, whereupon Massine began composing on it too. Massine seemed indefatigable and was now at the height of his powers. Each ballet he composed was better than the last; and such was the admiration they evidently evoked that he asked Diaghilev at this time to let his name appear on our programmes as *Maître de Ballet*. Diaghilev, however, replied that he must be patient. He must compose ten ballets before being accorded such an honour!

★   ★   ★

From Paris we went to Rome, arriving in February. Diaghilev, as ever, was intent on the confection of new works. Though we still had *Pulcinella* on the stocks, he was anxious to find fresh music in particular, and, burrowing in an Italian library, came upon the score of a little-known opera by Domenico Cimarosa, called *Le Astuzie Femminili*. It was in three acts and had a *finale* for dancers; and Diaghilev was much attracted by it. After cutting all the recitatives, with which it abounded, he handed the score to Respighi and invited him to re-orchestrate it. Although it was primarily an opera, it contained many passages that lent themselves to dancing; and it was Diaghilev's aim to lay special stress on these. At this point—for the first time in their now long collaboration—Diaghilev and Massine fell out, over the treatment of this opera. Massine was in favour of ending it with a *divertissement*. But Diaghilev disliked *divertissements*, and wanted a connected suite of dances. Their arguments were interminable, but Massine held out; and the *finale* of *Le Astuzie*, as produced, was in fact a *divertissement*. They had, of course, argued before on points of detail. But hitherto Massine had always yielded to Diaghilev's reasoning. So this was a new departure;

and whether or not it signified a rebellion on Massine's part, whether or not he had decided to assert himself, it marked in fact the opening of a rift between them, which was to widen as time went on. All the same, if these heated discussions had taken place at any juncture but this, I am inclined to think they would have led to no such consequences. For it happened that Diaghilev was in a state of distress. Margherita Poletti, the wife of his valet Beppo, had just died after an operation; and Diaghilev, who was very fond of her, was grievously shocked by her death. Such an event was very frightful to him; for he had an inordinate dread of death and would always, if possible, avoid the subject. It was for this reason that he would never, if he could help it, cross the sea. For someone had told him that he would die on water.

★　　★　　★

Before we left Rome, the management of the *Costanzi* invited us to return in 1921; and Diaghilev joyfully accepted the engagement, since to live in Italy made him feel young, he said; he loved it above all. From Rome we went to Milan, where we had never performed before. Our reception there was comparatively cool. The theatre was most indifferent and so was the orchestra; and we danced for once to half empty houses. We put down this lack of success to our impresario. Diaghilev, being preoccupied with the organization of our next season in Paris, had left all arrangements to him; and he had made little effort to prepare the ground for us. However, we just managed to pay our way.

★　　★　　★

Our next destination was Monte Carlo. It was all but six years since our last visit; and we were greeted very warmly on our return to the Casino. The sight of Monte Carlo made us think of the Ballet's early days—with Bakst and Benois, Stravinsky and Fokine, Karsavina and Nijinsky. Of all that famous band Karsavina alone returned with us; though Stravinsky also paid us a flying visit, to observe the progress of *Pulcinella*. Our present company were otherwise all new. But the spirit of our enterprise remained the same, preserved by its traditions from all decline. 'However much wine you may draw from a cask, when you refill it some of the old remains.' So Diaghilev would say, half joking, in this connection; and of the spirit of his Ballet it was indubitably true.

Monte Carlo was cram-full of visitors; and the theatre was always sold out for our performances. We had five new ballets to present to these audiences; the company were in excellent training; and their dancing was irreproachable. *Pulcinella* and the dances for *Le Astuzie* were both all but ready. Little of our time, therefore, was occupied with rehearsals. Diaghilev now relented about Massine's designation. As soon as the *mise en scène* and choreography of *Le Astuzie* were finished, his wish to be entitled *Maître de Ballet* was granted, and he appeared thenceforward as such on our programmes.

Our next season in Paris was to open on May the 8th; but we had undertaken to appear at a charity gala that was to be held there four days earlier; and just as we were due to leave, there occurred a railway strike in the south of France. I was at a loss what to do; for in those days there were no long-distance bus services, and it was impossible to ascertain what, if any, trains were running. Fortunately the son of the station-master was a *balletomane*, and he told us privately at what time a train—the only one—would be passing through Monte Carlo on its way from Italy to Paris. We therefore all assembled on the platform at 5 A.M., the appointed hour; but when the train duly steamed into the station we saw that it was packed full to the last inch. How we managed to add ourselves to its other occupants I cannot imagine, but we did somehow, and arrived in Paris well in time for the gala.

★   ★   ★

The programme of this gala was far from being supplied only by us. It also included Sarah Bernhardt, Ida Rubinstein, Zambelli (the *prima ballerina* of the *Opéra*) and a chorus of Russian singers. Our contribution consisted of *Schéhérazade* and *Les Sylphides*. It was now many years since Karsavina had first danced *Les Sylphides* in Paris; and her reappearance in the part delighted the public. Her chief supporters were Nemchinova and Tchernicheva, with Massine—handsome, elegant and poetic—in the sole male part, originally danced by Nijinsky. It had long been Massine's wish to appear in *Les Sylphides*. But Diaghilev had never thought him quite suited to the part and had refused to let him dance it as long as Gavrilov remained with us. Ida Rubinstein's share in the gala consisted in her once again playing Zobeïdé in *Schéhérazade*, the role she had created in the now distant past. But, strangely enough, she no longer seemed to fit it. It was as if, after so many years away from us, she had lost touch with our spirit. She was never to appear with the Diaghilev Ballet again.

★   ★   ★

For the first night of this our ninth season in Paris, although there were no new ballets in the programme, the auditorium of the *Opéra* was filled with an elegant audience. Russian Ballet seemed to have become an institution with the French: as a critic remarked, the spring would not be the spring without it. To Diaghilev the opinion of Paris on his aesthetic ideas was always decisive; it provided him with a criterion of true success or failure. Paris, on its side, was always eager to see his latest creations; and on this occasion what provoked most expectation was, naturally enough, *Pulcinella*, with its score by Stravinsky and its *décor* by Picasso.

When Picasso showed Diaghilev his designs, Diaghilev criticized those for some of the costumes; and this led to a quarrel between them that could only be patched up by Madame Sert, who was a friend of both. Whether in the end Picasso altered the costumes I am not sure. But, as they turned out, I personally never thought them either very interesting in themselves or congruous with the set. Thanks to its being founded on music by Pergolesi, Stravinsky's score was a great deal more tuneful than usual, and therefore much easier to dance to. Massine's choreography, inspired by the *Commedia dell' Arte*, was excellent: at once poetic and amusing. The cast was a small one and the dances were mostly solos; but the interest was most ingeniously sustained. Pulcinella was played by Massine himself, with Woidzikowsky as his double; and both were brilliant. The chief women's parts were danced, admirably too, by Karsavina, Tchernicheva and Nemchinova.

We gave *Le Astuzie Femminili* for the first time on May the 27th. The singers included Mafalda de Voltri, Angelo Masni-Pieralli and Aurelio Anglada: a strong cast chosen by Diaghilev during our stay in Italy. The production was by Massine and culminated in the *divertissement* on which he had insisted, all the items of which were extremely well composed and danced. The scenery and costumes were by José-Maria Sert —this being the third production he designed for Diaghilev. Nevertheless the opera failed to produce the impression expected. Its reception was indeed favourable; but Paris was far from being carried away by it; and Diaghilev was disappointed.

There was a feature of this season in Paris that I dwelt on when dis-

156

cussing it with Diaghilev in retrospect, namely that in both our two latest productions the music was by Italian composers, Pergolesi and Cimarosa, and the *décor* by Spanish painters, Picasso and Sert. 'Yes. Only the choreography was Russian,' said Diaghilev. 'But what can we do? How can we find young Russian musicians and painters abroad? Oh, how I long to be back in Russia: to breathe in its air and gain new energy from its soil! But shall I ever be able to? I wonder.'

This season in Paris was, then, quite satisfactory. Nevertheless Diaghilev was faced with serious financial worries. For in these post-war years the cost of living continually rose; the company found it hard to make ends meet; and they requested Diaghilev to raise their salaries. Although he entirely sympathized with their demands, his budget would not allow of his meeting these in full. However, by careful scrutiny of expenditure he contrived at least to meet them partially.

★   ★   ★

This summer, as in the days before the war, having finished in Paris, we moved to London, and now found ourselves once again at Covent Garden, where we had not appeared for seven years. Our performances were to alternate with those of operas, a restful arrangement that we much appreciated. Ballet was becoming quite a habit in London. Both our new productions were well received, the Cimarosa, indeed, better than in Paris. But *Le Chant du Rossignol* was not much liked; and we only gave it twice in consequence.

This season at Covent Garden had an unfortunate ending. A misunderstanding about money arose between Diaghilev and the management. Diaghilev was much irritated and consulted his lawyer; and the lawyer suggested that, unless the matter were duly settled, we should refuse to give the last performance. But it proved impossible to settle it in time; so that Diaghilev was forced to carry out his threat and cancel the performance at an hour's notice. Alas, this proved a fatal mistake, both as regards the management and the public. What had been the right course in Buenos Aires was the contrary in London. For a last performance in London is usually a great occasion, and for this one not only was the house sold out, but a profusion of bouquets had already arrived at the stage door for the dancers. To disappoint his admirers so was to risk causing no little offence. But Diaghilev realized this only at the eleventh hour; and by that time it was too late: the harm had been done.

The Diaghilev Ballet

★   ★   ★

The company now dispersed for the holidays, Diaghilev going as usual to Venice. He was much exercised over engagements for the autumn and winter. With the impoverishment of Germany and her neighbours, a mid-European tour, such as would have solved the problem in pre-war days, was out of the question; and he was still undecided, when one of our employees suggested a tour of the English provinces. The idea was not one that much appealed to Diaghilev, and he was doubtful of its wisdom. However, since he had nothing else in prospect, he agreed; the tour was arranged; and after our holidays we reassembled in London.

Diaghilev's doubts soon proved well founded. Our provincial tour was not a success. The public we confronted showed little interest in ballet and found our performances merely bewildering. Had it not been for a final fortnight in Liverpool we should scarcely have been able to carry on; and our financial position was hardly improved by our agent in Birmingham, who made off with our takings.

In the meantime Diaghilev had been considering what the pro-gramme should consist of for our next season in Paris. While we were still in London before setting out on our ill-fated tour, he had sent me a telegram, being still in Paris himself before rejoining us, instructing me to start once again rehearsing *Daphnis et Chloë*. This was regarded by the company as an evil omen. It reminded them of our listless days in Lisbon, when in 1917 our fortunes had sunk so low. It was therefore a positive comfort when Diaghilev on his arrival in London counter-manded his first order and told me to rehearse *Le Sacre du Printemps* instead. But how were we to do so? After so many years Nijinsky's choreography had been completely forgotten, and we had no means of restoring it. There was nothing for it, as Diaghilev saw, but to resort to Massine for an entirely new version. Massine duly agreed to undertake one, and assumed the task with his usual energy. Only a few days remained before we set out from London. But by the time we did so he had a scheme of work already mapped out.

★   ★   ★

It was some consolation for the ill success of our English tour that Diaghilev had meanwhile arranged with the management of the

Théâtre des Champs-Élysées for us to perform there in the course of December. The question was: what new ballets to show? As I have indicated, Diaghilev's first idea was a revival of *Daphnis*, which had the advantage of a distinguished score by Ravel. But then for some reason he had veered away from it, and plumped instead for *Le Sacre du Printemps*. Seven years had now passed since the great anti-Stravinsky demonstration; and Diaghilev judged that *Le Sacre* would no longer strike the public as revolutionary. Massine's new version was accordingly decided on, and was danced for the first time on December the 15th. It was conducted by Ansermet, the Stravinsky specialist, and, sure enough, this time it was received very favourably, both at the *répétition générale* and on the first night itself.

Massine's choreography was highly expert, but to my mind lacked pathos, in which it differed notably from Nijinsky's. It was as if Massine had paid greater heed to the complicated rhythms of the music than to its meaning; and the result was something almost mechanical, without depth, which failed to be moving. Nijinsky's version, comparatively helpless though it was, had better captured the spirit of the music, and whereas it had brought out the general theme and, in particular, the contrast between the two scenes, these somehow became obscured in Massine's composition. This no doubt was partly accounted for by the fact that Diaghilev abolished the first set for this production. The whole ballet was now performed in the other, which represented the ancient Scythian Steppe under a lowering black and yellow sky. The only solo dance in the ballet, that of the doomed maiden, before performed by Piltz, was now interpreted by Lydia Sokolova. Few dances can ever have been longer or more strenuous.

It was at about this time that I began to notice a change in Diaghilev. He was inclined to be irritable and often lost his temper—a thing that had never happened before. I mentioned this to Zuykov, who always knew what was happening. 'Quarrelling with Massine,' replied Zuykov laconically. And then, only two days later, during a lighting rehearsal, while I was alone with Diaghilev, he suddenly asked: 'What would you think if Massine suddenly left us?' This was so unexpected I merely looked surprised; so Diaghilev went on: 'Yes,' he said, 'we are to part.' As soon as I could collect my thoughts, I answered that as a dancer Massine could certainly be replaced. But as a choreographer—to replace him at all quickly would be extremely difficult. 'You think so?' said Diaghilev, as if not so sure. Then, looking at his watch, he asked me to continue by myself; after which he stood up and went away, leaving me much perturbed.

Nevertheless nothing further happened immediately. Our tenth season in Paris ran its customary course; and the only evidence Diaghilev exhibited of the private conflict that was distressing him was that he showed less than his usual interest in the details of our performances. He looked more and more sombre, however; and it was clear that his relations with Massine were rapidly deteriorating. Knowing Diaghilev as I did, I felt sure we were heading for a crisis that might affect the whole future direction of the Ballet. It was therefore in an atmosphere of painful tension that, at the very end of the year, we at length left Paris for Rome.

CHAPTER THIRTEEN

1921

WE opened in Rome on New Year's Day, being joined there by Catherine Devillier, a character dancer from the *Bolshoy* Theatre in Moscow. Diaghilev was always on the look-out for talent fresh from Russia. Devillier did not, however, remain with us very long.

We made a point of showing the Romans *Le Astuzie*, which, though Italian, was new to them; and it proved, as we had hoped, very much to their taste. *Pulcinella*, on the other hand, was presented only towards the end of the season, and we were unable to give it more than one performance on account of Massine's then leaving the company.

It was now a whole year since Diaghilev and he had had their first difference of opinion over the Cimarosa; and although in the interval their relations had clearly worsened, I did not believe, until he actually did so, that Diaghilev would act on his decision to part with Massine. One day in Rome he sent for me, however. I found him in a state of great agitation. 'I am definitely parting with Massine,' he declared. 'I have come to the conclusion that we can no longer work together. His contract has expired; and I should like you, as *régisseur*, to inform him before today's rehearsal that I have no more need of his services, and that he may accordingly consider himself at liberty.' Diaghilev's face was flushed as he told me this, and he could not keep still, but kept walking up and down the room. I knew, as before over Fokine, that it was useless to argue or make any attempt to over-persuade him. So I remained silent; on which, realizing that I did not agree, he continued even more heatedly. Hadn't he, he cried, done everything for Massine? Hadn't he *made* him? What had Massine's contribution been? 'Nothing but a good-looking face and poor legs!' And now, when, owing to Diaghilev, he had become the dancer and choreographer he was; when, working together, they could have created the most wonderful things—

everything had collapsed and they must needs part company!—His voice was full of pain and bitterness. He grew more and more agitated, and continued his pacing to and fro. Then he poured himself out a glass of wine, which he drank off quickly, and, suddenly controlling himself: 'So, my dear Sergey Leonidovich,' he said, 'go and deliver my message, please. We'll talk further about this later on.'

I felt much dejected on leaving Diaghilev after this interview. This was the second time he had called on me to perform an unpleasant duty of this kind. But at least to Nijinsky I had only had to sign a telegram; whereas now I was forced to tackle Massine face to face!

★   ★   ★

Massine looked preoccupied when he arrived at the rehearsal. I immediately took him aside and gave him Diaghilev's message. He was clearly quite unprepared for it and looked most astonished. Then without saying a word he left the room. I cancelled the rehearsal without giving the company any explanation, and went back by myself to my hotel. That night Massine called on me and asked me in detail what Diaghilev had said. I told him as much as I could, adding that I was convinced no power on earth could make Diaghilev revoke his decision. Massine agreed that this was probably so; after which we shook hands and said goodbye.

Once Massine had departed, Diaghilev somewhat regained his equanimity; but the company continued to be amazed at this sudden turn of events, which they greatly regretted. Then, when our performances in Rome were over, we left for France, never, as a company, to see the Eternal City again.

★   ★   ★

Massine's departure ended the third period in the history of Diaghilev's Ballet—a period that for length and fertility may be compared with the first period of Fokine. It had been Fokine's achievement to widen the scope of the classical choreography in which he had grown up. He had introduced new *forms* of dancing, with more complicated movements and grouping, and had established an even balance between the *corps de ballet* and the soloists. Massine, as a next step in the development of choreography, basing himself not on the classical canon direct, but rather on that canon as modified by Fokine, introduced movements more complicated still, and also more mannered and broken up, thus creating his own characteristic style. When he left our company he was far from having said his last word; and that was the pity of his break with Diaghilev. He was indeed then just reaching maturity, and with Diaghilev's collaboration might have risen to even greater heights than he had already attained.

In parting with Massine Diaghilev placed himself in an awkward position. For he was obliged to discover some other choreographer, since new ballets were always expected during his Paris seasons. He therefore surveyed the talent in the company, and fixed for this role of choreographer on a dancer named Slavinsky—who, though young and gifted, was entirely devoid of any knowledge of choreography. When asked by Diaghilev for my opinion of his choice, I replied by enquiring what ballets he intended Slavinsky to compose; and found that what he had in mind was a ballet on some music suitable for dancing that had been written by Prokofiev, a Russian composer of the new generation. Now I knew that Prokofiev's music was inclined to be difficult, and felt sure that Slavinsky would be unable to cope with it, if not for lack of talent, at least for lack of experience. But Diaghilev countered this objection by saying just as he had once put Larionov in charge of the youthful Massine, so now there was no reason why he should not put him in charge of Slavinsky. The ballet was to be a modern treatment of a Russian fairy tale, and to be called *Chout* (a French spelling of the Russian *Shût*, meaning 'The Buffoon').

★   ★   ★

Our first destination on leaving Rome was Lyons, where we gave a ten-day season. This was marked by a number of notable *débuts*—of the various dancers who now took over the large number of parts that Massine had been dancing. Thus Idzikovsky now achieved a long-cherished ambition of dancing the Poet in *Les Sylphides*, while Zverev began playing the Negro in *Schéhérazade*, and Woidzikowsky Amoun in *Cléopâtre*. Diaghilev seemed well satisfied with all three.

Then from Lyons we went to Spain, at the special request of King Alfonso, who had made Diaghilev promise him this visit at their meeting in London. Diaghilev himself went to Paris on business, having arranged to rejoin us later in Madrid. In the month that had elapsed since the departure of Massine he had begun to recover his normal good spirits and to display once more his usual energy and enterprise.

The Diaghilev Ballet

I was glad to arrive in Madrid well in advance of our opening night, since there were still a number of Massine's parts in which I had to rehearse new dancers, and in some cases they experienced considerable difficulty in learning them. *Le Tricorne* presented the greatest problem. The part of the Miller was given to Woidzikowsky. Possessing a remarkable memory for steps, he learnt it quickly enough and danced it admirably. There was a something, however, that seemed to elude him —a certain *brio* in the attack, the peculiar Spanish nobility of carriage, with which Massine had contrived to endow his performance.

★　　★　　★

When Diaghilev arrived in Madrid in time for our first night, he was accompanied by Valentine Nouvel and a young man, till then unknown to me, called Boris Kochno, whom Diaghilev had taken on as his personal secretary. Nouvel of course I was well acquainted with from the far-off days of our 'committee' in St. Petersburg; and I was delighted to hear that he was now to manage our administration. For Barocchi had left us some time before; on which Diaghilev and I had divided his duties between us. I had often told Diaghilev that, in addition to my other duties, I really could not cope with administrative responsibilities. As long as Massine was with us, moreover, he had rehearsed his own ballets; whereas since his departure I had been saddled with these as well. This appointment of Nouvel, accordingly, came to me as a blessed relief.

Diaghilev, we were pleased to find, had entirely recovered and was full of news. Lydia Lopokova, for instance, had reappeared and was to rejoin us; Larionov was taken with the idea of *Chout*, which he was to start work on with Slavinsky as soon as possible; and Prokofiev had finished the score, which was precisely what was needed. 'But we must think of other new things,' said Diaghilev. '*Chout* won't be quite enough by itself.'

★　　★　　★

At our first night in Madrid we had a vociferous reception. The absence of Massine seemed scarcely to be noticed—except by the King, who asked Diaghilev what it meant. What counted now were the ballets rather than individual performers; and Madrid was enchanted with what to it were our new creations, *La Boutique Fantasque, Les Contes*

Russes and, above all, *Le Tricorne*, with its Spanish music and *décor*. The audiences in Madrid could not get over our mastery and execution of their own intricate Spanish steps; and though I privately missed the presence of Massine in this ballet, Woidzikowsky as the Miller was astonishingly effective.

We were again fascinated by the traditional dancing at the little popular cafés and night-time cabarets: the so-called *Cuadro Flamenco*, to the accompaniment of guitar, castanets and voice. Diaghilev used to go to them with us, and after one particularly striking performance conceived the plan of transporting a *Cuadro* just as it stood to Paris and London, where he felt sure nothing of the kind had ever been seen. This would also have the merit of providing a second new item for his next programme.

★   ★   ★

The middle of April saw the end of our performances in Madrid, where, oddly enough, the Diaghilev Ballet were never, any more than in Rome, to appear again. Our next destination was Monte Carlo. In contrast with what had occurred the year before, during this season no new ballets were to be shown; and we were able to concentrate on the production of *Chout*. Larionov had begun work with Slavinsky in Madrid; and I watched the progress of their operations with interest. A scenario had already been sketched out by Larionov in Paris. It was composed of six scenes, of which these two somewhat inexperienced masters were now engaged in assembling the component parts, as if for a mosaic, bit by bit. Slavinsky's contribution seemed to consist in doing what he was told to do by Larionov. However, the work was finished before we left Monte Carlo. When Diaghilev saw it, his enthusiasm was, to say the least, moderate; and afterwards, as we sat on the terrace, he asked me what I thought of it. I said I thought the production thin: it had the air of being by a student of dancing. 'Yes,' he agreed. 'The best part is the music. The next best is the *décor*; and the worst is the choreography. However, at least it's ready; so we're all right for the moment. But it takes us nowhere. We must find a choreographer.' Leaving out of account the quality of this new production, with it and *Cuadro Flamenco*, it was true, we were 'all right' for Paris. Meanwhile for the *Cuadro* Diaghilev had arranged for Picasso to design a set and some costumes; and the cast had all been carefully chosen while we were still in Spain. Among them was a very beautiful girl, Maria Dalbaicin, and when

engaging her Diaghilev intended her also to dance the Miller's Wife in
Le Tricorne. He had always wished Spaniards to dance the chief parts in
this work, and so now brought her to Monte Carlo to begin rehearsals. I
saw, however, from the first moment she started that technically it was
beyond her. But Diaghilev insisted on her going on with it; and as I was
busy with the preparation of Massine's *Sacre* for Paris, I had no time to
argue and was forced to submit. I handed Dalbaicin over to my assistant
Kremnev. But in spite of our labours she had still not learnt the part by
the time we left for Paris.

★   ★   ★

When Diaghilev had lost Fokine in 1913 he had been able to make up
for a lack of new productions by presenting a programme of ballets
alternating with operas (in which the chief parts were sung by Chaliapine), whilst also experimenting in choreography with Nijinsky. Now,
however, on his loss of Massine, he had no such resource: Russia was
closed to him. He therefore decided to make his season in Paris short,
and during it to show only ballets of proved appeal to the Paris public,
together with *Chout* and *Cuadro Flamenco* as novelties. He also took
especial care over advance publicity, in which the main emphasis was
laid on Prokofiev's music for *Chout*, the attractions of the *Cuadro* and the
merits of some of the leading dancers. We were to give our season this
time at the *Gaieté Lyrique*.

This was not a particularly distinguished theatre. But, when occupied
by us, that seemed to make little difference. At the first performance we
gave both *Cuadro Flamenco* and *Chout*; and the former created a positive
furore. Such dancing had never been seen in Paris; and Picasso's *décor*,
which he had painted himself, was altogether enchanting; it represented
the interior of a small Spanish theatre, with spectators in boxes painted
on wings at either side. As for *Chout*, as Diaghilev had expected, the
music was commended, but little notice was taken of either the *décor* or
the choreography. But such was the enthusiasm aroused by the rest of
our programme, and *Cuadro* in particular, which was performed every
night, that this eleventh season of ours in Paris went off very well,
despite the absence of Massine.

We became, however, somewhat painfully conscious of Massine's
existence while in Paris. After leaving us he had signed a contract for
South America, and since he then found it difficult to collect dancers to
accompany him, began laying siege to some of ours. They succumbed

to this pressure to quite a serious extent, and the day before our season in Paris ended, announced that they would be leaving. Diaghilev was incensed. Moreover, their defection embarrassed him. For our next season, in London, was due to begin almost immediately.

★   ★   ★

Owing to his differences with the management of Covent Garden Diaghilev could not expect to return there this year. So he instead accepted an offer by Charles Cochran of the Princes Theatre, then recently rebuilt. Unfortunately this theatre was very small for us. Not only were we uncomfortably cramped on the stage; but the accommodation for performers was so restricted that some of the company had to dress and make up in other premises, specially rented.

The outcome of the London season did not worry Diaghilev. He was entirely confident of its success. We began with ballets that were all well known, and left the more problematical *Chout* for later presentation. On the other hand, we showed *Cuadro Flamenco* from the first; and it was even more liked in London than in Paris. It was not until June the 8th that we gave *Chout*, at a *répétition générale* conducted by Prokofiev. He was greeted as an interesting and talented composer; but the ballet, with Devillier, Sokolova and Slavinsky in the leading parts, failed, as in Paris, to make any great impression. The third new work that we showed in London was the Massine version of *Le Sacre du Printemps*. It was better received than its predecessor in 1913; but the English public still seemed to Diaghilev unaccountably slow in appreciating Stravinsky's score.

The great 'sensation' of the season, however, was the return of Lopokova. She was received with wild excitement: the London public seemed utterly subjugated by her charm. Maria Dalbaicin, in contrast, had no such success. She had by now mastered her steps in *Le Tricorne*, but, despite her good looks, made no effect as a dancer.

The season was thus in the main most satisfactory. Yet the problem remained: for new ballets a choreographer was necessary. The only alternative was to revive old works; and that we in fact took it was in part due to an accident. It happened that a musical play called *Chu Chin Chow* was then running in its third year at His Majesty's Theatre. Diaghilev was amazed at the possibility of such an enormous run, and one day he said to me half jokingly how much he wished he could discover a ballet that would run for ever—that would be happiness! I replied that not only was such a thing quite impossible, but it would bore him to death. 'Not at all,' he retorted. 'You'd run it and I'd do something else!'

'In that case, why not put on *Coppélia*?' said I. 'It's one of Petipa's best ballets and lasts a whole evening.' This conversation evidently set his mind working. He kept returning to the subject, till at last one day he said he had thought of the ideal solution. This was a production of another of the Petipa ballets, *La Belle au Bois Dormant*. This appeared to me an excellent plan, which should provide an issue from our temporary embarrassment.

Once having made up his mind, Diaghilev went into action. By great good luck the Alhambra had had another failure and was available for the autumn. Mr. Wolheim, our agent, accordingly opened negotiations for it, and in a comparatively short time an agreement was duly drawn up, between Diaghilev on the one hand and Stoll on the other. By the terms of this contract, whereas Diaghilev was to have complete artistic control of the production, Stoll was to finance it, the capital he sank in it being repayable from the box-office takings. I remember the arrival of this document at Diaghilev's hotel. He was rather excited and immediately read it anxiously through. Next he placed it on a small table in front of him and, making the sign of the Cross over it, said with a sigh, 'Well—what will be will be!' Then he signed it, very carefully.

★   ★   ★

The contract once signed, Diaghilev was faced with having to do a great deal of work in a very short space of time. His first problem was the scenery and costumes; and here he badly missed Benois, since Benois had a special knowledge of the Louis XIV period, in which *The Sleeping Princess* (to give the ballet its English title) was to be set. However, he had by now made peace with Bakst, and therefore sought his help instead. But Bakst had not entirely forgotten the cause of their quarrel—the *décor* of *La Boutique*—and was not easily persuaded. Moreover, he foresaw how colossal an undertaking this would prove. Designs for no less than five sets and about a hundred costumes would be required; and there was very little time to do them in. Nevertheless, in the end, he consented.

Then there was the music. Diaghilev began by studying Tchaikovsky's score. He deleted everything he considered dull, and replaced these excisions with material from other compositions of Tchaikovsky's. He also asked Stravinsky to re-orchestrate the Prelude and Aurora's *variation* in Act III; and the score was undoubtedly much improved by these alterations.

Finally, there was the choreography and the question of dancers. Diaghilev's first step was to engage Nicolas Sergeev, a former *régisseur* of the *Mariinsky*, who now lived in Paris and, being thoroughly familiar with all the ballets of Petipa, was clearly the best person to restore *The Sleeping Princess*. As for a ballerina to dance the title role, at about that time several famous ballerinas from the *Mariinsky* emigrated to Paris, namely Vera Trefilova, Liubov Egorova and Olga Spesivtseva; and Diaghilev decided to invite, not one of them, but all three. Vladimirov, the *premier danseur* of the *Mariinsky*, had already joined us, and another most excellent dancer, Anatol Vilzak, was now asked to join us too. Diaghilev believed that a ballet such as *The Sleeping Princess* could be adequately performed only by dancers brought up in the traditions of the *Mariinsky* and of Petipa—in which opinion, of course, he was perfectly right; and to complete the tale of such dancers he engaged Madame Carlotta Brianza to play the wicked Fairy Carabosse; thereby achieving a link with the original production of the ballet in 1890, in which Madame Brianza had created the part of the Princess herself. Madame Brianza was also to take over the daily lessons hitherto given to the whole company by *Maestro* Cecchetti. For the *Maestro* had grown too old to cope with them any longer, and, at the end of our season at the Prince's, had left us, though he remained on in London and still taught pupils in private.

This year we were only able to go on holiday for a month, after which we reassembled in London to start rehearsing. Our company was considerably enlarged for this production; and among its new members was a young beginner named Patrick Kay—who was later to become celebrated as Anton Dolin.

Many of our dancers, who were used to the difficult and intricate movements characteristic of Fokine's and even more of Massine's choreography, were astonished, and even somewhat disappointed—especially in the *ensemble* numbers—by the classical simplicity characteristic of Petipa. They could not understand why so many rehearsals should be required: a whole two months to revive such an easy ballet, particularly since the leading dancers all knew their parts already. But

The Diaghilev Ballet

Diaghilev was of another opinion. He held that this, if any, ballet required thorough rehearsal, for the very reason that it *was* so simple, and judged that it would take time for the dancers to acquire the period features of Petipa's style. Diaghilev took an active part in the *mise en scène*, directing much of it himself, and though what he aimed at primarily was a reconstruction of this ballet in its original form, he was prepared, where it seemed advisable, to introduce fresh matter. It was hence that Bronislava Nijinska came to take a hand in the choreography. She had left the company at the same time as her brother, and had returned to Russia, where she had done some productions. But she happened to arrive in London about the time of our starting rehearsals; and though he had not of course seen any of her compositions, Diaghilev invited her without more ado to arrange some new numbers in *The Sleeping Princess*. She did this most successfully, the best known of these numbers being the afterwards celebrated Dance of the Three Ivans. It was clear even from such modest creations that she was possessed of a certain knowledge and experience; and Diaghilev at once scented in Nijinska a possible choreographer in succession to Massine.

A propos of the Three Ivans, Diaghilev met with some criticism from his friends for introducing such a dance into this ballet at all. Was not a Russian peasant dance incongruous, they said, at the court of a King of France? But Diaghilev replied that in a ballet anything was possible; and in the event this dance of Nijinska's turned out one of the most successful in the whole *divertissement* with which the ballet closed.

During the period of preparation Diaghilev displayed amazing energy. He entered into every detail of the production, endeavouring to make it as perfect as possible. I was reminded of his activity in 1909, when preparing his very first season in Paris.

I was often asked in later years how it was that after ten years spent in guiding ballet through a succession of new phases, Diaghilev should have chosen at this juncture, as it were, to go back and restore a work of the type that his own productions had superseded. My answer was double. In the first place, *The Sleeping Princess* provided a solution to the problem we were faced with in no longer having a choreographer at our disposal; and in the second, Diaghilev was genuinely attracted by the opportunity of showing Europe an example of the old Petersburg school of ballet, on which he himself had been brought up from childhood, and which formed the foundation he had built on himself.

So, on November the 2nd, 1921, *The Sleeping Princess* was revived in

170

PLATE XII

LIUBOV TCHERNICHEVA

The Diaghilev Ballet

London. To watch a full-length ballet was a new experience for the English public; but, such were the ingredients of this one, it undoubtedly produced an unforgettable impression. In the first place, there was the music—Tchaikovsky at his most melodious. Then Bakst's scenery and costumes were nothing less than superb. His two architectural scenes in particular, one in white marble and the other in gold, were not only superlatively drawn and painted, but supplied a perfect background for the magnificent costumes. As far as the Ballet was concerned, incidentally, *The Sleeping Princess* was Bakst's final creation—and, not long after, he departed this life.

Aurora at the first performance was danced by Spesivtseva, and Prince Charming by Vladimirov. The other leading dancers were all in it too: Lopokova as the Lilac Fairy; Tchernicheva as a Lady of the Court in a wonderful eighteenth-century hunting costume; and Woidzikowsky incomparable as one of the Three Ivans. Sergeev had been most successful in reproducing Petipa's choreography and in contriving to preserve its very definite style.

From the opening night onwards the ballet was performed daily, the title role being taken by various ballerinas in turn. This part was first shared between Spesivtseva, Lopokova and Egorova; and in mid-December a fourth ballerina joined them in the person of Trefilova. During December King George and Queen Mary saw a performance; and on January the 5th we celebrated *Maestro* Cecchetti's fiftieth anniversary as a dancer. In the first production of *The Sleeping Princess* in 1890 at St. Petersburg Cecchetti had played the Fairy Carabosse; and so Diaghilev suggested that he should play it on this occasion too. The *Maestro* consented and gave a wonderful performance; and in the interval there was a celebration during which he received wreaths of laurel, flowers and a number of presents, both from Diaghilev himself and from various members of the company.

CHAPTER FOURTEEN

1922

DIAGHILEV was particularly pleased at having Spesivtseva in our cast. I had not seen her since 1915, since, although she had danced with the company in the following year, it had been in the United States during the period of Nijinsky's control. In the interval she had become highly accomplished. She was also lovely to look at, and both in her appearance and in some of her movements reminded me of Pavlova, though she lacked Pavlova's power of dominating an audience. The ballerina who had most success in the part of Aurora was Trefilova, a true exponent of the Petipa tradition. Next in my estimation came Egorova, who though she too had all the *Mariinsky* style at her command, was somehow less effective. As for Lopokova, though she danced Aurora with her usual charm, I did not think her naturally suited to the part. Finally, Aurora was also danced by Nemchinova, but only a few times, since Diaghilev did not think her sufficiently experienced. The ballet, incidentally, was conducted in turn by Eugene Goossens and Gregor Fitelberg.

★   ★   ★

Our hopes of a long run for *The Sleeping Princess* were, unfortunately, disappointed. After Christmas our receipts began to drop; and though this was at first regarded as part of a seasonal fluctuation, they failed to pick up. Stoll and Diaghilev were much concerned and tried various experiments in publicity, but without effect. Diaghilev had banked on a run of at least six months, during which, he had reckoned, he would be able to pay Stoll what the latter had advanced. But it soon became clear that this would not prove possible.

The time for long runs of ballet had not yet come. It still appealed to a relatively restricted public, whose support was soon exhausted. Stoll suggested that Diaghilev should bring over the scenery and costumes of some of his other ballets, which were stored in Paris, and revert to his usual triple bills in alternation with performances of *The Sleeping Princess*. But Diaghilev judged it prudent to reject this proposal. For though it was already clear that, if *The Sleeping Princess* were taken off before he had discharged his debt, Stoll would sequester *its* scenery and costumes, it seemed to Diaghilev foolish to attempt an avoidance of this calamity by risking the like seizure of this other material too. Nevertheless, when it was finally decided to end the run of *The Sleeping Princess*, what distressed him most was the knowledge that, owing to this action of Stoll, he would be unable to show the ballet in Paris. For to do so had been his dearest wish, whereas now he had small hope of its ever being revived at all.

During the last days of *The Sleeping Princess*, indeed, Diaghilev invited some of his friends to the theatre. 'Watch this performance,' he said to them with a bitter smile. 'It will not be repeated many times more; and you will never again see such a perfect *ensemble, or* such choreography, *or* such a *décor*. This is the last relic of the great days of St. Petersburg.'

We eventually closed down on February the 4th, after a hundred and five consecutive performances. It cannot thus be said that *The Sleeping Princess* was a failure. It had enchanted the audiences that came to see it; but in those days the public for ballet was too small to maintain for very long a single spectacle repeated nightly as this had been. Diaghilev left London before the end of the season. To see the curtain descend for the last time on *The Sleeping Princess* was more than he could bear. He instructed me to give the company a month's leave, but to keep them together as much as I could.

★   ★   ★

Diaghilev had counted on continuing in London at least until April, and then taking us to Monte Carlo. But this plan being now upset, he was at a loss how to employ the company during the period thus left unoccupied, since no new engagement could be arranged at such short notice. Moreover, at about this time Massine returned to London from South America; and since most of the dancers he had engaged for his tour there had meanwhile left him, he was in search of others and now seized his chance to approach some of ours. While these were on leave, unfounded rumours had been spread abroad that the Diaghilev Ballet was closing down; and as a result of Massine's advances four of our leading dancers, Lopokova, Sokolova, Woidzikowsky and Slavinsky, all elected to join him, though I did my best to dissuade them. Considering that they had, so to speak, grown up and come to the fore in Diaghilev's company, this action on their part was both irresponsible and inconsiderate; for they could not but know that their defection must injure us. Needless to say, Diaghilev, on hearing of it, was highly indignant—in particular with Lopokova, who had thus deserted him for the third time in her career. Spesivtseva also left us after *The Sleeping Princess* was taken off—not to join Massine, but to return to Russia. I did all I could again to deter her from doing so, promising her a brilliant future under Diaghilev's auspices; but she was deaf to all my eloquence, and yielded, as once before, to other influences.

I thus spent two most unpleasant months in London, never knowing what blow might not fall on us next. Great was my relief, therefore, when at last the day came on which I received Diaghilev's instructions: to bring what remained of our company to Paris first, and thence later to Monte Carlo.

★   ★   ★

As I have mentioned, Diaghilev had intended showing *The Sleeping Princess* in Paris at the *Opéra*, where we were due to appear again in the late spring. Its untimely end had therefore upset his calculations; and though the arrival of Bronislava Nijinska held the promise of fresh choreographic achievements, it was essential to find something he could put on immediately. Fortunately he had an inspiration. Some time before, at a private party, he had heard some ballet music, with songs, by Stravinsky, who had been commissioned to write this work by the hostess at this gathering, Princesse Edmond de Polignac, a friend of Diaghilev and a patron of young and advanced composers. This ballet was entitled *Le Renard*; and, since it was her property, Diaghilev now obtained Madame de Polignac's consent to produce it at the *Opéra*.

In addition to this, Stravinsky was now hard at work on a one-act opera, the libretto of which was by Boris Kochno. Kochno, who had become Diaghilev's secretary in the previous year, was a well-educated and intelligent young man, given to writing poetry and eager to contribute to the work of the Ballet. This opera, which was called *Mavra*, was his first essay at a libretto; and Diaghilev decided to include it also in the Paris season.

He had thus for presentation two new compositions by Stravinsky. But he considered them insufficient: another new and more important

The Diaghilev Ballet

ballet must also figure in the programme. Now 1922 was the centenary of the birth of Petipa; and Diaghilev was burning to show Paris a specimen of his art. The idea, therefore, not unnaturally occurred to him of selecting some of the best dances from *The Sleeping Princess* and presenting them as a suite. The result was a brilliant ballet *divertissement*, which he entitled *Le Mariage de la Belle au Bois Dormant*, or, more shortly, *Le Mariage d'Aurore*. Since he had no funds for a new *décor* for it, he decided to use that of *Le Pavillon d'Armide*. This was most suitable, and, as it had not been used since before the war, would be unfamiliar to most spectators. *Le Mariage d'Aurore* was destined in the event to become one of our most popular spectacles.

★　　★　　★

Our Paris season, however, was to be preceded by one at Monte Carlo, where we arrived ten days before we were due to open. We were overwhelmed with work. I had to rehearse a number of ballets that had not been danced for the best part of a year; and not only had they been to some extent forgotten, but some of the dancers who had before taken part in them had left the company while we were out of work in London. Then Nijinska had to start on the composition of *Le Renard*; and although there were only a few characters in the ballet, Stravinsky's music presented the usual difficulties. Diaghilev was at first somewhat anxious about *Le Renard*, but soon perceived that Nijinska was very well able to cope with the production. As regards our season, we gave in all twelve performances, for which the theatre was always full, to the satisfaction of the Casino management. Then, having finished at Monte Carlo, we moved to Marseilles, where we gave five performances at the Colonial Exhibition.

Diaghilev himself went direct from Monte Carlo to Paris. Before he left he told me that, according to all accounts, a venture that Massine had embarked on in Paris was doing none too well. This had not very much surprised me in any case; but hardly had Diaghilev arrived in Paris before he sent me an express letter, which read as follows:

DEAR SERGEY LEONIDOVICH,

I must let you know what has just happened to me at the *Opéra*. I was summoned to the theatre by Monsieur Rouché, who told me when I arrived that Massine was waiting outside in the passage. His object was to ask whether I would take him and all his dancers back into the company. He would not mind what salary he was offered. At the same time he knew that without them my season in Paris would be impossible!

I told Rouché that I would give him an answer in a few days' time. It will be in the negative. So that's the position. Yours

SERGEY DIAGHILEV.

Attached to his own letter was a copy of his promised reply to Rouché. It stated that he saw no reason for accepting Massine's offer. Thus did Diaghilev take his revenge.

★　　★　　★

This season at the *Opéra* was highly successful. It was our twelfth in Paris and we opened on May the 18th. Our two new ballets were strikingly contrasted: nothing indeed could have been less like than *Le Renard* and *Le Mariage d'Aurore*. *Le Renard* was described as a '*Ballet Burlesque avec Chant*' and was treated by us in much the same manner as *Le Coq d'Or*: that is to say the singers—for it was in fact a short, sixteen-minute opera—did not perform on the stage, but in this case were concealed in the orchestra pit, while the action was presented by dancers corresponding to the voices. There were only four characters, two of which, the Fox and the Cock, were danced respectively by Nijinska and Idzikovsky. Nijinska's choreography, her first essay in it under our auspices, was considered by Diaghilev to be most satisfactory.

The evening began with *Le Mariage d'Aurore*, which was brilliantly performed by all the dancers concerned. The Aurora was Trefilova, who thus made her *début* in Paris; and the ballet consisted of a kind of parade, which permitted the performers to show themselves in classical numbers. It was conducted by Fitelberg, whereas *Le Renard* was conducted by Ansermet.

After this first performance, which had an excellent reception, Diaghilev concentrated on the production of *Mavra*, Stravinsky's opera. He presented it first to his friends at the Hôtel Continental on May the 29th, and then to the public a week later, on June the 3rd. On the latter occasion it formed part of a 'Stravinsky Evening', being presented together with *Petrushka* and *Le Sacre du Printemps*. Unfortunately it fell completely flat. Nevertheless, as it had many good points, including an attractive *décor* by Léopold Survage, we continued to give it till the end of the season. It was very well sung and well conducted by Fitelberg.

The Diaghilev Ballet

★   ★   ★

So successful was this season of ours at the *Opéra* that the management would have liked to prolong it had they been able. Their arrangements, however, made this impossible; so Diaghilev was persuaded by his friends to take another theatre, the *Mogador*, which was free. He did this against his better judgment, being aware that it is seldom good policy to change theatres; and his hesitation proved not unjustified, since our performances there were far from being so well attended as those at the *Opéra*.

We were joined by Karsavina at the *Mogador*, where we also gave several ballets not included in our previous programmes. *Pulcinella* was one; and in connection with its revival Diaghilev's almost morbid taste for everything fashionable very nearly produced what I feel sure would have proved a fiasco. For it happened that a Russian named Sakharov and his wife were at that moment enjoying a vogue in Paris as dancers; and merely because they were the latest thing, Diaghilev conceived the grotesque idea of engaging Sakharov to take Massine's part in *Pulcinella*. But Sakharov was not what we considered a dancer at all: he possessed none of the requisite technique and could not possibly have danced *Pulcinella* successfully. Nevertheless it was only with the greatest difficulty that I dissuaded Diaghilev from pursuing this fantasy.

★   ★   ★

At the end of our season at the *Mogador* the company were given a three weeks' holiday. But there now in fact set in for us another very uncertain period. Engagements for the autumn and winter had been hard to secure at the best of times; and this year they were made more so by our being precluded from returning to London owing to our financial imbroglio with Stoll. Diaghilev managed, indeed, to arrange various dates for us in several places here and there in Europe. But this was no solution for our ultimate existence; and our future for the moment looked depressingly doubtful.

The first of these dates was again at Marseilles, where we paid a second visit to the Colonial Exhibition. On this occasion we gave several outdoor performances, two of them in the daytime, in the full glare of the sun. The crowd that watched them was large and variegated. A few of the spectators were even mounted on camels; and we attributed the immobility in which these animals surveyed us to an intelligent interest in our odd behaviour.

We went next to Geneva and then to Ostend, and finally, via Paris, to San Sebastian. Nouvel was in charge of the company during this tour. Diaghilev did not accompany us, but remained in Paris. On reaching Paris, accordingly, I went as usual to report to him. I was feeling dejected: our prospects still seemed bleak; and I fully expected to find him equally so. But not at all. He was drinking his breakfast coffee and greeted me most merrily. Why was I looking so glum, he asked, and without waiting for an answer, said 'Cheer up: I've something to tell you!' He then began by observing that the Ballet simply could not continue as it was, perpetually running into crisis after crisis. Some way out must be found; and he thought he had found it. I was, of course, all ears. 'Something has happened,' he went on. 'Something that may make all the difference to our future existence. The Prince of Monaco has recently died, and he's been succeeded by Prince Louis II!' This entirely bewildered me, as Diaghilev observed. So he went on to explain that the new Prince had a daughter; this daughter was heiress to the Principality; and her husband, the Prince de Polignac, was a nephew of his close friend, Princesse Edmond de Polignac. 'Well,' said Diaghilev, 'the young couple are cultivated. They're fond of the arts and of our Ballet in particular. So: my idea is to establish ourselves at Monte Carlo, as a base for the winter from November to May. Madame de Polignac has promised to help; and I see no reason why this should not come off.' (It was Diaghilev's way, I may add in parenthesis, seldom to say *my* Ballet, but either *our* Ballet or the *Russian* ballet.) He went on to explain his scheme in greater detail. This was that we should start every winter with a season of ballet lasting till the Italian opera season opened, when we should dance in such operas as had ballets in them. The advantage of the scheme in general was twofold: it would give the company employment throughout the winter, and allow Diaghilev ample time to devise new productions. I had begun to congratulate him when he interrupted me. 'Unfortunately there's a slight obstacle in the way of this admirable plan,' he said. 'At the moment the Casino have engaged an Italian ballet company to dance first on their own and then in the operas. So my scheme could not take effect till next year.'

'And in the meantime we should starve!' I put in.

'Yes, if we had to wait, we certainly should,' said Diaghilev. 'That's why I've suggested an interim arrangement. I've suggested that this year we should work *with* the Italians—just *some* of the company, that's to say. And what's more, the young Polignacs highly approve, and are going to press the Casino to accept.'

'But shouldn't we then be at the orders of Offenbach and Belloni?' I asked. (Offenbach was the director of the Italian opera at Monte Carlo and Belloni that of the Italian Ballet.) 'Wouldn't you be afraid of that?'

'Oh, *you*'ll have to deal with *them*!' laughed Diaghilev. 'I shan't appear. I'll be behind the scenes!'

I would willingly work with the Devil, I thought, if only this excellent plan could be realized.

⋆　　⋆　　⋆

Before any more was heard of this scheme, however, I had travelled all over the place, on the rest of our tour. San Sebastian, which we had not visited since 1918, was as attractive as ever: we always felt as if at home in Spain; and once more found in King Alfonso our most faithful of spectators. Next, on our way to Bordeaux, we stopped at Bayonne for a single performance in the lovely once-Royal Theatre; and from Bordeaux, where both the theatre and the attendance were poor, we went first to Geneva and then to Belgium, this kaleidoscopic tour coming to an end at Liége.

⋆　　⋆　　⋆

It thus came about that we were in Brussels when we learnt to our delight that the contract had been signed: the Casino had agreed to all Diaghilev's proposals. And so the Ballet at last acquired a permanent base. We were to stay in Monte Carlo for six whole months in the year. As two other months were always set aside for leave, there would remain only four to fill up with other engagements; and this, we felt sure, would prove easy enough. Monte Carlo, moreover, was an ideal place for us to work at new ballets in. It was equally ideal both for the storage and repair of all our paraphernalia, and, since excellent paint-rooms were available, for the painting of new scenery. We were fully aware of all these advantages—to which were to be added the sunshine and the delightful climate.

After our visit to Belgium we returned to Paris; and there Diaghilev proceeded to reduce the size of the company. By giving notice to some of the weaker dancers (to eliminate whom was the chief aim of this operation) he cut the number he retained to thirty. We also now lost one of our 'stars', namely Vladimirov, who chose to leave us at this juncture.

On arrival at Monte Carlo I at once called on Monsieur Offenbach, whom I already knew. He was a charming old man, a descendant of the composer. I subsequently introduced our whole company, one by one, both to him and to his colleague, Signor Belloni. The latter, as I have mentioned, was the Director of the Italian ballet company, with whom it had been agreed that we were now to co-operate.

CHAPTER FIFTEEN

1923

BELLONI received me somewhat coldly. He knew little about us and mistakenly imagined that since the Diaghilev company were given to dancing modern ballets, they would be quite incompetent in the classical style. As soon as he proceeded to examine them, however, and discovered to his surprise that they were able to execute every step he suggested, his opinion, very naturally, entirely changed, and his attitude with it: he became most friendly.

Our company took part in his Italian ballets for about two months, and quite enjoyed it. For the choreography was very simple, and cost them little effort to execute perfectly. There followed next the season of Italian operas, in which, by Diaghilev's arrangement, we were also to dance when necessary. Belloni still required our services, moreover, for the matinées he now gave several times a week at the *Palais des Beaux-Arts*. So the winter went by for us in constant activity.

We had been five months in Monte Carlo before Diaghilev at length arrived, accompanied by his 'suite' in the persons of Nouvel, Kochno, Larionov and P. Korebut-Kubatovich, the last being a middle-aged cousin of Diaghilev. They were followed shortly afterwards by some newly engaged dancers, who were to fill the depleted ranks of the company. The first to appear were five young men, former pupils of Nijinska, for whom, at Diaghilev's suggestion, she had written to Russia. On putting these five through their paces, we were disappointed to find them very weak and inexperienced. The best of the party was E. Lapitsky. The worst was a boy named Serge Lifar. When Diaghilev first saw them soon after their arrival, he made a face, and remarked that they seemed hardly worth the trouble and expense involved in bringing them so far to join us.

When Diaghilev showed me his projected programme for our coming seasons in Monte Carlo and Paris, I pointed out that some of the ballets he had included could not be done unless we engaged still more dancers;

PLATE XIII

ALEXANDRE BENOIS

LÉON BAKST

MICHEL LARIONOV

PABLO PICASSO

The Diaghilev Ballet

and knowing that I should be obliged shortly to go to London on private business, I suggested that I might approach some of those who had deserted to Massine and were now out of work. Diaghilev at first protested at this proposal; these defections still rankled with him and he was loth to forgive them. But in the end he relented and said I might do this; and I duly returned from London bringing with me Sokolova, Woidzikowsky and Slavinsky, all three of whom I was delighted to have back with us.

★   ★   ★

It was Diaghilev's plan to present only one new ballet during his next season in Paris—namely yet another work of Stravinsky's, which was to be entitled *Les Noces*. This had been thought of, and Stravinsky had begun composing it, a long time before: unless I am mistaken, it had been discussed as far back as the days of Nijinsky. The score was written for four pianos plus some wind and percussion instruments. Diaghilev took a particular interest in *Les Noces* and was anxious that the choreography should match the score in originality. Although the subject was 'realistic'—it was a traditional peasant wedding ceremony—he wished the dancers' movements to be highly stylized, the women, for instance, dancing largely on 'points', with Russian icons as their main inspiration. This choreography was much discussed between him, Stravinsky, Nijinska, who was actually to devise it, and Larionov and Goncharova, who were to design the scenery and costumes.

★   ★   ★

Nijinska accordingly began working on *Les Noces*, whilst I, on my return from London, busied myself with preparations for our season in Monte Carlo. This was to open in April; and a few days before it started Diaghilev informed me that the *Princesse Héritière*, who, as I knew, was much interested in the Ballet, wished to attend one of the rehearsals of *Le Mariage d'Aurore*, which she had seen in Paris. A visit by the Princess to a ballet rehearsal was an unprecedented occurrence in Monte Carlo. Fortunately the rehearsal went very well; Diaghilev presented the leading dancers, whom the Princess already knew 'from the front'; and the company all found her most gracious and charming. This first visit, moreover, was soon followed by others, to rehearsals of *Le Sacre* and *Les Noces*; and, Monte Carlo being the small place it is, the interest thus displayed in our activities by a member of the Royal Family went far to ensure our ultimate success. The season in fact went extremely well, and resulted in the conclusion of a further contract with the Casino, for another season lasting from November 1923 to May 1924, in the course of which Diaghilev was to present not only ballets but operas as well.

★　　★　　★

Since our financial obligation to Stoll was still unsatisfied, we were again unable to give a season this year in London. On leaving Monte Carlo, therefore, on our way to Paris, we went first to Lyons, where the ballet was now beginning to be popular, and thence to Switzerland.

When we eventually arrived in Paris, we found it excessively crowded. It was next to impossible to find anywhere to stay. Moreover the cost of living had risen uncomfortably, with the natural result that the company demanded an increase of salary. A number of them indeed threatened to resign unless it were granted; but this was not at all the way to approach Diaghilev in such matters. His reply was to call the whole company together and explain that he was not in a position to pay them more. He added that if those who were dissatisfied should resign, he would quite understand. But no-one did so.

★　　★　　★

Our thirteenth Paris season was to be at the *Gaieté Lyrique*. This was a theatre that none of us very much liked. By the time we reached Paris *Les Noces* had been thoroughly rehearsed. The music, however, as always with Stravinsky, was difficult for the dancers to assimilate. In order, therefore, to give them a general hearing of this complicated and unusual score, such as they could not obtain at ordinary rehearsals, Diaghilev asked Princesse Edmond to hold an 'orchestra' rehearsal at her house for the benefit of both the company and her friends. This she did; and it proved most helpful. When it came to the dress rehearsal on the stage, however, the music presented us with another problem. For the two double pianos on which it had largely to be performed could not be fitted into the orchestra pit. There was no alternative, therefore, but to place them on either side of the stage, near the proscenium.

We gave *Les Noces* its first performance on July the 13th; and its success was far greater than we had expected. It even reminded us of our triumphs

The Diaghilev Ballet

of 1909. All eight performances were received with equal enthusiasm.

The ballet was in four scenes: the consecration of the bride; the consecration of the bridegroom; the leave-taking of the bride; and the wedding festivities. The scenery was by Goncharova and was exceedingly austere, but highly effective as a background for the dancers. It consisted of a plain backcloth and wings, together with one or two central 'flats', in which windows of varying colours were inserted to indicate changes of place. The choreography had in it reminiscences of both Fokine and Nijinsky, yet was not in the least imitative: Nijinska had her own, very personal, style. The music was stirring and, though hard to follow, deeply moving. Diaghilev was delighted with this ballet and its triumph; and thenceforward Nijinska was known as '*La Nijinska*'.

★   ★   ★

After the conclusion of our season Diaghilev was invited by a committee that had been set up by the French Government for the restoration of the Palace of Versailles to give a performance in the famous *Galerie des Glaces* in aid of the fund they were collecting for this purpose. Diaghilev was much excited by this proposal; but the *Galerie* being very long in relation to its width, to contrive a satisfactory setting in it was something of a problem. His solution was to devote two-thirds of the hall to the audience, and one-third to the stage. The latter consisted of a large rostrum at the back of which a wide staircase rose almost to the ceiling. There was, of course, no curtain; the orchestra was concealed beneath the staircase; and the sides of the rostrum and staircase were decorated with flowers and plants in a manner suggested by actual records of similar performances in this very hall under *Le Roi Soleil*. For the last three days before the performances the company spent the whole day at Versailles rehearsing, and on the day of the dress rehearsal were to be seen strolling about the gardens in Louis-Quatorze wigs and costumes, fully made up.

This memorable performance took place on June the 30th. It began with an overture played by the invisible orchestra; and then the dancers descended the great stairs in two columns to the strains of Tchaikovsky's *Polonaise*—for the ballet we were giving was, of course, *Le Mariage d'Aurore*—lengthened for the occasion by the addition of new dances and some songs. The success of this performance was enormous, and so were the receipts. The audience was of the most distinguished, including President Poincaré, the whole Cabinet and most of the Diplomatic

186

Corps. Since there was no electric lighting in the great forecourt of the Palace, it was lit by huge flaring torches, which cast over the departing crowd and their carriages a strange flickering glare, as if from the past.

★　　★　　★

While the company now went on holiday, Diaghilev remained in Paris, both to make arrangements for an autumn tour and to look out further music for new ballets. He thus discovered in some library a score by the French composer Montéclair (1666–1737), which he decided to use for the ballet eventually entitled *Les Tentations de la Bergère ou L'Amour Vainqueur*. Nor, he saw, would one new ballet be enough, since our next season at Monte Carlo was to be a long one. He therefore invited two young French composers, Francis Poulenc and Georges Auric, each to write another, and had it also in mind to do a fourth, *La Concurrence*, by Satie, which, however, was never performed during his lifetime. He thought further that it would be good policy, as well as employing all this French music for his ballets, to choose French works for the operas he was also to give at Monte Carlo.

I learnt of all these plans in a letter Diaghilev sent me while I was in London for my holiday. I was struck by the total absence of anything Russian from the suggested programme—it was evident that we were drifting away from Russia more than ever. Diaghilev also gave me various instructions in this letter, and added, in a postscript, that, 'provided he made no conditions', I might re-engage Patrikeyev (*i.e.* Patrick Kay, *alias* Anton Dolin). Patrikeyev had been with us during the run of *The Sleeping Princess*, but had left at the end of it. Diaghilev had heard that his dancing had greatly improved and hoped to improve it still more if he rejoined us. The stipulation about his making no conditions, however, made any approach to him slightly awkward, since I knew that he now aspired to solo parts, which we might not, perhaps, feel able to allot to him. I therefore suggested to the future Dolin that he should settle his re-engagement direct with Diaghilev. While in London I also saw Idzikovsky and signed another contract with him.

★　　★　　★

The company had already reassembled in Paris on August the 15th when I received a telegram from Diaghilev instructing me to rehearse

The Diaghilev Ballet

Le Pavillon d'Armide. This rather surprised me, since not only had this ballet not been done for years, but its scenery and costumes were being used for *Le Mariage d'Aurore.* However, this instruction was almost immediately countermanded, and that exquisite creation of Fokine was thereafter buried for good.

Diaghilev returned to Paris with Nijinska. After the austere simplicity of *Les Noces,* and in view of the universal success of *Le Mariage d'Aurore,* Diaghilev was thirsting to exhibit another gorgeous spectacle; and it seemed to him that *Les Tentations de la Bergère* might provide just the opportunity he needed. Nijinska was accordingly asked to compose a ballet on the Montéclair music in the manner of its period; and this she did, basing her creation on classical steps, and guided carefully by Diaghilev as regards details of style. For a whole month we rehearsed every day, not only this but our old *répertoire* as well. The heat in Paris was stifling; and the dancers were half exhausted. But Diaghilev insisted on our continuing till the *Bergère* was ready, and by the end of the month ready it was.

★   ★   ★

After this it was a relief to escape to Switzerland, where we appeared in turn at Geneva, Lausanne and Berne, showing *Le Mariage d'Aurore, Cléopâtre, Schéhérazade* and *Pulcinella,* the last of which was a novelty in these places. The orchestra was in the hands of our old friend Ansermet and was always beautifully conducted. Then from Switzerland we moved to Antwerp, and thence once again to Monte Carlo. We had been eagerly looking forward to returning thither; and now, since the Italian Ballet was no longer in existence, we felt that we practically owned the place. Monte Carlo was, in fact, to be our permanent home as long as Diaghilev was alive.

★   ★   ★

Our season at Monte Carlo was to start in November and continue right through the winter. We were bound in the course of it to show a large variety of ballets, but it was decided to defer presentation of our new works till January, when Monte Carlo usually filled up with visitors.

Diaghilev now conceived the idea of reviving some of our oldest ballets, such as *Narcisse, Daphnis et Chloë* and *Le Lac des Cygnes.* As

Narcisse had not been danced since 1919, and neither *Daphnis* nor the *Lac* since 1914, my task in reviving them was far from easy. The *Lac*, with its simple choreography by Ivanov and Petipa, was not too difficult; but *Daphnis* was extremely complicated and none of our dancers remembered it at all. I had therefore to fall back on my own unaided memory. Fortunately this had been exercised on the two previous occasions when, having nothing else to do, the company had rehearsed *Daphnis* without ever performing it; and when Diaghilev saw how we had succeeded in restoring it, he was pleasantly surprised: it surpassed his expectations.

As a result of my long experience as a *régisseur* I have come to the conclusion that there are lucky ballets and unlucky. *Daphnis et Chloë* was an unlucky ballet. Somehow it never could stick in our *répertoire*; and now again, having been so painfully resurrected, it was given only two or three times and then dropped. Yet it had lovely music, settings, costumes and choreography. There seemed to be some malignant fate overhanging it.

Meanwhile Nijinska had begun work on the two new French ballets: *Les Biches* by Poulenc and *Les Fâcheux* by Auric; and this autumn was marked also by two interesting additions to our cast. One of these was Patrikeyev, who arrived with Diaghilev from Paris, and was now reintroduced to the company under his new name: Anton Dolin. His re-engagement had been pressed by Serafima Astafieva, who had danced with us in the past. She had since set up as a teacher in London, and Dolin had there become her pupil. She had met Diaghilev in Paris to further Dolin's suit; and, as a result of the discussion that I had advised him while in London to pursue with Diaghilev direct, the latter had re-engaged him, to dance at first in the *corps de ballet*, but with a promise that in due course he should be promoted to solos.

Our other new-comer was a charming young Irish girl, who nevertheless went by the resounding French name of Ninette de Valois.

PLATE XIV

VERA TREFILOVA

CHAPTER SIXTEEN

1924

OUR season at Monte Carlo had opened on November the 25th, but as I have mentioned, we deferred the presentation of our new productions till January. During the remainder of the season Diaghilev showed no less than seven such productions; and our programme altogether was rich and varied. Among the visitors who thronged Monte Carlo in January were a number of critics and journalists who were eager to see our new ballets on account of their music, especially that of the young French composers, and their *décors* by various celebrated painters. Diaghilev thus achieved one of his major aims: to make Monte Carlo into a centre of advanced artistic life.

On New Year's Day we gave one of the French operas Diaghilev had chosen, namely Gounod's *La Colombe*, a little-known work, together with our resuscitation of *Daphnis et Chloë*, in which Daphnis was danced by Dolin. During his two months' sojourn with the company Dolin had made great strides; and although we thought him scarcely quite ready to take such a responsible part, Diaghilev was anxious to lose no time in exhibiting his latest creation in the way of dancers; and Dolin in fact gave an excellent account of himself. He was good-looking and his movements were graceful and well-defined. His chief fault was a tendency to be mannered, which Diaghilev was aware of and did his best to check. His partner as Chloe was Sokolova. But I did not think her suited to this part.

As for our other two revivals, in *Narcisse* the title role was danced by Slavinsky and Echo by Tchernicheva. Incidentally, Tchernicheva and Karsavina were the only dancers ever to perform this part, and both excelled in it. For the chief part in *Le Lac des Cygnes* Diaghilev invited Trefilova, the best of all Princess Auroras even at the *Mariinsky*; and she amazed everyone at Monte Carlo by her extraordinary *fouettés*.

Our next first night was that of *Les Tentations de la Bergère*. The *décor*

The Diaghilev Ballet

for this was by the Spanish painter Juan Gris. Although most pleasing in colour—its was mainly in blue-grey and gold—unfortunately it was extremely cumbrous, and, with its platforms of various heights, faced Nijinska with difficult dancing problems. The weak point of this ballet, which taken as a whole was interesting and effective, was Montéclair's music, which turned out rather dull and monotonous. On account of its complicated and cumbrous set we later found it impossible to give the *Bergère* as often as we should have liked, and eventually dropped it altogether. This was a pity, since Nijinska's choreography was admirable. The part of the Shepherdess was danced by Nemchinova and that of the Shepherd by Woidzikowsky, with Vilzak as a supremely elegant *Marquis*.

Next came another Gounod opera: *Le Médecin Malgré Lui*, with incidental dances arranged by Nijinska. It was in these that I began to notice the efforts of a young dancer who stood out by his performance in the *corps de ballet*. He was clearly bent on improving his work and standing. He was well made and had an attractive face with a slightly *retroussé* nose. The future showed that I was justified in singling him out. It was Serge Lifar, who had first attracted any notice he had received by disappointing us with his incompetence.

This opera went very well, much assisted by a delicious *décor* by Benois. Benois had only recently returned from Russia, when I had been particularly pleased to see him and discuss old times. Owing to the war and the revolution, however, it was a whole ten years since we had seen him; and during that long time Diaghilev's taste had completely changed and he did not admire Benois any more. I remember how Benois stood with me in the wings and said with a shrug, 'Diaghilev no longer likes my *décors*. I can't understand it.' But I could understand it, well enough. Diaghilev in the interval had moved to the left; and work such as Benois's now seemed to him academic.

Later in that same week we gave our second new ballet, *Les Biches*; and it turned out the greatest success of the season. It was 'modern' in character, as befitted the music. For Poulenc was one of the famous *Six*, who then constituted the musical advance-guard of Paris. It had no plot; and Nijinska's choreography, which was charmingly varied and gay, consisted in fact of a suite of dances: *Rondo*; *Chanson-Dansée*; *Rag-Mazurka*; and '*Jeux*'; arranged for a cast of three men and a number of girls. The *décor* was by Marie Laurencin; the scenery mostly white with patches of pale blue and other pale colours, which likewise predominated in the costumes. The ballet as a whole was superficial, without much meaning; but it was entertaining and greatly enjoyed.

★   ★   ★

As part of his attempt to make this season at Monte Carlo as interesting as possible, Diaghilev also revived Massine's *Las Meninas*, which had only been danced before in 1917, and the suite of dances from *Le Astuzie Femminili*, composed by him in 1920. The latter, which was lengthened by the addition of some new numbers, was now entitled *Cimarosiana*. It was presented in an attractive setting by Sert, representing a terrace overlooking a panorama of Rome, and was most successful, both now and later. *Cimarosiana* was followed in the list of our productions by yet a third Gounod opera: *Philémon et Baucis*. This was again decorated by Benois—who was never, incidentally, to design another production for Diaghilev. Next, a week later, came *Une Éducation Manquée*, a one-act opera by Chabrier. It was performed in a delightful *décor* by Gris, and being the opera best liked of all by the public, was afterwards included by Diaghilev in his spring season in Paris. Finally, on January the 19th we gave the ballet *Les Fâcheux*, so called after a comedy of Molière's from which the scenario was adapted by Boris Kochno. The French composer of the music, Georges Auric, was another member of the group known as *Les Six*. The *décor* of this ballet, by the painter Georges Bracque, was extremely attractive, chiefly in yellows, greens and browns. The scenery, however, was executed so that it had the appearance of a sketch; and though Diaghilev liked this, it received some adverse criticism. As for the choreography, its composition was attended with disagreements. Nijinska did not consider Kochno, with whom she was supposed to co-operate, experienced enough to plan a ballet, and was inclined very often to disregard his suggestions. Then, on watching a rehearsal, Diaghilev would not approve what he saw; and this would result in long and heated arguments between him and Nijinska, which would go on and on till rehearsals would have to be cancelled and the dancers sent home. Nijinska would then do her best to carry out Diaghilev's instructions; but this not only wasted a lot of time, it also caused her to lose interest. These disputes were, to my mind, the more regrettable in that the ballet had seemed to me to be progressing quite happily; whereas the interference of Diaghilev and Kochno was not by any means always well directed. They suggested, for instance, that Dolin should dance a *variation* on 'points' like a ballerina, imagining that this would be strikingly effective. But when it came to his doing so at performances, the public, not unnaturally, regarded this merely as a 'stunt'. In these somewhat unfortunate circumstances it is not surprising that the composition of *Les Fâcheux* was less satisfactory than it might have been—though, as Massine was also to try his hand without any greater success at another version later, it may be that this also was an 'unlucky' ballet. Its performance by the cast, on the other hand, was brilliant; and with them Diaghilev was delighted, particularly, apart from Dolin, with Tchernicheva as Orphise and Vilzak as Évaste.

★　　★　　★

Our season, which had proved exceptionally full and interesting, came to an end on January the 30th. But the company had still to take part, as during the previous year, in the ordinary opera season, under the direction of G. Guinsbourg (a Frenchman quite unconnected with our former colleague, the Baron, of whom we had heard nothing since the Russian Revolution). Diaghilev, together with his particular friends· and supporters, now left Monte Carlo. But a few days before his departure he came to my wife and told her that the *Princesse Héritière* wished to find a teacher to give her lessons in ballet dancing; and 'I've recommended *you*, Liubov Pavlovna', said Diaghilev. So the following day he escorted her to the Palace; the Princess duly took her first lesson; and my wife continued to teach her to the end of our stay, finding her most apt and diligent.

★　　★　　★

To my surprise Diaghilev seemed somewhat doubtful of our prospects for the following year at Monte Carlo. But I eventually discovered the reason. Successful as our performances had been, they did not exactly meet the requirements of the Casino. Diaghilev's ambition of making Monte Carlo into an advanced art centre, the influence of which would radiate in all directions, had no real appeal for the management, on whom we depended. Moreover, Guinsbourg scented in Diaghilev a dangerous rival, and was bent on preventing him from giving another of his mixed opera-and-ballet seasons. In this opposition he had the support of local public opinion, which resented the sacrifice of its favourite light operas to what it regarded as Diaghilev's 'high-brow' productions. As a result the Casino management decided to revert to their former policy of presenting light operas in the autumn, 'grand' operas during the winter and ballet in the spring.

In the meantime Guinsbourg was much assisted by our participation in his productions, which involved Nijinska in the composition of innumerable incidental dances. But though his season did not end till April, from the middle of March our full-length ballet programmes began to alternate with his operas; and this greatly annoyed him. However, when Diaghilev returned to Monte Carlo from Paris at the end of March, I found that he had already decided in future years to present nothing but ballets at the Casino, eschewing the production of operas altogether. This was to fall in with Guinsbourg's wishes. But by now Diaghilev was resigned to the shortcomings of the Casino management. He had scarified them in his letters from Paris; but when he rejoined us, he was in excellent spirits; and the only evidence of his changed feelings for Monte Carlo was a complete lack of interest in what we should show the benighted place this year, which was in striking contrast with the intense care he usually devoted to this problem. In the end he even derived a certain satisfaction from presenting the Monte Carlo audiences with the old-fashioned ballets that particularly appealed to them, but that he himself now held in indulgent contempt.

★ ★ ★

Diaghilev's readiness to abandon the production of operas at Monte Carlo in future was partly due to the presence of Dolin in the company. For Dolin, he saw, had in him the makings of a first-rate dancer and even, it might be, of a choreographer; and the possibility of developing his talents was enough to concentrate all Diaghilev's interest once again on the ballet.

When he came to draw up the programme for our season in Paris, however, Diaghilev realized that our existing *répertoire* contained nothing calculated to show off Dolin's accomplishments to their best advantage for his *début* before the Paris public. He therefore invited Jean Cocteau to compose the scenario for a new ballet specially for Dolin's benefit; at the same time commissioning H. Laurens to design the scenery, and Darius Milhaud, yet another of *Les Six*, to write the music. The ballet was to be entitled *Le Train Bleu*—after the train in which the *beau monde* were then wont to travel from Paris to the *Côte d'Azur*—and to be

described as an '*opérette dansée*'. Its setting was to be a bathing beach
and its action inspired by various games and sports.

On the day of his return Diaghilev acquainted Nijinska with his plans
for *Le Train Bleu*, informing her that he would like it to be ready for our
season in Paris. Nijinska was very busy; and seeing how many other
ballets we were obliged to rehearse, there was all too little time. However, she dutifully began work on this too.

★   ★   ★

On finishing at Monte Carlo we went to the *Teatro Liceo* in Barcelona,
where nothing seemed to have changed during our five years' absence.
Our greatest success in Barcelona was *Le Tricorne*; as in Madrid, our
Spanish audiences could not get over our mastery of their national
dancing. We also gave *Cléopâtre*, *Thamar*, *Petrushka* and *Daphnis et Chloë*—
the last of which, that ill-fated work, the company were never to dance
again. Then on May the 2nd we went to Holland, visiting The Hague,
Amsterdam and Rotterdam, but giving only eight performances in all.

★   ★   ★

We were to return for our season in Paris this summer once more to the
Théâtre des Champs-Élysées. Its director was now Monsieur Hébertot,
with whom, though Diaghilev had been on bad terms with him at one
time, he had composed his differences the year before, with the result
that Hébertot had offered him this engagement.

For some reason Diaghilev now designated his company *Les Ballets
Russes de Monte Carlo*, and was furious at my saying I did not care for the
name. However, it only lasted a year. For he eventually quarrelled with
the Casino management, whereupon we became once more *Les Ballets
Russes de Serge de Diaghilev*.

We arrived in Paris a fortnight before our opening. Although we were
to give only a dozen performances, there was a great deal of preparatory
work to be got through, including the rehearsal of such difficult ballets
as *Le Sacre*, *Petrushka*, *Les Noces* and *Pulcinella*; moreover, *Le Train Bleu*
had still to be completed. On the other hand, we were to enjoy the
relief of not performing every evening consecutively, but of alternating
with operas, and even plays, presented by Hébertot. Seeing that all our
new ballets for this season had music by French composers, we made a

PLATE XV

OLGA SPESIVTSEVA

LYDIA SOKOLOVA

VERA NEMCHINOVA

FÉLIA DOUBROVSKA

point of including at least one Russian work in every programme. Thus on our first night, on May the 26th, we gave *Les Noces* as well as *Les Tentations de la Bergère* and *Les Biches*. Of these *Les Biches* was the most successful. To our surprise, since it was as well danced as ever, *Les Noces* failed to repeat its triumph of the previous year. At later performances *Les Fâcheux* won only moderate applause; but *Une Éducation Manquée* was liked; and *Le Sacre*, about which we were always slightly nervous, passed off without any hostile demonstration. As for *Le Train Bleu*, I think we never had so poor a *décor*: I was amazed that Diaghilev should ever have accepted it; and I fancy it was because he later realized its inferiority that he asked Picasso to design an act-drop—depicting two gigantic running females—which could at least remain on view during the playing of the overture. The costumes were by the famous dressmaker Chanel, and were indeed no more than fashionable bathing-dresses and '*costumes de sport*'. The score by Milhaud was quite attractive but lacked the lightness and frivolity appropriate to an '*opérette dansée*'. The ballet's best feature was Nijinska's choreography, ingeniously based on movements characteristic of various games. The chief part, of the '*Beau Gosse*', was admirably danced by Dolin, whose British upbringing helped him to endow it with real character. His performance indeed was highly accomplished and met with much deserved applause. Diaghilev had, in fact, achieved his design of making Dolin into a first-rate dancer.

★   ★   ★

Though this season of ours in Paris met with an appreciative response from the public, Diaghilev began at this time to be more and more frequently attacked for deflecting the ballet from its proper course. He was reproached for abandoning the classical tradition; for eliminating plots and reducing ballets to mere suites of dances; and for an inconsiderate pursuit of what in the arts was at any moment merely fashionable. In the judgment of Fokine, who in his day had been a bold reformer of the classical school, these latest ballets made no appeal to the heart; they possessed neither sense nor beauty; they consisted of gymnastic exercises rather than of dances; and their leading object was to surprise. There was much truth in his observations. I myself frequently insisted with Diaghilev on the need in ballets for plot and dramatic development. But he was merely irritated by such remarks, replying that one must move with the times; that ballets such as

198

Cléopâtre and *Schéhérazade* were as dead as mutton; and that what he was in search of were new forms of expression.

★   ★   ★

At the end of the Paris season we went on holiday, to reassemble on September the 1st for an extensive tour of Germany. Knowing how sadly the war had impoverished Germany, and imagining that the Germans must all be imbued with resentment, I was filled with misgivings about this tour and said so to Diaghilev. He assured me, however, that our agent, who had had much experience of touring and was entirely reliable, had guaranteed that we should cover our expenditure. Our tour in fact turned out to have been efficiently organized; but we observed a great change in the country: it seemed shabby and untidy and its people no longer friendly to foreigners. Nevertheless, wherever we performed, first in Munich and afterwards in eight other towns, we were always both well received and intelligently criticized. The favourite ballets, as before the war, were those with a plot such as *Schéhérazade*, *Le Tricorne* and *Les Contes Russes*. The Germans, in return, provided us with some entertainment by their habit of referring to *Herr Doktor* Diaghilev.

The *Herr Doktor* eventually joined us in Berlin, and at our first meeting sprang a new problem on me. It appeared that he had asked our London agent, Wolheim, to approach Sir Oswald Stoll again about our sequestrated property. The conditions on which Stoll was ready to arrive at a settlement, however, were such that Diaghilev was reluctant to agree to them. 'He wants us again at the Coliseum, for twenty-four weeks,' he said. 'But I don't know. In 1918 it was different: then we had no alternative. But now . . . the Coliseum. . . .'

'It's not the place that makes the man; it's the man that makes the place,' I replied. 'Until we settle our quarrel with Stoll, we shall never be able to return to London.'

Whether or not as a result of this conversation, soon after Diaghilev's return to Paris, we learnt that he had decided to accept Stoll's offer: we were to appear again at the Coliseum as soon as we had completed our tour in Germany.

★   ★   ★

Our first performances at the Coliseum were given on November the 22nd: *Cimarosiana* at the matinée and *Le Train Bleu* in the evening. Both ballets were liked, *Le Train Bleu* the better of the two; and everyone was much impressed with Dolin's soaring leaps. The company not having been in London for almost four years, the public were delighted to have us back. The customary quiet of our London life was soon disturbed, however, by rumours that Nijinska was about to leave us. I refused to pay any attention to them at first; but eventually asked Diaghilev whether they had any basis; on which he told me, quite calmly, that they were perfectly true. I was horrified, and pointed out that, if Nijinska left us, we should find ourselves again in the hopeless plight we had been placed in before, on Massine's departure. But Diaghilev seemed singularly indifferent to my arguments. He said he would speak to Nijinska again; but without waiting for him to do so, I went to her myself and did my best to dissuade her. All she said, however, was that my entreaties were useless. She had been deeply offended by Diaghilev, I gathered; but precisely how she declined to specify. I subsequently discovered that Diaghilev had done with her exactly what he had earlier done with Fokine: he had begun rehearsing, in secret, with someone else. In this case, moreover, his partner was none other than young Serge Lifar, who had been Nijinska's own pupil. Lifar was obviously devoid of any knowledge or experience; and, quite apart from the surreptitious manner in which Diaghilev had done this, Nijinska had good reason to take umbrage on that account. I imagine, however, that what had really occurred was that Diaghilev had ceased to be satisfied with Nijinska's choreography, and had begun looking round for someone to replace her. He had at one time, I knew, had hopes of Dolin; but I had noticed that, having once launched Dolin as a dancer, he had recently ceased to take much interest in his progress. He had therefore, I take it, turned his attention to Lifar, but, as before with Nijinsky, had wished to keep the experiment secret, until he was certain that it would prove successful. This is mere speculation on my part, however.

During our season at the Coliseum we received several notable additions to the company. The first was of four young Russian dancers, two girls and two men, all former pupils of the *Mariinsky*. They had only recently come from Russia in a batch, having been allowed to leave Leningrad for a tour of Germany. As soon as he heard of them Diaghilev had invited them to join us. Their names were Alexandra Danilova, Tamara Gevergeva, Nicolas Efimov and Georges Balanchivadze. They were all excellent dancers, and though at first somewhat provincial in manner, soon adapted themselves to our more sophisticated ways. They had no pretensions and willingly danced anything they were given. This was an attitude that appealed to Diaghilev; and we, for our part, were all very pleased to welcome them as colleagues.

The next new arrival was a former member of the company, namely Vera Savina, Massine's first wife. She had left us on her marriage in 1921; and we had been sorry to lose her, as we considered her most talented.

The last new-comer was for us a somewhat strange one: a little girl of no more than fourteen. She, like Dolin, was a pupil of Madame Asta-fieva, and, despite her extreme youth, Madame Astafieva pressed Diaghilev to take her. Diaghilev at first refused. But Madame Astafieva was nothing if not insistent and made Diaghilev and myself go and see her *protégée* at a lesson. The child certainly danced well, but was extremely thin and under-developed physically; and though we both thought her promising, I could not imagine how we could possibly use her. Nevertheless Diaghilev was in the end persuaded by Madame Astafieva to take her. 'We'll give her a chance to grow and study,' he said, 'and when she *has* grown and studied a little—then we'll see.' The little girl's name was Alice Marks; but this was instantly changed to Alicia Markova.

CHAPTER SEVENTEEN

1925

THE departure of Nijinska brought the fourth period in the choreographic history of our Ballet to an end. All four periods had one thing in common, the tradition of the St. Petersburg school of dancing, which had been carefully preserved by the older dancers, by Diaghilev and by myself. It was thanks to our so preserving it that the company were able to maintain the style and character of all the various works composed during these four periods, however widely they might differ one from another.

Nijinska bequeathed to us six major ballets. Her style was nearer to the purely classical than that of her predecessors in our company and may perhaps be best described as 'neo-classical'. This was partly why Diaghilev ceased to care for it. For he was never tired of repeating that it was essential for choreography to explore new paths and keep in line with contemporary aesthetic developments.

As I have mentioned, on becoming dissatisfied, on this account, with Nijinska, he had begun looking elsewhere in the company for possible choreographic talent. There were actually three of its members in whom he thought this might be developed; for, as well as to Dolin and Lifar, his attention had been attracted to the new arrival, Georges Balanchivadze—or Balanchine, as for convenience he came to be called. Diaghilev's aspirations for Dolin as a choreographer were soon abandoned. He used often to tell me that Dolin's aesthetic reactions were completely unlike our own, as Russians. His intelligence and temperament were distinctively British, and in matters of art he, as it were, spoke another language.

As for Lifar, he was still very young, and had yet to develop his powers as a dancer. He displayed the ability to become one. But only after having done so could he acquire the artistic knowledge that alone might enable him to become a good choreographer.

The third candidate, Balanchine, was more obviously gifted, as he had shown by some dances he had already composed, which had been performed by his wife, Tamara Gevergeva. Moreover, since he was fresh from Russia, Diaghilev was interested in all he had to say about the ballet at Leningrad, and in particular about the productions of the choreographer Golizovsky, whose main aim was the achievement of sculptural effects, for which he was wont almost to denude his dancers of all clothing. Diaghilev greatly enjoyed these conversations, in the course of which he came to consider that of all the available dancers Balanchine was the most likely to make a choreographer such as we needed. At the same time he perceived, what was less welcome to him, that Balanchine's ideas were already, so to speak, crystallized, and that he would consequently prove too independent to act as a mere instrument for the realization of Diaghilev's own conceptions. However, in order to test Balanchine's capacity further, it was arranged that he should take Nijinska's place in composing some of the dances for the Monte Carlo operas.

★   ★   ★

We arrived in Monte Carlo from London at the beginning of January, and opened at once with a gala performance in celebration of the Monégasque National Day, at which we gave *Les Tentations de la Bergère* and *Cimarosiana*. From then up to February the 1st, when the Italian opera season started, Diaghilev exercised his right of giving regular performances; and all went well till the last few days of this period, when the company suddenly went on strike. It began by some of the dancers announcing to me that, owing to a rise in the cost of living, they must ask again for an increase in their salaries. I, of course, reported this at once to Diaghilev; on which he undertook to consider their request and to do as much to meet it as his finances would allow. But this answer appeared not to satisfy the company. They called a meeting, presided over by Schollar and Vilzak, who, as soloists remunerated on a different scale, were entirely disinterested in the result of this move; and it was resolved at this meeting that unless Diaghilev gave them a definite promise to raise their salaries, they should not perform on the following night. I was asked to convey this resolution to Diaghilev; but when I called on him I found that he already knew about it and was highly indignant at the dancers' behaviour. I warned him that they were quite capable of carrying out their threat; to which he answered that he did not care if they did. I insisted, however, that he should speak to them himself; and after some hesitation he agreed to do so.

He arrived at the meeting looking extremely angry. 'I'm very much astonished at your behaviour,' he began. 'You've already been told that I intend considering my budget and seeing what I can do for you. What more can you expect? You each of you have a separate contract with me. Very well—if you refuse to perform this evening I shall regard your non-attendance as a breach of contract and shall sue you for damages—which I should in fact have suffered, by having been forced to cancel the performance.' On which, turning his back on them, he left the room and returned in my company to his hotel. He asked me to let him know what happened, since he did not propose going to the theatre himself.

It was almost nine o'clock when I arrived at the theatre, and time to ring up; but few of the dancers had put in an appearance. The Duke of Connaught was in the audience, and as the minutes passed and we failed to begin, the management sent round to ask why. By this time, however, the other dancers had begun arriving; and I somehow contrived to start the performance half an hour late. My difficulty was increased by the absence of Schollar and Vilzak, who had to be replaced at the last minute in solos. Next morning they were both told that they had broken their contracts and were therefore dismissed; and they accordingly left us. As for the malcontents who had launched the protest, their grievances were duly redressed, as soon as Diaghilev found he could afford it.

★   ★   ★

After the last of our performances, on January the 30th, Diaghilev's friends told him how much they disliked the prospect of seeing no more of our ballets for two whole months, while, according to the terms of our engagement, we were taking part in the Guinsbourg operas. The management of the Casino, however, said that they were prevented by their agreement with Guinsbourg from allowing us to perform at all during that period; and nothing more would probably have been done had not the *Princesse Héritière* requested Diaghilev to stage a special performance at a large party she was giving. Diaghilev was, of course, delighted to accept her invitation, and made up a suitable programme out of some of our best items performed by our best dancers—which ended, incidentally, with a valse specially composed by Balanchine for our child prodigy, little Alicia Markova. And the success of this selection of separate dances gave him the idea of arranging a series of 'Concert-Performances' during the period of our exclusion from the theatre. These performances took place in the *Nouvelle Salle de Musique* attached to the Casino, and were presented without scenery, in front of plain black velvet curtains. Occasionally the scene would be indicated by a placard, with 'A Palace', 'A Street', 'A Garden' written on it: *à la* Shakespeare, as Diaghilev used to say; and for orchestra we had two pianos and a string quartet. These performances seemed to be just what the public wanted; and the *Nouvelle Salle* was always full for them. But their success was not at all to the taste of Monsieur Guinsbourg; and in virtue of some clause in his contract with the Casino, he prevailed on the management to prohibit them in the following year.

Balanchine, meanwhile, was showing himself to have a real talent for composition in the dances he invented for performance in the operas. A case in point was the remarkable *Lezginka* he composed for Tcherni-cheva and Woidzikowsky in the Russian opera *Le Démon*, by Rubinstein, which had to be repeated at every performance. Diaghilev, therefore, now commissioned him to devise new choreography for Stravinsky's *Le Chant du Rossignol*, since Massine's version of 1920 had been seldom performed and had by this time been quite forgotten.

★   ★   ★

It was too soon, however, for Diaghilev to rely entirely on Balanchine; and when Kochno, who was beginning to play an important part in the counsels of the Ballet, heard that Massine was offering his services to us once more, he was insistent that we should accept them. Diaghilev and Massine accordingly met. But their interview was not very cordial; and during the whole period of Massine's renewed engagement, Kochno acted, not only as an intermediary between him and Diaghilev, but also as sole direct collaborator with Massine and the author of his scenarios; Diaghilev disclaiming any personal interest in Massine's creations. At the same time Diaghilev was well aware that, as regards the public, it was a great advantage to us to have Massine back again after his five years' absence.

Two novelties were on our list this year in the shape of two scores, one by Georges Auric (his second), and the other by a young Russian

The Diaghilev Ballet

named Vladimir Dukelsky, the latter being a discovery of some of Diaghilev's friends. We all considered Dukelsky a most attractive person; and some of our young ladies even detected in him a likeness to Pushkin. It was his ballet, entitled *Zéphire et Flore*, that Massine began rehearsing, when, while we were still in London, he reappeared on our horizon. I cannot say whether it was Diaghilev or Kochno who first thought of this theme for a ballet, except that Diaghilev, when discussing fresh productions, had expressed a wish to stage a ballet of the kind formerly danced by the private companies, recruited from among their peasants, that Russian nobles had taken to maintaining in the reign of Alexander I. The subject of Zephyr and Flora had been used by the celebrated ballet-master Didelot in 1795, with music by either Kovas or Bossi; and it was intended that we should recreate the atmosphere of that period in our new production to Dukelsky's music.

★   ★   ★

Balanchine's composition of *Le Chant du Rossignol* was almost ready, when Massine arrived in Monte Carlo to continue rehearsal of *Zéphire et Flore*. He was also to produce our other new ballet to Auric's music, which was called *Les Matelots*. Since he had another engagement elsewhere, Massine could not stay with us very long; and it was lucky, therefore, that both these ballets had small casts, since that greatly reduced the amount of work involved in their creation. Despite his appearing to be much pressed for time, however, he asked me to arrange some rehearsals of the first ballet he ever composed, *Le Soleil de Nuit*, in which, he said, he wished to make some alterations. This rather surprised me, since I had always thought *Le Soleil de Nuit* excellent as it was; but since I imagined that Massine had first consulted Diaghilev, I allotted him the rehearsals he had asked for; with the result that he altered practically the entire choreography. By the time Diaghilev returned from Paris, Massine had already left; and on hearing about *Le Soleil de Nuit* Diaghilev was as astonished as I had been: Massine had said nothing to him of his intention. He accordingly asked to see the new version and watched the rehearsal of it attentively. During its progress he sat quite silent; but as soon as it was over said loudly, so that everyone could hear: 'I should be obliged, Sergey Leonidovich, if you would revert to the original version of this ballet. This new one is no good at all!' I could not help being pleased at his decision, since I entirely agreed that *Le Soleil de Nuit*, of which I was particularly fond, had been spoilt by the alterations. On thinking over this peculiar incident I came to the conclusion that Massine's object had been to assert his independence of Diaghilev's, and possibly also of Larionov's, influence which had so closely conditioned his early work. But it was a strange way of going about it.

★   ★   ★

Diaghilev decided that *Zéphire et Flore*, before receiving its *première* proper in Paris, should be 'tried out' during our season in Monte Carlo. For the leading parts in it were to be taken by Dolin, Lifar and a new girl named Nikitina, and the two last were both relatively inexperienced. The performance in fact went smoothly, but the ballet failed to produce any great impression. As far as I could judge there were several reasons for this ineffectiveness. In the first place, the scenery and costumes by Bracque were attractive but quite unsuited to the subject: indeed I wondered how Diaghilev could have passed the designs, and could only suppose he had been mesmerized by the artist's celebrity. Then Dukelsky's music suffered from similar defects: it too was interesting but ill suited to the plot. Finally, there was Massine's choreography: though he made good use in it of the young dancers, it seemed deficient in both style and inspiration and devoid of any fresh ideas. As for the dancing, Lifar's technique had enormously improved during the previous two years, but he was still somewhat raw and uncertain. The only performers who were entirely satisfactory were Dolin, with his sure, well-shapen movements, and the executants of a charming *variation* for four Muses, namely Tchernicheva, Danilova, Doubrovska and Sokolova. Diaghilev was, of course, fully conscious of the shortcomings of *Zéphire et Flore*, which very clearly disappointed him; and when he left Monte Carlo he was still considering how it might be improved before being shown in Paris.

★   ★   ★

After leaving Monte Carlo we went, as in 1922, to Barcelona. Our season there was again highly successful, and the only drawback to our usual delight at finding ourselves in Spain was that the management insisted on our giving four ballets an evening instead of our customary three. This involved our finishing very late at night, and was exceedingly tiring not only for the dancers but also for the public. Barcelona still remained faithful to its old favourites such as *Schéhérazade* and *Cléopâtre*, and seemed little interested in such newer creations as the *Bergère* and *Le Train Bleu*.

I noticed while we were in Barcelona that Diaghilev was again look-ing worried. A few days before the end of our season there, as I was walking down the Ramblas, I heard him call out my name, and, on turning round, saw that he was sitting alone at a table in a café—which was for him a most unusual proceeding. He asked me to sit down, and after a few casual remarks said that he wished to talk to me about Dolin—who would be leaving the company at the end of our season in London. So that was it! But this was most unwelcome news. Dolin, to say the least of it, had become a very useful member of the company. At that juncture, indeed, he was all but indispensable: he was young, good-looking and danced extremely well; and his participation greatly enhanced the attraction of our performances. When I asked Diaghilev *why* he was leaving, all that he did was to shrug his shoulders; but though I had not expected this development, it did not altogether surprise me. For Diaghilev had lately been showing more and more interest in Lifar, and was clearly bent on giving him parts at least as important as Dolin's. So Dolin, I thought, as I sipped my coffee, had evidently judged that this might injure his career; and since his career was, very rightly, of major concern to him, he preferred, rather than jeopardize it, to seek his fortune elsewhere. During the long years of my collaboration with Diaghilev I had grown all too well used to these sudden upheavals. But I was sorry that Dolin should feel that he must leave us, just as he had begun really to blossom forth. It was clear to me also that Diaghilev was slightly fearful of the consequences, and had chosen to warn me in advance, so that I too might have the chance of considering how Dolin's departure might best be made up for.

From Barcelona we went back to London for the second part of our engagement at the Coliseum. This was to last from June the 18th to August the 1st; but in the middle we were to have a break of one week, during which we were to give a short season in Paris.

★   ★   ★

This curious arrangement, whereby our summer season in Paris, to which Diaghilev usually attached particular importance, was sand-wiched between the two halves of our London engagement, was due primarily, of course, to our having to discharge our obligation to Stoll. But the extreme shortness of our appearance in Paris—we were to give only six performances—apparently owed something also to a change of attitude in Diaghilev. For—why precisely I could not make out— nothing in his view at this time was bad enough for Paris: he was continually cursing the Paris public; and there was even a moment when, by way of punishment, he threatened not to indulge them with our presence at all! He afterwards relented so far as to *allow* them a season, but, even so, it was to be as short as possible—just long enough, but no longer than what was required, to remind 'those rotten Parisians' that the Ballet still existed. I enquired more than once what had so incensed him against Paris. But he would only frown and say it was a long story.

For this week in Paris we were again at that unattractive theatre, the *Gaieté Lyrique*; and we were faced at the outset with a *contretemps*. Our conductor, Eugene Goossens, could not at the last moment come with us to Paris. However, we telegraphed to Monte Carlo for Marc-César Scotto, who was familiar with our *répertoire* and in the event conducted for us quite satisfactorily.

Whatever resentment Diaghilev may have cherished against Paris at this time, he took infinite pains to make sure that all went well; and Paris for its part clearly conceived it a duty to come and see us; for the theatre was packed out at all six performances.

Since its performance at Monte Carlo Diaghilev had done his best to improve *Zéphire et Flore*, the first of our novelties to be presented. But though its cast of young people, and to some extent Dukelsky's music, were considered charming, this ballet remained an obstinate failure. On the other hand, Balanchine's new version of *Le Chant du Rossignol*, in which he made his real *début* as a choreographer, was much liked, by both Diaghilev and the Parisian audiences. Since this ballet had not been seen for five years, and then in another dancing version, it virtually ranked as a new creation; and in coping with the difficulties presented by the Stravinsky score and to a lesser degree by the pseudo-Chinese setting, Balanchine showed himself to be most promisingly talented. Sokolova again played Death, as which she was this time extraordinarily moving, and I again played the Emperor—a part that Diaghilev was good enough to rank as the best of my exceedingly limited *répertoire*! On this occasion the Nightingale was danced by little Markova, whose highly stylized antics greatly diverted the audience.

On the same night as *Le Rossignol*, that is June the 17th, we also gave

The Diaghilev Ballet

a first performance to our other entirely new ballet, *Les Matelots*. The music, as I have mentioned, was by Auric, whom, of the composers he had commissioned scores from the year before, Diaghilev admired the most. The scenario was by Kochno, with assistance from Diaghilev himself; but it was exceedingly slight, in accordance with Diaghilev's dictum, with which I personally disagreed, that the public were bored with plots and only liked dances. *Les Matelots* certainly had plenty of dances and little story. Variety was provided by constant changes of scene: there were no less than five *tableaux*, and by Massine's choreography, which was lively and admirably ingenious. The ballet was in fact a great success and was excellently danced by Woidzikowsky, Slavinsky and Lifar as the three sailors, Spanish, American and French, and by Nemchinova and Sokolova as the two girls. Diaghilev was so pleased with the 'hit' scored by *Les Matelots* that he forgave Paris whatever it was she had been guilty of.

It was in *Les Matelots* that Lifar first attracted special attention. His youth, his good figure and his elegant interpretation of the French sailor all made an impression; and Diaghilev was congratulated by his friends on his new discovery. When, however, we presented *Les Matelots* a week later on our return to the Coliseum, it provoked no such enthusiasm as in Paris—an interesting example of the difference between French and English taste.

Then on August the 1st we all went on holiday. Dolin, as arranged, left the company; and Diaghilev re-engaged Vladimirov to take over some of his parts.

★　　　★　　　★

After the holidays we reassembled in Paris, where we intended to rehearse before returning yet again to London. But it was then arranged that we should travel via Belgium, and give a few performances in towns there on our way. In the course of this year the company had acquired a number of new dancers, whom I had had no time to rehearse in any way adequately. Moreover, during their holiday most of the rest of the company had got out of training from lack of lessons. Since, therefore, our projected rehearsals in Paris had been cut short, we were scarcely in a condition to show ourselves in public. We opened at Antwerp with *Le Mariage d'Aurore*, a difficult ballet; and when the soloists began I all but swooned with horror at what I saw. I think the Diaghilev Ballet never danced so atrociously. Diaghilev was in front, but did not come round as usual. Instead he sent Kochno to say that he wished to see everyone at the next day's rehearsal. This was a storm signal. However, a general summons of this kind was by no means unusual. Two or three times a year Diaghilev would inform the assembled dancers that their performances had been falling off; and these minatory harangues always proved instantly effective. As a rule, however, I was sent for first and harangued on my own. I was not strict enough with the company, I would be told; I had not been imposing enough fines on delinquents. He expected his *régisseur* to be merciless: a watch-dog, a pitiless Tartar! I always listened to this invective without answering back, and then ventured the counter-thesis that, far from being a Tartar or anything so fierce, a *régisseur* was appointed to *assist* the dancers. Needless to say, this was all to no purpose. But the usual procedure was for us first to conclude this exchange in private, and then to go off and face the company together. Diaghilev would then lecture them in the most biting terms, but with complete self-control and without ever raising his voice. On this occasion, however, I had *not* been sent for; and when he appeared at the rehearsal he started venting his rage all round. When he at length ceased, there was a shamefaced hush, for the dancers were all conscious that they had deserved these strictures. But when he next turned on me and asked furiously how I could possibly have allowed such a performance, before I could answer, my assistant Kremnev stepped forward and said: 'Sergey Pavlovich, the reason why this has happened is simple. We're all out of practice, because of our holidays.'

'Oh, *are* you?' said Diaghilev, slightly taken aback. 'Well, then, I'd be obliged if you'd get *into* practice again, and as soon as possible!' After which he left the rehearsal.

★   ★   ★

We returned to London at the end of October to complete our series of seasons at the Coliseum. By the end of this third season Diaghilev would have discharged his debt to Stoll, and the scenery and costumes of *The Sleeping Princess* would become his property. These final weeks at the Coliseum were marked by one or two events that are worth recording. During the last year, while we had been in London, the company had again taken lessons with *Maestro* Cecchetti. But at the end of August he had finally left London for Milan, to take up an appointment at the

The Diaghilev Ballet

Scala, where it had always been his ambition to end his career. Cecchetti was therefore no longer in London when we returned; but at this juncture another former professor of dancing at the *Mariinsky*, where he had also been *premier danseur*, arrived from Leningrad—namely Nicolas Legat; and Diaghilev immediately engaged him in Cecchetti's place. The appointment, however, was not altogether a happy one, since Legat was an exponent of the French school of ballet; and arguments at once arose over the respective merit of this and the Italian school, to which, under Cecchetti, the company were accustomed.

The next notable event of this season was another return to our ranks of Lydia Lopokova. She returned from nowhere and imported her usual gaiety into our lives and performances alike. And then Diaghilev announced a new ballet. It was to be done at once, while we were still in London. He asked me to go round to his hotel and showed me a sketch, asking whether I liked it. I saw that it was signed 'Utrillo'—a painter whose work I greatly admired—and said, yes, I did. 'This is for the scenery of our new ballet, *Barabau*,' said Diaghilev. I had already heard that the young Italian composer Vittorio Rieti had written the music; and what Diaghilev had summoned me for was to allot the parts. The choreography was to be by Balanchine, of whom Diaghilev now had high hopes as a result of his success with *Le Chant du Rossignol*.

Barabau in fact turned out very well. Utrillo's sketch for the scenery was beautifully interpreted by a remarkable scenic artist, Prince A. Shervashidze; the music, consisting of simple Italian tunes, partly sung by a choir placed on the stage itself, was delightful; and Balanchine's choreography, apart from a not altogether satisfactory *finale*, was most interesting and original. There were three chief parts: Barabau himself, danced by Woidzikowsky—in this as always marvellously precise in his movements; the Peasant Woman, danced by Tatiana Chamié—an excellent comedy role; and a smart young Sergeant, danced by Lifar. Unfortunately we were unable to give *Barabau* as often as we should have liked on account of the chorus, who were very expensive.

We ended our long engagement at the Coliseum on December the 1st with two performances of *Le Mariage d'Aurore*. We received a most touching farewell from the public, who greeted every dancer with loud applause and overwhelmed the company with bouquets.

The following morning we left for Berlin.

CHAPTER EIGHTEEN
1926

IN Berlin it was at the *Deutsches Künstlertheater* that we were to give our season; and it was intended to last a fortnight. Our impresario expected us to do good business. Unfortunately, however, though the theatre was full for the opening performance, the public thereafter stayed away with such unanimity that hardly a soul came to see us. In view of our almost invariable success elsewhere this was extremely puzzling. But there it was; and at the end of our first week the receipts proved to have been so meagre that the impresario was unable to pay us. This placed us in a grave predicament, since we had too little money even to transport ourselves to Monte Carlo, where we were expected next. Diaghilev was indignant and left for Paris in the hope of raising funds, meanwhile handing over all the cash in his possession to Nouvel and myself. As it was the Christmas season, to make any business arrangement was particularly difficult; and our credit at the bank was exhausted. We naturally felt extremely despondent and regarded the New Year with misgiving. Several days went by without news of Diaghilev, during which we continued our dismal performances to empty houses; and then, the very day before we were scheduled to leave, Nouvel arrived at the theatre looking unusually brisk, and joyfully announced that the money was on its way and that we should consequently be able to leave as arranged. How Diaghilev could have made the necessary arrangements so quickly, and especially at Christmas, said Nouvel, he could not imagine. However—our relief was enormous; but we took leave of Berlin wondering what this peculiar failure of ours could have meant. Some of us supposed that we had gone to an unsuitable theatre; others that we should not have shown so many ballets that were the work of French musicians and painters, and should have concentrated on Russian works. That the character of our programme was so largely French would appear to have been the more likely reason, since hostility to France was still common in Germany—or perhaps it was merely that the latest developments of Diaghilev's taste in art were not appreciated in Berlin.

★ ★ ★

In any case it was a great comfort to be back in Monte Carlo. It was by this time almost the end of January; but we were able to give five performances before the opening of the opera season, including a gala in honour of the Prince of Monaco, at which we presented the two-act version of *Le Lac des Cygnes*.

But the pleasure of our return was spoilt at this juncture by a somewhat unpleasant incident. This was the sudden departure of Vera Nemchinova and Nicolas Zverev, two of our leading dancers, to take up an engagement, which we had heard nothing about, in London. Zverev did not even speak to me about it before they left. He merely sent me a short note stating that they had received a telegram from London and would be absent for the duration of the Casino opera season. As Nemchinova was one of the three leading dancers whom Diaghilev was obliged by his contract to provide for that season, her absence placed him in an awkward position. He was naturally enough extremely angry, and he had every reason to be so. Nemchinova and Zverev had both been in our company for ten years. I had brought Nemchinova from Russia in 1915, when she was still no more than a pupil; and Zverev had joined us at about the same time. Every opportunity had been given to both of them of studying under *Maestro* Cecchetti and developing their art under Diaghilev's critical eye, till they had become first-rate dancers. But they were both Tolstoyans, and Tolstoy's doctrine forbade its adherents among other things to sign contracts. Diaghilev had accordingly consented to rely on a 'Gentleman's Agreement' with them—an agreement which carried their engagement with the company up to July the 1st of this year (whereas we were now only in January). However, the religious, or philosophical, convictions that had been too strong to allow of their adding their signatures to a contract were evidently too weak to deter them from breaking it, when to break it suited their immediate interests.

The defection of Nemchinova opened the way to promotion for two hitherto lesser dancers: Danilova and Nikitina. During the year she had now spent with our company, Danilova had made remarkable progress and was by this time fully capable of taking Nemchinova's place. The

214

same could not quite be said of Nikitina. Her technique was indifferent and the parts she could fill were fewer. But Nikitina possessed a most valuable endowment: self-confidence, of which she commanded an apparently boundless supply.

★   ★   ★

As we were not particularly busy during this time at Monte Carlo, Balanchine and I thought we might slightly reduce the hours of our morning rehearsals, which usually lasted from ten to one. We did not, however, say anything to Diaghilev; and I had little fear that he would find out for himself, since, whenever he had little business to do, it was his habit to rise late, so that he seldom emerged from his hotel before one o'clock. Indeed, I used to visit him there every morning and indulge in general gossip, which he much enjoyed. One morning, however, on my calling as usual, I found him already dressed and almost ready to go out. He said he wished to attend Balanchine's rehearsal, and prevented me from following my first impulse, which was to dash ahead and give warning, by asking me to wait for him. I guessed that Balanchine and I had been betrayed; and when we reached the rehearsal-rooms, Diaghilev was duly told by Joseph, the one-armed porter, that the rehearsal had finished half an hour earlier. Great was my confusion! No more, however, was said. Only our rehearsal time was thenceforward cut no more!

★   ★   ★

One day not long after this incident, Diaghilev sent for me to go to his hotel. I saw at once that he was in a very good mood. 'You always maintain, Sergey Leonidovich,' he began, 'that ballets should have plots. Well—you'll be pleased to hear that our next ballet should answer your requirements.'

'Oh, good,' said I. 'What is it going to be?'

'Romeo and Juliet,' said Diaghilev triumphantly. 'Of course for ballet purposes it will have to be somewhat adapted, but still . . . The score has already been written, by an Englishman, Constant Lambert; and since Shakespeare used no scenery, neither shall we. What I've not yet decided is who will compose the choreography. That's what I wanted to talk to you about.'

I was interested to discover how it was proposed to adapt the plot, and was somewhat dismayed to find that its connection with Shake-

215

The Diaghilev Ballet

speare's tragedy was to be slender in the extreme. All it amounted to indeed was that, in the first place, the dancers were to be shown rehearsing various incidents from that famous drama, and that, in the second, the two principals playing the 'star-cross'd lovers' were, like them, to elope. However, as regards choreographers, 'Neither Massine nor Balanchine seem to me suited to this ballet,' said Diaghilev. 'So I thought of asking Nijinska.' This I entirely approved, and since, despite her quarrel with Diaghilev, Nijinska was apparently ready to work for him again, it was decided to present *Roméo et Juliette* at Monte Carlo in March, when she would be free.

As for other new works, Diaghilev had it in mind to do yet a third ballet by Auric and possibly another by Satie. It appeared that for the moment he could obtain nothing more from Stravinsky, and was hence obliged to resort to these French composers and the Englishman Lambert. Moreover, as will appear, he had already ordered a score from another English composer, Lord Berners.

★   ★   ★

The peace of our existence in Monte Carlo this year was again disturbed by the resignation of Legat as ballet-master. Diaghilev took to attending not only rehearsals but also lessons, and soon began to show signs of dissatisfaction with Legat's method, repeatedly asking me why the dancers in general, and Lifar in particular, seemed to make so little progress. I explained that Legat was less of a teacher than a coach—that is to say that he was better at teaching dancers actual parts than at improving their general technique—which was, of course, not very useful for the numerous very young people in our company whose first need was to continue their grounding. As for Lifar, his *pirouettes* and *double-tours* were still very poor; so much so that one day Diaghilev scolded him in front of the whole company, making them all acutely uncomfortable. I did my best to defend him, but without success; Diaghilev's irritation over his poor technique continued, but was at length transferred to Legat, whom he blamed for failing to show Lifar how to overcome his difficulties. Legat was deeply offended; and from that moment his relations with Diaghilev grew more and more strained till he finally resigned and would never thereafter have anything more to do with Diaghilev. On his resignation Diaghilev wrote to Cecchetti in Milan, asking him whom he would recommend as a teacher for the

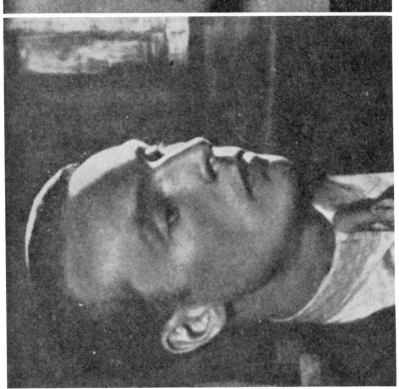

PLATE XVI

BRONISLAVA NIJINSKA

GEORGES BALANCHINE

The Diaghilev Ballet

company; and Cecchetti promptly replied saying that in his view Diaghilev could not do better than employ my wife, Liubov Tchernicheva, for the purpose. My wife in fact possessed a particularly thorough knowledge of both the French and the Italian methods of training for ballet-dancing, having first completed her own, under Fokine, at the Imperial Theatre School at St. Petersburg, and then worked, throughout her career in the Diaghilev Ballet, under Cecchetti. When Diaghilev duly offered her the post, she was honoured to accept it; and thereafter Diaghilev frequently watched her classes and complimented her on the way in which she contrived to improve her pupils. He was especially struck, for instance, with her success in developing Markova, whose *élévation* she so greatly improved that in Diaghilev's words 'she made her take wing and fly'. From the time of her appointment up to Diaghilev's death my wife remained the company's 'ballet-mistress'.

Another event of importance to the Ballet that took place at this time was the appearance of the British newspaper magnate, Lord Rothermere, as a keen admirer of our work. One day Diaghilev came to a rehearsal accompanied by a tall, burly man with quite a pleasant English-looking face. It was the custom on such occasions for the rehearsal to stop, on which Diaghilev would bow to the company and then shake hands with the *régisseur*, the choreographer and the leading dancers; after which he would sit down and the rehearsal would be resumed. This ritual was performed on this occasion as usual, except that Diaghilev also introduced us to the visitor, saying that Lord Rothermere was an ardent admirer of our Ballet and was always, when possible, present at our performances; he had been following our progress for years and would be much interested in seeing a ballet in the process of creation. Diaghilev and Lord Rothermere then sat down, and the latter, we observed, watched the rehearsal with the closest attention. Nor was this visit his last. On the contrary, he came more and more often, and gradually became a regular spectator of our activities, both at rehearsal and on the stage.

It was one of Diaghilev's characteristics never to mention money. But I knew that at this time he was in great straits for it, owing partly to our failure in Berlin and partly to the liquidation of his debt to Stoll; so that I was not surprised when, a few days before our season at Monte Carlo began, he told me that he had no money with which to stage new ballets. It was true that *Barabau* was ready and that *Roméo et Juliette* was not going to cost much; but they were not enough. 'Do you know what

218

I think I'll do?' said Diaghilev. 'I think I'll sell the curtain Picasso did for *Le Tricorne*, and his figure-paintings on the *décor* for *Cuadro Flamenco*, all of which are signed. I've already got a buyer in Germany; and the money will enable me to do some new productions.' He looked at me questioningly. I was sad at the idea of parting with the curtain for *Le Tricorne*, which I loved, and said I feared we might be criticized for presenting the ballet without it. Diaghilev laughed. 'Oh, in that case we'd say we were afraid it might get spoilt, if we went on using it,' he said, 'and so we'd put it away. No, I must sell it. So will you please produce it and the *Cuadro* pieces tomorrow? I'll do the cutting out myself.' The 'cutting out' he referred to was what made the sale of the *Tricorne* picture possible; for it had been painted as a comparatively small panel in the centre of a huge cloth. Diaghilev would have liked also to sell Picasso's curtain for *Parade* in the same way. But the design in that case covered the whole expanse of canvas; and no-one could be found to buy anything so vast.

★   ★   ★

For the part of Juliet in *Roméo et Juliette* Diaghilev succeeded in once again engaging Karsavina. Apart from his particular affection for her, he had been eager for Lifar to have her as a partner in this ballet. He was able thereby, as it were, to conjure up once again the Golden Age, when she had so often danced with Nijinsky. For despite his perpetual striving after fashion and modernity, Diaghilev had an immense respect for tradition, and greatly valued the older generation of dancers, insisting always that the young must appreciate their inheritance and learn from the past.

There was also another reason for his welcoming Karsavina's return at this juncture. For as I have mentioned, the sudden departure of Nemchinova had left him in an awkward position as regards the management of the Casino. Now, therefore, he could substitute Karsavina's name for Nemchinova's; and the exchange was not one at which the management could be anything but pleased.

We opened our season with *Les Matelots* and *Barabau*, neither of which had before been seen in Monte Carlo. Both were well received, *Barabau* in particular having an appeal of its own for the local Italian colony. Then, on May the 4th, followed the first night of *Roméo et Juliette*. This ballet had no *décor* in the accepted sense of the word. The curtain rose on an entirely bare stage—an effect that tended to embarrass the public,

The Diaghilev Ballet

who imagined that it had been brought up by mistake. However, as the dancers began appearing, and from what was stated in their programmes, the spectators soon realized that what was to be enacted was the rehearsal of a play. Such scenery as there was consisted of small flats, moved about by the dancers themselves, and representing, say, part of a hall, or a courtyard, or a balcony. The costumes were all alike and nothing if not simple—yellow tunics for the ladies and practice clothes for the men. The only characters who wore period costumes were Romeo and Juliet themselves. To make up for the absence of scenery there were no less than two act-drops, by the *Surréaliste* painters Max Ernst and Jean Miro; but their design had no relation to the subject, the music or the choreography. Diaghilev took enormous pains over lighting these act-drops; and at one of these lighting rehearsals, when I was as usual sitting next to him, he asked me if I did not think the first act-drop particularly lovely. What I saw hung in front of me was a huge plain pale-blue expanse of canvas, in the centre of which was painted a large disc resembling a gramophone record, of which three-quarters were distinct and the remainder lost in a haze. I certainly could not go into ecstasies over it and said so; at which Diaghilev all but lost his temper. 'I can't understand you,' he said. 'After all the years you've worked with me, and all you've seen, you don't seem to be able to grasp the idea of modern painting!'

'I just don't care for it,' I answered. 'And as for *Surréalisme*—it seems to me both pointless and ugly.'

Diaghilev thereupon got up. Just now, he said, there was no time. But one of these days he would prove to me, he undertook, that what I called 'ugliness' was really full of beauty.

As for the other elements in this ballet, the score, by Constant Lambert, was much like any other example of second-rate modern music and made no impression on the public whatever. Nijinska's choreography was difficult to assess. Indeed it could hardly be called choreography: it consisted mainly of exercises at the bar. There was a *pas de deux*, it is true, and a great deal of miming; but of dancing proper practically nothing. The whole conception of the ballet indeed seemed to be based on a desire to shock. Thus it was in two parts, between which, though the curtain was lowered, its bottom was kept some feet above the stage, so that the audience could see the dancers' legs as they moved across it; and at the end Lifar, as Romeo, appeared dressed as an airman, ready for elopement with Juliet by aeroplane. These 'modern' touches were apparently to Diaghilev's taste.

Diaghilev had hoped that Lifar's performance would prove as striking as Dolin's in *Le Train Bleu*. But though he looked very well, and, despite his technical limitations, danced well, he failed to produce any comparable impression. Karsavina was as enchanting as ever—very simple and sincere. But her part was not good enough choreographically to allow of her either making any great effect.

★   ★   ★

At the end of our season at Monte Carlo we went straight to Paris, where we were this year to perform at the *Théâtre Sarah Bernhardt*. A first night in Paris was always especially exciting; but the first night of this season, which fell on March the 18th, was made even more so than usual by our being warned before the performance by the police that the *Surréalistes* were expected to stage a demonstration during the performance of *Roméo et Juliette* against their colleagues Ernst and Miro for collaborating with a 'capitalist' such as Diaghilev. The house was as usual packed with an expectant audience. But behind the curtain the company could not but be somewhat apprehensive. We began with *Pulcinella*, during which there were no signs of disturbance. Then, in the interval, Diaghilev came behind and said that if any trouble occurred I was to ring down and put on the house-lights. Sure enough, it began as soon as the first act-drop was exposed: pandemonium broke out: shouts, hissing, stamping and a shower of leaflets from the gallery (signed 'Louis Aragon' and 'André Breton')—reminding me only too vividly of the first night of *Le Sacre* so many years before. However, this time we were under no orders against stopping whatever happened; and though the dancers in fact continued as long as they could hear the orchestra, when at length the hubbub drowned all sound of the music, I brought the curtain down, as instructed, and turned on the lights in the auditorium. This was then cleared by the police of the noisier demonstrators; order was restored; and the performance was resumed. The company fully realized that the demonstration was not directed against them; and, if anything, this scandal was rather useful to us on account of the publicity it received in the newspapers. As for the ballet, the public on the whole did not take it seriously, but were quite amused. Lifar scored a certain personal success, and so did Nikitina, who danced Juliet—for Karsavina had been unable to accompany us to Paris.

To complete the programme on this first night we gave *Les Matelots*, which was again very well received. Its success the year before had meanwhile suggested to Diaghilev the use in another ballet of all its ingredients except Massine's choreography: that is, that he should employ the same designer, Pruna; the same composer, Auric; the same librettist, Kochno, and some of the same dancers; while confiding the choreography, this time, to Balanchine. Unfortunately this combination failed to work as before; and *La Pastorale*, as the new ballet was called, was a disappointment to Diaghilev. It was in no less than twelve scenes; and the dancing was much hampered by the employment of a large number of small rostrums and screens on wheels, which were moved about in the course of the action. Neither Pruna's *décor* nor Auric's music was as good as for *Les Matelots*; and the subject itself was unhelpful to Balanchine's invention. The subject indeed seemed curiously unrelated to the name of the ballet. For the chief characters were a Film Star (danced by Félia Doubrovska) and a Telegraph Boy (danced by Lifar). It might, however, almost be said that the chief part in the ballet was played by the Telegraph Boy's bicycle. For this and Lifar seemed to be all but inseparable: it figured even in his and Doubrovska's *pas de deux*.

Meanwhile, earlier in the season than the first night of *La Pastorale*, we had shown Paris *Barabau*, which was also new to it; and both Utrillo's *décor* and Balanchine's choreography had been much admired. Moreover, we still had a fourth novelty, which was presented in the latter part of the season; and this was the most eccentric of all. Diaghilev had always been much attracted by the music of Eric Satie, the composer of *Parade*, and was anxious, while Satie, who had recently died, was still thought of as a contemporary, to add a second ballet by him to our *répertoire*. So when he learnt that a piano score of Satie's was in the possession of Comte Étienne de Beaumont, Diaghilev persuaded the latter to let him use it, and handed it over for orchestration to Darius Milhaud. The scenery and costumes were ordered from Derain; the choreography was again by Balanchine; and the ballet, which consisted virtually of no more than three dances, was entitled (in English) *Jack-in-the-Box*. It was danced by Danilova, Tchernicheva, Doubrovska and Idzikovsky. But in spite of their brilliant execution and the impressive list of collaborators responsible for it, *Jack-in-the-Box* was not a ballet for the general public, whom it rather bored. Its appeal was rather to a small circle, for whom it had 'snob' value; and it also received a certain amount of attention in the press. In this connection I may add that none of the new ballets we presented during this season in Paris possessed any wide appeal. They were not to be compared in this respect with, for instance, *Petrushka*, or *Les Noces*, which really stirred whatever audiences we showed them to, wherever it might be.

Throughout this season our orchestra was conducted by Roger Desormière.

★   ★   ★

Now that we were at last free of any obligation to Stoll and might appear in London where we chose, we felt that we had re-established what we liked to consider our proper routine, consisting of three main seasons: in Monte Carlo, in Paris and in London. It was now five years since we had last appeared in London otherwise than at the Coliseum; and our return to an ordinary theatre was awaited with interest. Diaghilev had a double ambition: to remain independent of any management and, of choice, to instal himself at His Majesty's, one of the most attractive theatres in London, with a pleasant auditorium and a good stage, which, though not large, was large enough to take our scenery satisfactorily. For this, however, he naturally required finance; and so he asked Lord Rothermere to subsidize him, on the understanding that Diaghilev would refund the sum advanced at the end of the season. Rothermere duly consented; and with his assistance Diaghilev succeeded in organizing one of the most brilliant seasons we ever had.

We presented a programme of twenty ballets, four of them new to London, with a cast headed by Trefilova, Karsavina and Lopokova. On the opening night we gave *Les Noces*, which London had not yet seen; and since Stravinsky's music had by this time become familiar through *L'Oiseau de Feu*, *Petrushka*, *Le Sacre du Printemps* and *Le Rossignol*, it was very well received. Next, a week later, we gave *Roméo et Juliette* with Karsavina; and here the public were interested both by the Shakespearian association and the fact that the score was by an English composer. Our season was to last five weeks; and we aimed at presenting a new ballet every Monday. For our third *première*, accordingly, we chose *La Pastorale*. After its presentation in Paris Diaghilev had cut a number of the cumbersome rostrums, and improved the ballet otherwise; so that the English audiences unexpectedly took to it. Finally, the last event of note during the season was what Diaghilev called a '*Festival Eric Satie*'. This consisted of a performance, as the middle item of the evening's programme, of our two Satie ballets, *Parade* and

Jack-in-the-Box, plus some piano pieces by the same composer played by Marcelle Mayer. The effect was perhaps one of extravaganza; but it nevertheless created a good deal of interest.

As regards the season as a whole, the men of the company, Woidzikowsky, Idzikovsky, Slavinsky, Lifar and Balanchine, tended to be outshone by the exceptionally brilliant galaxy of female 'stars': Trefilova, Karsavina, Lopokova, Tchernicheva, Sokolova, Danilova and Doubrovska. In London our orchestra was again conducted by Goossens.

Fortunately the season was not only an artistic, but also a financial, success, which enabled Diaghilev to fulfil his undertaking to repay Rothermere the money he had advanced. The result of this was that Rothermere at once offered his help in the organization of another London season in the autumn.

★　　★　　★

From London the company went to Ostend, where they gave two performances, and thence to Le Touquet. At Le Touquet they stayed a month, performing under the management of René Blum (brother of the celebrated French politician), during which Nouvel was placed in charge, while I went away for a rest.

It was pleasant for once to escape from our daily routine of rehearsal and performance. But I felt somewhat lost; and my mind was for ever churning over the affairs of the Ballet. In a vague way I was disturbed about Diaghilev himself. I tried to disentangle my latest impressions, which were much confused. I thought over the many meetings and talks I had had with him in recent months, and concluded that a change had come over him: he seemed to have lost some of his interest in the Ballet and to be always half thinking of something else. He had indeed repeatedly said that he would like to disband the existing company and form a smaller one, for more 'intimate' work. He had also complained bitterly and often of being starved artistically. Moreover, another passion that had always possessed him, a passion for book collecting, seemed now to have been gaining a greater hold on him than ever. I had remarked the delight in his face when he would tell me how he had acquired some rare edition. For the time being, at any rate, such discoveries clearly meant more to him than the Ballet.

Supposing that my understanding of this development in Diaghilev were right, there were two questions that especially exercised me: what was it that had caused him to lose interest in the Ballet; and what effect might this decline of interest be expected to have on its fortunes? When I recalled the first years of its existence, I perceived that what Diaghilev had then enjoyed was not the organization and management of our enterprise, but the opportunity it afforded him for the exercise of his creative aesthetic talents. He was unable to become a choreographer himself, but had succeeded, given the right dancers, in realizing his ideas with their co-operation. His collaboration first with Fokine and later with Massine had produced wonders. But neither in Dolin nor in Lifar had he found the particular qualities demanded for a similar creative partnership. Moreover, he was growing older—he was now fifty-four—and no longer possessed the energy and enthusiasm to keep him for ever in search of new talent to develop. There was now, it was true, Georges Balanchine. But Balanchine had arrived from Russia with his ideas already formed; and though Diaghilev could still guide and correct him, he was unable to use him as a medium of creation. As for the continued existence of the Ballet, I came to the conclusion that this was pretty well assured. For even though Diaghilev might have grown less keen on it, he was almost bound to maintain it in being, even if only to provide him with the means of book-buying!

Quite apart from all these considerations, also, I reminded myself that Diaghilev was essentially changeable. His collector's passion might any day be overwhelmed in a renewed passion for the theatre. Perhaps all that was needed for such a process was the discovery of some young and exceptionally gifted choreographer!

I was considerably cheered indeed to receive a number of letters from Diaghilev not long after, from Venice, outlining his future plans and giving me instructions for work. I learnt from these that our autumn season in London was now definitely fixed, and that he was busy with the planning of the new ballet it was essential for us to present in the course of it. He asked whether Balanchine had succeeded in securing any new dancers from Russia; whether Woidzikowsky had duly returned from Warsaw. . . . Altogether, for the time being I was reassured.

★　　★　　★

The new ballet mentioned by Diaghilev in his letter was to be thoroughly English, in accordance with Lord Rothermere's wish that we should include such a work in our programme. It had been first thought of the summer before, when Diaghilev had met Lord Berners—'not a bad composer' in his estimation—in Venice, and had engaged him to provide the score. It was inspired by the pantomimes that had been a favourite form of entertainment in London in the early years of Queen Victoria and was to be entitled *The Triumph of Neptune*. Finally, it was to be in twelve *tableaux* so entirely disconnected that any one of them might be omitted—as some of them subsequently were (the ballet being found to be far too long)—without injury to the rest. Having so much scenery and a large number of costumes to correspond, it would be a highly expensive production.

We began rehearsals in Paris; and once again Diaghilev effected a 'purge' of the company, engaging a number of new dancers to replace those discharged, the most notable of whom was a substitute for Nikitina, who had now left us, in the person of Vera Petrova from Warsaw. These alterations in the composition of the company involved me in a great deal of work. For we had little time in which to rehearse the new-comers in our old *répertoire* as well as preparing *The Triumph of Neptune*, and I was determined at all costs to avoid a repetition of the Antwerp disaster. I therefore decided that we should open our season in London with the ballets that were easiest for our new recruits to learn.

Our London season was to be under the joint patronage of two Royal personages, the *Princesse Héritière* of Monaco and H.R.H. The Duke of Connaught. The theatre we were to perform at was the Lyceum, for which I personally did not much care. Diaghilev was much exercised about the composition of our programme. It was barely three months since we had closed at His Majesty's; *The Triumph of Neptune* was not yet ready; and it was imperative that we should not merely repeat ourselves. We therefore fell back on various ballets not seen in London for some time, the first of which was *Le Lac des Cygnes*, last performed there as long before as 1914. This we now gave in a one-act version, consisting of the old first act slightly altered by the excision of some dull passages and scenes in mime. The Princess in this version was danced by Danilova and the Prince by Lifar.

Our second such revival was *L'Après-Midi d'un Faune*, which had last been performed in London even longer before, in 1913, in the days of Nijinsky. The Faun in this revival was danced by Lifar, and the first nymph by Tchernicheva. Lastly, we revived *L'Oiseau de Feu*, not seen in London since 1921, in a new *décor* by Natalia Goncharova. Diaghilev had told me in Monte Carlo that he proposed ordering this from her as

Plate XVII

ALEXANDRA DANILOVA

soon as he could afford it. I much preferred the original *décor* by Golovine; but Diaghilev was always averse from copying what had once been fresh. These three revivals were all most successful, particularly *L'Oiseau de Feu*, in which Danilova and Lifar once again took the chief parts of the Bird and the Prince, with Tchernicheva as the Enchanted Princess. Its new *décor*, which was much admired, served to make *L'Oiseau de Feu* almost an original production.

The Triumph of Neptune required much time to prepare; but it was finally presented, all too near the end of our season, on December the 3rd. As I have mentioned, the music was by Lord Berners; and the scenario was by the English poet Sacheverell Sitwell. The *décor* was taken from specimens in a collection of Victorian coloured prints chosen by Diaghilev and admirably adapted and painted by Prince Shervashidze; and the choreography was of course by Balanchine. There were three principal *tableaux*: 'Cloudland', 'The Frozen Forest' and 'The Triumph of Neptune' itself. In 'The Frozen Forest' scene, which contained the best *variation* for the ballerinas, they were brought on on wires, in the period manner; and Diaghilev was much diverted by this Victorian contrivance. Balanchine not only composed the choreography, but also danced the part of the tipsy Negro, in which he was brilliant. The other chief parts were those of the Fairy Queen, danced by Danilova, and of Tom Tug the Sailor, who was the hero and appeared in every scene, danced by Lifar. *The Triumph of Neptune* was much to the taste of the London public; and it was a great pity that, since our season ended on December the 11th, we could not perform it more often than we did. During this season our orchestra was conducted by Henri Defosse. He was a particularly talented conductor of ballet, and the only one ever engaged by us with whom Diaghilev never quarrelled over *tempi*.

One night towards the end of this season, when I was standing as usual in the prompt corner, keeping an eye on the performance, Diaghilev came and sat down on my chair. 'Massine's asking to come back to us again,' he said, smiling. 'What do you think?'—and, before I had time to answer, went on: 'I don't think we really need him. Besides, he'd be expensive and upset our budget.' I disagreed. I told him I thought Massine would be a most desirable addition to the company, provided, that was, that he would come for such and such a salary—and named quite a modest figure. 'My dear Sergey Leonidovich, you're joking,' said Diaghilev. 'He'd never come for anything like that!'

'Well, there's no harm in seeing,' said I. 'You suggest it, and if he agrees you'll have another good dancer in the company. You try.'

Diaghilev got up. 'All right,' he said. 'I will'—and a few days later he told me that Massine *had* agreed, and would join us in Turin, where we were dancing next.

CHAPTER NINETEEN

1927

O N our way from London to Turin we stopped in Paris. Diaghilev was already there, and when we met he told me that Olga Spesivtseva had rejoined the company. It may be remembered that she had left us in 1922, after the untimely demise of *The Sleeping Princess*, despite my efforts to retain her. I was delighted to hear of her return.

It had been arranged that we should give fourteen performances at Turin. This was really too many for so small a city. But we were guaranteed against loss by the *Società degli Amici di Torino*, so that we were not alarmed at the possibility of poor houses.

Massine was already in Turin when we arrived. There were no parts he could take immediately; but he began coming daily to my wife's lessons with the rest of the company.

The theatre in Turin was quite a pleasant one, and we enjoyed performing in it. Since this was our first visit, however, the public, not having seen our ballets before, were inclined to find them somewhat above their heads; and so, although our performances went quite well, they were far from creating any great stir.

This season at Turin is distinguished in my memory as much as anything by the tiresome obstinacy of our conductor, Inghelbrecht. Inghelbrecht was no doubt an able musician; but as a conductor of ballet he was lamentable. Nor would he take the slightest notice of complaints either from the dancers or from Diaghilev. It was a rule with us that all *tempi* were fixed by Diaghilev. No-one else was permitted to interfere. When, therefore, at a rehearsal in Turin of *L'Après-Midi*, Inghelbrecht took the music at so breathless a speed that the cast could not dance to it, I had no alternative but to stop the rehearsal, since I had no right to criticize his *tempo*. However, Diaghilev was as usual watching the rehearsal from the stalls. But when he duly pointed out that Inghelbrecht had been going much too fast, the latter flew into a rage and shouted that he knew perfectly well at what speed the works of French composers should be taken! Diaghilev replied quite calmly that this was no doubt true in general; but that in the case of *L'Après-Midi* the *tempo* for the ballet had been fixed by Debussy himself. However, Inghelbrecht was not to be mollified and an altercation ensued; and though Diaghilev eventually won his way, Inghelbrecht thenceforward refused to speak to him. Not long after, consequently—and to our great relief—he was replaced by Roger Desormière.

Not, however, before his conducting had given rise to another somewhat painful incident. The ballet in this case was *Le Lac des Cygnes*—in which the Prince and Princess were danced respectively by Lifar and Spesivtseva. The trouble this time arose because, being now under a self-imposed oath not to speak to Diaghilev, Inghelbrecht chose to ask Massine at what speed various passages in the score should be taken; and Massine, who did not really know, made several wild and quite misleading guesses. The result was that at the performance the orchestra played so slowly that poor Spesivtseva, who anyhow had little ear or sense of time, was completely thrown out. Lifar made desperate signals to Inghelbrecht; but the latter entirely ignored them; and the whole performance was reduced to chaos. Diaghilev was enraged, and after retur•ing to his hotel telephoned asking me to go round. Foreseeing a storm, I tried to escape it by alleging that I was already in bed; but Nouvel, who was speaking for him, said that Diaghilev insisted on seeing me. When I reached the hotel I found Diaghilev, Nouvel, Kochno and Lifar all sitting in the empty restaurant.

'Well, what do you say to tonight's *Lac des Cygnes* as danced by our principals?' asked Diaghilev, offering me some coffee.

'Not very good,' I answered.

'Not very *good*!' he protested. 'It was *shameful*! However badly a ballet may be conducted, it can always be danced in *time*. But Mademoiselle Spesivtseva, if you please, contrived to finish her *variation* no less than *two bars late*! And as for Monsieur Lifar, I *died* of shame at the sight of him! During the whole existence of our Ballet, *never* have people danced in such a fashion! I have asked you to come round so that I may say this to Monsieur Lifar in the presence of my *régisseur* . . .' and so on and so on for about forty minutes, while Lifar sat and listened without uttering a word. When he did in the end stop, Diaghilev turned to me and said in the most amiable tone: 'Thank you. Now you must please go to bed. I'm sorry to have disturbed you at such an hour. I imagine that Lifar has never forgotten his *début* with Spesivtseva.

★　　★　　★

From Turin we went to Milan. It had always been one of Diaghilev's great ambitions for the Ballet to perform at the Scala; and at last the great day had come. He chose our programme with particular care: it was to consist of *Cimarosiana*, *Le Mariage d'Aurore*, *Le Lac des Cygnes* and *L'Oiseau de Feu*. But, alas, he chose all wrong! He should have chosen *Petrushka*, *Schéhérazade* and the Polovtsian Dances; then we should pretty certainly have been a success. As it was, though our performances filled the theatre, the Milanese were evidently disappointed. The famous Russian Ballet in the classics, so tame and sober! They had expected a tremendous display of passion, in which the notorious Slavonic temperament should find vent in scenes of the wildest licence! Our reception was almost cold; and Diaghilev was greatly upset.

Whilst in Milan we of course met our beloved old *Maestro* Cecchetti. We were shown into his class by the Director of the Scala, who was more than a little disconcerted when with one accord we all fell on the *Maestro*'s neck and began embracing and kissing him. The director looked in bewilderment at Diaghilev, who had to explain that Cecchetti had given the whole company lessons for no less than fifteen years.

★　　★　　★

At Monte Carlo, to which we next returned, the company, as usual, were to begin by taking part in the operas. This did not involve much work except in the case of Puccini's *Turandot*, for which a number of dances in the Chinese style were required. These were performed by Danilova, Tchernicheva, Woidzikowsky and Balanchine; and Balanchine, who also arranged them, received high praise for them from Guinsbourg.

Diaghilev, meanwhile, had gone to Paris to make plans for new productions. He now had two choreographers, Massine and Balanchine, in the company; and since Balanchine was busy with the opera work, whereas Massine was unoccupied, the first ballet to be undertaken he allotted to Massine. This was a new version of *Les Fâcheux*, of which he liked the *décor*, but, as I have mentioned, had been disappointed with the choreography, by Nijinska. Massine was always an energetic worker and at once applied himself to this task. Yet for some strange reason he too was to fail in the attempt to infuse some interest into *Les Fâcheux*.

★ ★ ★

Counting the exhibition he had arranged in 1906, and the music and opera seasons he had arranged in 1907 and 1908, this next season in Paris was to be Diaghilev's twentieth; and although he was averse from the celebration of anything like an anniversary, he was anxious to make it particularly full and interesting. It was fortunate, therefore, that just at this moment two new works should fall into his lap, one by Stravinsky and the other by Prokofiev. We had produced nothing new by Stravinsky for four years; so Diaghilev was all the more delighted to be able to include this latest composition of his in his Paris programme. It was, however, not a ballet but an opera: *Oedipus Rex*. The Prokofiev work *was* a ballet, so far nameless; but Diaghilev accepted it at once. The third novelty, for Paris, was to be *The Triumph of Neptune*. But there were to be yet two others, namely a new ballet ordered from the young French composer, Henri Sauguet, and another of Satie's. Moreover, the revised version of *Les Fâcheux* and the re-staged *Oiseau de Feu* could both to some extent be classed as novelties too.

On Diaghilev's return to Monte Carlo rehearsals for all these productions were begun at high pressure, the more so since the ballet by Sauguet, which was named *La Chatte*, was to be presented first at Monte Carlo itself. The choreography of this was confided to Balanchine; but Diaghilev had not yet decided who was to undertake the Prokofiev. I gathered from his description that the staging of the latter was to be unusual: it was to be in the so-called 'Constructivist' style then fashionable in Russia; and Diaghilev wished the choreography to be in keeping. He at first had hopes of bringing over the choreographer Golizovsky, about whom he had heard from Balanchine; but these gradually faded; and after some further deliberation, considering that of the available talent Massine's was the most suitable, he finally entrusted the ballet to him. Fortunately, although Balanchine was by now busy on *La Chatte*, the latter required only a small cast; so I was able to supply both choreographers simultaneously with as many dancers as each required.

Diaghilev's next problem was the production of *Oedipus Rex*. He could not decide who should do the *décor* and kept reverting to the subject. Since the opera contained no dances, it lay outside my province. But it appeared to me extravagant to order scenery and costumes for a work that was to be performed no more than three or four times: and I said so to Diaghilev, who seemed inclined to agree. The next day I met him on the terrace looking uncommonly pleased with himself.

'Well—I've thought of the way to do *Oedipus*,' he said. 'We'll simply give it a concert performance—no *décor*, and the cast in evening dress, sitting on the stage in front of black velvet curtains. Musically it will even gain.'

I congratulated him on this bright idea.

Meanwhile the scenery for *La Chatte* was being made. I had not seen the designs, and so when I called at the studios about repairs to something else, and found the place full of large wire constructions covered with celluloid, I asked Origo, our property master, what on earth they were.

'Oh, didn't you know?' said Origo. 'In his next ballet Monsieur Diaghilev's going to have a laboratory on the stage. This is the scenery for *La Chatte*.'

And so it was. The designs were by Gabo and Pevsner: very 'modern' indeed; and I must say that, for one of Aesop's Fables, I thought them rather odd.

At about the same time I was shown a photograph of the Constructivist set we were to use for the Prokofiev ballet, which was to be given the somewhat obscure title of *Le Pas d'Acier*. It had been designed in Russia by the painter Yakoulov as long before as 1920, and seemed to me dreadfully depressing.

★   ★   ★

Since Guinsbourg still objected to our performing at the *Salle de Musique* while his opera season was in progress, Diaghilev appealed to the Casino management to allow him an increase in the number of our performances in the spring, and somehow contrived almost to double it. This meant that we had to put on more productions than we should have otherwise, both new works and revivals. The 'novelties' we had ready were *Neptune*, *Jack-in-the-Box* and the Goncharova staging of *L'Oiseau de Feu*, while *La Chatte* and Massine's version of *Les Fâcheux* were to be performed as soon as ready. As for dancers, we also had two actual newcomers in Spesivtseva and Petrova, while Massine almost ranked as one after his long absence from our ranks as a dancer. Spesivtseva (whose name was now simplified for Western tongues into Spessiva) appeared not only in our 'classics' but also in *Roméo et Juliette* and *Zéphire et Flore*. Petrova proved a brilliant substitute for Nemchinova in *Les Biches*, and also took over many of the parts hitherto danced by Sokolova, who, to our distress, had fallen seriously ill.

Les Fâcheux, though the sight of Massine's new choreography was eagerly awaited, unfortunately again fell pretty flat, as I have indicated. *La Chatte*, on the other hand, caused no little excitement, so unlike was it to anything we had ever till then presented. Its youthful French composer, Henri Sauguet, had never before written anything for the stage, but since he was a disciple of Satie, his music was to Diaghilev's taste. It also went well with a Constructivist production; and it was this which Diaghilev, abetted by Balanchine, was now especially eager to try. The subject of *La Chatte* was simple. A young man falls in love with a cat, and prays Aphrodite to transform her into a woman. But Aphrodite, having done so, seeks to test the passion this new-made woman now displays for the young man. She therefore causes a mouse to appear; when the woman immediately leaves her lover and chases it. She is thereupon changed back into a cat; and the unfortunate young man expires from disappointment. When the curtain rose the audience was confronted with the celluloid structures I had seen in the property room, set against a background of black American cloth. In the centre of the stage stood the figure of Aphrodite; but since this was itself one of the structures in question, the identity of the goddess was not instantly apparent. However, the set was lit in the most effective manner; and Balanchine's choreography was full of invention, particularly as regards its poses, which were highly 'sculptural'. *La Chatte* was undoubtedly the best work he had yet done. Moreover, it gave a wonderful opportunity to Lifar, who had indeed far more to do than Spesivtseva, though their *pas de deux* showed them both to great advantage. Their costumes, incidentally, were also partially made of celluloid—but of a somewhat finer variety than that used for the scenery.

We gave *La Chatte* for the first time on April the 30th; and its success, for Monte Carlo, was immense.

★　　★　　★

On our way from Monte Carlo to Paris we gave a few performances first at Marseilles and then at Barcelona.

235

The Diaghilev Ballet

Despite Diaghilev's known horror of anniversaries the company after many discussions decided that, all the same, they could not let the opening of his twentieth season in Paris go by without marking the occasion with some kind of celebration in his honour. This was to take the form of an address glorifying his achievements—accompanied by a present of some description. But rumours of what was afoot got about; and as soon as they reached Diaghilev he appeared at a rehearsal and begged them to drop the project.

'Ladies and gentlemen,' he said, 'it has come to my knowledge that you intend celebrating my twentieth season in Paris. I am deeply grateful to you for the thought; but I implore you not to act on it. I truly do not want any "benefits" or addresses. I am afraid I abhor jubilees in general and my own in particular. A jubilee is the beginning of an end: something that rounds off a career. But I am not ready to give up. I wish to continue working. . . .' He paused a moment. 'I wish to remain always young.'

Some of the company attempted to argue with him. But it was of no avail: they had to give in.

Meanwhile our performances in Barcelona—the scene of this declaration—were going well. On May the 17th we gave a gala performance as part of the celebrations marking (alas for Diaghilev!) the twenty-fifth anniversary of King Alfonso's coronation—though these celebrations, which were of course staged for the most part in Madrid, prevented the King for once from coming to see us. Massine at length appeared here again in the best of all his roles, the Miller in *Le Tricorne*, delighting the Spaniards with his wonderful interpretation. The Miller's Wife was danced by Tchernicheva; and Eugene Goossens conducted.

Meanwhile Massine had continued his composition of *Le Pas d'Acier*; and the ballet was now all but ready. He had been considerably helped, while we were still at Monte Carlo, by various suggestions made by Prokofiev, who had visited us on several occasions and played the music through himself. Diaghilev was very fond of Prokofiev, with whom he had long talks whenever the latter came on visits from Russia. Feeling his exile as he did, Diaghilev was eager for any news he could glean of artistic and cultural developments in Russia; and *Le Pas d'Acier* brought him nearer to understanding them. Once again a terrible nostalgia for Russia overcame him, and he pined to go back. He even sounded the authorities through Prokofiev, and gained the impression that his return would be welcomed. But suppose he should eventually wish to revisit

236

Europe, would he be allowed to? There was no guarantee; so he stifled his longing and never went.

★   ★   ★

'Only those who know their Paris well can appreciate the hold on it possessed by the Diaghilev Ballet. To conquer Paris is difficult. To hold it in subjection through twenty seasons is a feat. Never in the city's history has there existed a theatrical enterprise that summer after summer has enjoyed such unparalleled success.'

So wrote one of the Paris newspapers on the day of our opening.

This year we were at the *Théâtre Sarah Bernhardt*, and our first performance took place on May the 27th, when we gave *Neptune, L'Oiseau de Feu* and *La Chatte. L'Oiseau de Feu* was conducted by Stravinsky; and it was intended that the title role should be danced by Spesivtseva. Diaghilev was anxious that Spesivtseva should score a success. He even wrote to *Le Figaro* about her (never having done such a thing before), explaining that though Paris had seen her already at the *Opéra*, her proper setting was our Russian Ballet. But some fatality seemed to dog Spesivtseva in all her dealings with our company. On the eve of the first performance she injured one of her feet so seriously that there was no chance of her being able to take part in the season at all. Her accident, moreover, placed Diaghilev in a quandary, as regards *La Chatte* in particular. For although the Cat was not a strenuous or complicated part, it had to be appropriately cast. But Danilova was unsuitable; and Markova still looked too much of a little girl. Hence when Lifar suggested Nikitina, who, though no longer in the company, happened to be in Paris, Diaghilev agreed on account of her appearance, little though he really liked her. The success of *La Chatte* was immediate: it reminded Diaghilev, so he said, of nothing so much as the instantaneous success, in the old days, of *Le Spectre de la Rose*.

Our next *première* was *Oedipus Rex*. The theatre was packed with an audience excited at the prospect of a new work by Stravinsky. But in the event it produced little impression. Compared to *L'Oiseau de Feu*, which was in the same programme, it seemed very tame. We gave it exactly three times, after which it was heard no more; so that it was just as well that Diaghilev had not spent much on its production.

The next novelty so far as our company was concerned was what for Paris was no more than a revival. In 1924 Comte Étienne de Beaumont had organized a season under the title *Soirées de Paris*, for which Massine had composed a ballet called *Mercure*. It was to music by Satie, with a *décor* by Picasso. It was this we now put on again. It was described in the programme, not as a ballet, but as '*Poses plastiques*', and was in three *tableaux*. But to my mind—and I fear likewise to the public's—*Mercure* was utterly nonsensical.

Then, last of all, came *Le Pas d'Acier*. Diaghilev had been warned that on the first night there might be a demonstration of protest on the part of Russian *émigrés* in Paris against our production of a 'Bolshevik' ballet; but nothing in fact happened. *Le Pas d'Acier* had no plot. It had two *tableaux* representing scenes of contemporary Russian life, the life of the peasants in the countryside on the one hand, and that of the workmen in the factories on the other. The scenery remained unchanged. It consisted of a very high rostrum set in the centre of the stage, with steps leading up to it on either side. On the front and sides of the rostrum were placed a number of wheels, levers and pistons, all built in plain unpainted wood. The whole stage also was crammed with objects of various kinds so that it was almost impossible to move. The back cloth was grey; and the general effect, though ugly, was yet forceful and exciting. Prokofiev's music, particularly the *finale*, was extraordinarily powerful. The choreography, on the other hand, seemed to be out of key with this very 'modern' score: it was in the nature of a *divertissement*, in the composition of which Massine seemed to have been hampered both by the music and by the lack of free space on the stage. The second *tableau* was better than the first; and Massine's arrangement of the *finale* was decidedly impressive. For this, as the movements of the dancers became more and more energetic, the wheels were set revolving and the levers and pistons moving backwards and forwards; the lights went on and off with perpetual changes of colour; and the curtain came down to a tremendous *crescendo* from the orchestra. *Le Pas d'Acier* produced quite a stirring impression on the opening night, but was by no means so well thought of as Diaghilev had expected. It had neither unity nor meaning, and was purely mechanical except for the *finale*, which alone exhibited some life. I was astonished to observe that Diaghilev did not very much mind its comparative failure. Perhaps he had already understood what it lacked. Otherwise the polite silence maintained by the critics over *Le Pas d'Acier* would have roused him to storms of indignation.

On the last day of our season the company assembled on the stage and presented me, as their oldest colleague, with a most touching address, which every one of them had signed. This was to commemorate the close of our twentieth season in Paris. Then two of the ladies made me a present of a most excellent gold watch, which I wear to this day. This little ceremony was as unexpected as it was moving; and I was deeply touched by this attention on the part of the company.

★ ★ ★

Almost immediately after closing in Paris we paid another visit to London. Diaghilev had accepted Lord Rothermere's offer of further assistance on the same terms as before. Unfortunately His Majesty's was not this time available; and so we had to content ourselves with the Princes, a theatre I always disliked on account of its shallow stage and general lack of space. The season was once again under the patronage of the Duke of Connaught.

We opened with *La Chatte*, which was no less well received than in Paris. Neither of our other new ballets, *Mercure* and *Le Pas d'Acier*, both of which we gave in the latter part of the season, were, however, at all liked. Nevertheless we continued to give *Le Pas d'Acier* on account of Prokofiev's music. As in Paris, there were no protests, but neither was there any enthusiasm. Besides these new works we included twenty-two older ballets in the programme, which was therefore widely varied; and in the course of the season we gave no less than three gala performances. The first was a Stravinsky 'festival', at which Stravinsky himself conducted *Petrushka*, *Pulcinella* and *L'Oiseau de Feu* (to the dismay, incidentally, of the dancers, who never knew what *tempo* he might adopt next); the second was in honour of the King of Egypt; and the third, at which we showed *Les Sylphides*, *Neptune*, *La Chatte* and the Polovtsian Dances, in honour of our old patron, the King of Spain.

This season was again most satisfactory as regards finance; and Diaghilev was able as before to refund Rothermere his advance. He also arranged a small ceremony on the stage, at which he presented him, amid the applause of the company, with a copy, handsomely bound in morocco, of the first programme of the Russian Ballet.

★ ★ ★

As soon as the London season was over, I went for my holidays to Monte Carlo. About a month later I heard from Diaghilev that he would be joining me, being obliged to interrupt his usual stay at Venice in order to come and sign a contract for the following winter with the Director of the Casino, who had apparently been too busy during our spring season to prepare it for signature then. On account of the excuses the Director had then made, Diaghilev was somewhat anxious about this contract, suspecting the Casino of not really wishing to renew his engagement. When he arrived he was altogether in rather a nervy state. He also had a badly cut finger, and the cut would not heal; he put this down to his being diabetic; and we had to visit a doctor before he would believe that it would get better. Since Diaghilev was quite alone during his visit, I used to spend all day with him, and we had many interesting conversations. When discussing future productions, he told me that he had been to see Stravinsky, who was then living in Nice, and had heard him play the score of another new ballet. Diaghilev was enchanted with it, he said. It was surprisingly unlike Stravinsky's usual work, simple and melodious, rather in the manner of Glinka. It was scored entirely for strings, with no wind or percussion. . . . While he was in the midst of describing this music to me, a letter from the Casino was handed to him. It asked him to attend a meeting. A few hours later I learnt that the contract had been signed. Diaghilev was able, therefore, to leave Monte Carlo reassured.

★ ★ ★

The autumn was mostly occupied for us by a mid-European tour, covering five countries. It began with visits to various towns in Germany, not, however, including Berlin, since we had fared so ill there the year before. In Vienna, our next destination, we gave three performances at the *Operntheater*, where we had first appeared in 1913, showing *Le Tricorne*, *La Chatte*, *Les Biches*, *La Boutique Fantasque* and the Polovtsian Dances, all with great success. From Vienna we went to Brno in Czechoslovakia, and thence to Budapest; completed the tour in Geneva; and then returned to Paris. During this tour Diaghilev allowed Markova to dance *La Chatte*, in which she did extremely well. Lifar was delighted with her as a partner, since she was so easy to lift in their *pas de deux*!

On our return to Paris Monsieur Rouché, the Director of the *Opéra*, invited Diaghilev to give two gala performances on December the 27th and 29th. We had not appeared at the *Opéra* for five years; so Diaghilev was very pleased to accept. Among the ballets we gave at these two performances were some of our oldest and some of our newest: *L'Oiseau de Feu* and the Polovtsian Dances, on the one hand, and *La Chatte* and *Le Pas d'Acier* on the other.

CHAPTER TWENTY

1928

THE New Year thus found us in Paris. On the orthodox Christmas Eve Diaghilev telephoned to invite my wife and me to supper with him at a Russian restaurant. He said he wished to see a small Russian girl who was dancing there in the cabaret show. The child turned out to be about nine or ten years old, thin and swarthy, with lively black eyes. She performed some Russian dances very well. Diaghilev watched her attentively and said, 'Excellent!—but too mannered. That will spoil her dancing later on.' Five or six years later this little girl was to become well known as Tamara Toumanova.

Before returning to Monte Carlo, we had to fulfil engagements at both Lyons and Marseilles; so we arrived there later than was our wont. I observed that Diaghilev was cross with Monte Carlo, as he had once been cross with Paris. He even said he was not going to show any new ballets there this year. He was indeed in a bad mood altogether. His thoughts seemed to be elsewhere than on the Ballet; he was gloomy and taciturn, and only livened up into his accustomed good humour when tackled on the subject of books. His love of book collecting had grown more marked than ever. Any new find afforded him enormous pleasure. One day, when summoned to see him, I found him carefully turning over the pages of a book, which he handed to me.

'You like old books as well,' he said. 'They were my original love, before I took to the theatre. And now I seem to be returning to it.' He sounded almost apologetic, as if this were an excuse for his neglect of the Ballet. 'Why I sent for you, though,' he went on, 'was to discuss a charity performance the Grand Duke Michael has asked me to organize.'

Knowing that the company were exceptionally hard pressed at the moment, I asked whether this performance could not be postponed.

'Well,' said Diaghilev, 'the thing is I don't want to refuse the Grand

The Diaghilev Ballet

Duke on account of his wife, Countess Torby. It's her charity, you see, and she's a descendant of Pushkin; she's got eleven of his letters; and she's promised to leave me one in her will.'

That was enough: I understood immediately. Whatever else might be put off, not so the charity performance. Strange to relate, Countess Torby died the next year; and the promised letter became Diaghilev's property. Moreover, not content with this, he later induced the Grand Duke to sell him the other ten—a transaction that made him, for a moment, the happiest man in the world. His love of books, I could not help feeling, supplied something he was beginning sadly to miss. For the decline of his interest in the Ballet was largely due, as I mentioned before, to his continued failure to find a collaborator capable of interpreting his ideas. Lifar was by now an accomplished dancer. But Diaghilev was disappointed in him as a person. Not only would he often now lose patience with Lifar; he also considered him to be sly and scheming, too ambitious and too fond of self-advertisement. Not that Diaghilev condemned ambition as such. Only it had to be of another quality. Lifar, then, was not the person he needed; and failing such a person, Diaghilev's loss of enthusiasm for the Ballet was inevitable. Nevertheless the Ballet was also his livelihood—and ours; and if for no other reason he would maintain it still out of a sense of obligation to all of us.

★   ★   ★

During our next season in Paris, for which plans had now to be laid, Diaghilev decided to present only two new ballets: *Apollon Musagète*, as Stravinsky's latest composition had now been entitled, and a work by a new young Russian composer, Nicolas Nabokov. The scenario for the latter, as our scenarios now usually were, was the invention of Boris Kochno, and was based on an ode by the eighteenth-century Russian poet Lomonosov, being for this reason called, simply, *Ode*. From the first Diaghilev entirely dissociated himself from this second production, leaving it wholly in Kochno's hands. He had taken by this time to referring to Kochno as his successor: 'the Young Oak' he used to call him, and now wished to see how Kochno would manage without his guidance, while he himself concentrated his attention on the production of *Apollon Musagète*. In the event Kochno found *Ode* far from easy and repeatedly sought Diaghilev's help with it. Diaghilev, however, was firm and always refused it, half as a joke, saying that Kochno must himself find the solution to whatever problem it might be. As for the choreography of these ballets, *Apollon* was allotted to Balanchine, and *Ode* to Massine. A vocal chorus was required for *Ode*; so we thought we might as well plan our programme to include other ballets including choruses, such as *Les Noces, Barabau* and *Pulcinella*.

While we were rehearsing in Monte Carlo, Diaghilev went to Paris and London to make arrangements for our forthcoming seasons. On March the 28th, a few days before our opening at the Casino, I received a long letter from him in which, after dealing with such current matters as salary payments and advertising, he announced the astonishing and painful news that Lord Rothermere, for no apparent reason, had suddenly refused to back our next London season. The agent Wolheim had taken it for granted that all would again be well, but had heard nothing till March the 16th, when his Lordship had merely sent a telephone message to say that he was not prepared to do anything for the Ballet this year. Diaghilev was now, so he wrote, doing his best to avert a catastrophe (for it was already very late in the year to make new arrangements).

In the light of his attitude to the Ballet during the two previous years, this *volte-face* on the part of Lord Rothermere seemed as odd as it was unwelcome. I felt sure there was more behind it than met the eye; and I was soon to discover that this was so.

★　　★　　★

By the time Diaghilev returned to Monte Carlo our season had already begun and we were doing extremely well—which was fortunate in view of the set-back to our plans for London. Diaghilev was in better spirits than I had expected. According to him 'somebody'—and he had a shrewd idea who—had worked on Lord Rothermere and turned him against us. However, there had been nothing Diaghilev could do about it but try other sources of support, and his efforts appeared to have been successful, so that our London season was almost certain to take place after all.

As we were obliged to give many more performances than usual this year in Monte Carlo, in order to lend variety to our programme Diaghilev decided to revive some of the older items in our *répertoire*, including *Cléopâtre* and *Schéhérazade*, neither of which had been danced for some time. Diaghilev would now refer to them as 'youthful

The Diaghilev Ballet

peccadilloes'; and was quite put out to find that, whenever we gave them, the box-office receipts were particularly high.

★ ★ ★

Between our Monte Carlo and Paris seasons this year we went on tour, performing for the most part in Belgium, at Antwerp, Liége and Brussels, but ending up at Lausanne. We began in Brussels at the *Palais des Beaux-Arts*. This was an enormous new building, just finished; and we were invited to perform there for its opening. It had no stage, how-ever; only a concert platform; so we had to choose ballets that could be shown without *décor*. We then moved to the *Théâtre de la Monnaie*, where our first night was spoilt by a most tiresome incident. The theatre was used as a rule for operas; and I found that the flies were chock-a-block with scenery. I explained to the *régisseur* in charge that *The Triumph of Neptune* had nine quick changes of scene, which it would be impossible to work without a due amount of flying-space. But he absolutely refused to remove a thing; and what I was afraid of duly occurred. At the first change of scene the back-cloth stuck in the flies and I had to bring down the curtain in order to release it; and so it went on with every change in turn. The ballet, consequently, seemed perfectly endless, and was, need-less to say, a dismal failure. If ever I wished to murder anyone it was that *régisseur* of the *Théâtre de la Monnaie*!

The rest of our performances in Brussels, including one of *Le Sacre du Printemps*, went very well. At Lausanne our old friend Ansermet con-ducted us once again—still as handome as ever, though now slightly grey at the temples.

★ ★ ★

The programme of our twenty-first season in Paris was neither so large nor so exciting as that of the year before. This, however, did not seem to affect the enthusiasm of the public. Our first night was on June the 6th, when we showed the new Massine ballet *Ode*, between *Le Pas d'Acier* and *Les Noces* (an entirely Russian bill).

The subject of *Ode* was most unsuited to a ballet. Only the cinema could perhaps have done it justice visually. A statue of Nature comes to life and shows a young student some of the wonders Nature can perform. But the student is not satisfied. He wishes to be given a feast also of Nature's beauty, and not only this, he wishes to take part in it himself.

244

PLATE XVIII

ANTON DOLIN

The Diaghilev Ballet

But his intervention destroys the harmony of the vision; and Nature is petrified once again into a statue. Such a scenario faced both Massine and the designer, a young Russian, Tchelichev, with problems neither succeeded in solving. The music alone realized something of the idea and, especially in the choral passages, created a feeling of mysterious power.

There were only two principal parts in *Ode*: Nature and the Student. Nature had to be represented by a tall handsome woman. But since it is a necessary qualification in a ballet dancer *not* to be of more than medium height, we had to find an outsider for this part who was at the same time capable of treading the boards with a modicum of grace; and duly engaged a certain Mademoiselle Ira Beliamina. The Student was played by Lifar. But the part was a dull one with very little dancing; and it was scarcely his fault that he could do nothing with it. *Ode* indeed was a failure: for once the harmonious collaboration of librettist, composer, choreographer and designer failed to produce a work of much value. Diaghilev, I found, was curiously indifferent to this disappointing result of all their efforts: I never understood quite why. He had himself, it is true, taken no hand in it: only at the final rehearsals had he made one or two constructive criticisms, when it was already too late for them to have much effect on the production as a whole. Incidentally *Ode* was the last of Diaghilev's ballets for which Massine composed the choreography.

In contrast to *Ode, Apollon Musagète* was a very great success. It was conducted by the composer, and Diaghilev considered it the best of all Stravinsky's works, for the limpidity and calm of the music, which particularly moved him. He was also very well pleased with Balanchine's choreography. It had some rather ugly patches; but on the whole it was very well composed and consistently interesting. This ballet had no proper story. Indeed it was described on the programme as 'a piece without a plot'. It was therefore a mere succession of dances, of which the birth of Apollo was perhaps the most effective. His mother Leto was seen standing on a rock, beneath which was a grotto; and from this Apollo emerged in swaddling bands, of which he was then divested by a pair of goddesses. The *décor* was by the French painter Bauchant, and though little reminiscent of classical Greece, was beautiful and effective. The chief characters were Apollo himself, danced by Lifar, and three Muses, danced by Tchernicheva, Doubrovska and Danilova. They wore somewhat unbecoming costumes; but their *variations* were excellently

246

arranged, as was also the *finale*, ending with the descent of a chariot in which Apollo was borne off to Olympus. *Apollon Musagète* received very favourable press notices, although Balanchine's part in it was adversely criticized by some amateurs of the pure classical style.

To enhance the attraction of this season in Paris Diaghilev invited the famous Moscow ballerina, Sophie Fedorova, to rejoin us; and so, after nineteen years, she once again delighted Paris in the Polovtsian Dances.

★   ★   ★

Meanwhile, as he had hoped, Diaghilev had succeeded in extricating himself from the difficulty in which he had been placed owing to the strange behaviour of Lord Rothermere by engaging the help of certain of his friends in Paris and of Sir Thomas Beecham in England. In fact the situation had been brilliantly retrieved; and we even found ourselves back at His Majesty's, which Wolheim had succeeded in leasing for us. The Duke of Connaught again lent us his patronage; and we opened on June the 25th before a highly fashionable audience. In those days the stalls and boxes in London would still be filled by ladies in evening gowns and men in tail-coats; and the sight of such elegance was always a stimulus to the dancers. The company in any case loved performing in London. They found the audiences much more responsive than in Paris; and individuals were flattered at being singled out. In Paris attention was fixed almost exclusively on composers, designers and choreographers, the performers, with rare exceptions, being relegated to the background. In London, on the contrary, much the most notice was taken of *them*; and the public were quick to adopt their special favourites.

Our opening programme consisted of *Cimarosiana, Apollon* and *L'Oiseau de Feu*; and here again *Apollon*, conducted by Stravinsky, was pronounced a success. Then, in the way of new works, we next presented *Las Meninas*, having discovered that though Massine had composed it so long before, London had never yet seen it. Our third *première* was of course that of *Ode*; and since audiences in London are always exceedingly polite, and, even when they do not much care for what is performed, are always anxious to applaud the performers, even *Ode*, though as a ballet it clearly failed very much to please, was nevertheless quite well received.

In the meantime, on our arrival in London Diaghilev had gaily announced that we were immediately to start rehearsing a ballet for presentation during the season itself. The music had been chosen from various works of Handel, and had also been orchestrated, by Sir Thomas Beecham, who would conduct all its performances himself. I was horrified. I did not see how this could possibly be managed at such short notice and while we were anyhow up to our eyes in work with performances. But Diaghilev as usual was not to be withstood, and insisted that Kochno should forthwith devise the subject and Balanchine the choreography. Since no special *décor* could be prepared in the time, the scenery of *Daphnis et Chloë* must be brought over from Paris; and as for costumes, some of those from the *Bergère* would be just the thing. And so, in next to no time, this ballet was put together and presented on June the 16th, under the title *The Gods Go a-Begging* (*Les Dieux Mendiants*) —when a minor miracle occurred. For far from appearing half-baked, as might have been expected, *The Gods Go a-Begging* presented an extraordinarily satisfying combination of subject, choreography and *décor*; and its success was prodigious. The Gods were Woidzikowsky and Danilova, with Tchernicheva, Doubrovska and Tcherkass (a rising new man) as courtiers. Sir Thomas Beecham's conducting was superb; and the ovation at the end was tremendous. During the all-too-short remainder of the Ballet's career, *The Gods Go a-Begging* was never out of the programme.

At the end of this season Massine announced that he was again leaving us. But Diaghilev received this news with entire indifference. Massine's two latest ballets—*Les Pas d'Acier* and *Ode*—had both been disappointing; and as a dancer he had anyhow been sharing parts with Woidzikowsky, who had by now attained a rare perfection. Diaghilev, therefore, no longer considered Massine's collaboration essential; and so, quite amicably, we parted with him. I did not share Diaghilev's view of Massine's departure. I regarded him as a serious loss to us.

★   ★   ★

Before we dispersed for our holidays at the close of our London season, I pointed out to Diaghilev that his contract with Balanchine had expired and should be renewed. But Diaghilev said that Balanchine would be visiting him in Venice and that he would renew it then. Yet when we all met again in Paris after the holidays, and I enquired whether he had remembered to do so, he astounded me by fiercely abusing Balanchine: he felt very much, he said, like not renewing his contract at all! What the cause of this sudden change was I could not fathom. But I forbore to ask questions and merely said that all I wished to know was whether he proposed to retain Balanchine or not. If he did, then I would arrange the contract myself. 'Do as you like,' said Diaghilev, after a pause—and so to my relief, since, with Massine gone, Balanchine was our sole stand-by for choreography, the contract was safely renewed.

★   ★   ★

During our summer season in London Diaghilev had arranged for us to try another tour of the English provinces in the autumn. Sir Thomas Beecham was to accompany us and conduct *The Gods* and certain other ballets. We accordingly started off on this tour on November the 12th, visiting four of the largest towns in turn. The Russian Ballet, however, though by now an established feature of life in London, was still unfamiliar to the provinces; and the result was that though we usually had good houses on our first nights, our other performances were extremely ill attended—except, that is, when Beecham conducted (for he was evidently a greater attraction than we were), and fortunately he did so at least once or twice a week.

During this tour Diaghilev, who was always eager to promote young talent, first gave Alicia Markova the opportunity of distinguishing herself in two classical *pas de deux*—one in *Cimarosiana* and the other the famous *Oiseau Bleu* from *Le Mariage d'Aurore*. She was partnered in the latter by Tcherkass, who, as I have mentioned, had already taken a chief part in *The Gods* and was now beginning to be entrusted with other responsible parts, his manner and grace of movement being very much to Diaghilev's taste.

This tour was clouded for all of us by the sad news of the death of our dear *Maestro*: he had died on November the 13th. The news was conveyed to us while in Manchester by Diaghilev, to whom it was a grievous blow.

★   ★   ★

While we were still on tour, at Edinburgh, Diaghilev left us, to pay a visit to Paris. His object was to see a new ballet enterprise, launched at the *Opéra* itself by no less a person than Ida Rubinstein. After her short career in our Ballet, Ida Rubinstein had from time to time put plays on in Paris, invariably taking the chief part herself. But this time she had turned to ballets, proposing to dance the chief part in some, if not all, of them too. What was more, since she had ample means at her disposal, she had been able to command the services of a number of Diaghilev's former collaborators, including Benois, Ravel, Auric, Sauguet, Massine, Nijinska, Vilzak and Schollar. Not unnaturally, therefore, Diaghilev was somewhat disquieted, scenting in this enterprise a possible competitor with ours. However, his fears were soon dispelled; and he returned to us entirely reassured. His descriptions of the new venture, and of the part played in it by Ida Rubinstein herself, were indeed quite annihilating. He was indignant that people such as Stravinsky, who had also had a share in it, should deign to connect themselves with an undertaking so inferior.

★   ★   ★

Yet, however little he might think of the Ida Rubinstein venture, Diaghilev was taking no chances over our next appearance, which was to be, like hers, at the *Opéra*. For our first night, on December the 20th, he chose *The Gods Go a-Begging* and announced a 'Stravinsky Evening' for Christmas Eve, when we gave *L'Oiseau de Feu*, *Apollon* and *Petrushka*, the last with Karsavina. For the third performance, again, Beecham came over specially to conduct the Handel; and in fact these three performances were so outstandingly successful that Rouché asked Diaghilev to add a fourth, on January the 3rd.

When inviting Karsavina to dance once again in *Petrushka*, Diaghilev was haunted by the memory of her *début* in this ballet with Nijinsky; and from that he was led to wonder whether, if Nijinsky were to be shown *Petrushka* again, it might not produce so strong an impression on his mind as perhaps to set him on the way to recovery. So, on December the 27th, the unfortunate Nijinsky was brought to the *Opéra*, where, very gently, as if he were some precious object that might easily be broken, he was escorted by Diaghilev across the stage to a box. Diaghilev told me afterwards that Nijinsky watched the performance with great attention, but made no sound and would not answer when spoken to; and that when the ballet was over, he did not wish to leave. During the interval Diaghilev led him on to the stage and, bringing him up to me, said: 'Don't you remember, Vasya? This is Grigoriev.' I put out my hand, which he took very slowly, without saying anything. He just smiled, but quite vacantly. At that moment there appeared a photographer, who took us in a group: Diaghilev, Karsavina, Nijinsky, Benois, Lifar, Kremnev and myself. This, alas, was our final farewell to Nijinsky.

PLATE XIX

SERGE LIFAR

CHAPTER TWENTY-ONE

1929

WE had a party in Paris on New Year's Eve; and everyone was very merry. Diaghilev had not been in such good spirits for some time: not only was he exceedingly pleased with our recent successes; he was also relieved at finding that we had nothing to fear from the Rubinstein enterprise. Moreover, he had recently made a new discovery, not indeed of a choreographer through whom to work, but of a young and talented composer and pianist: a young Russian named Igor Markevich; and this had had the effect of somewhat reviving his interest in the ballet at the expense of his interest in books. I wished him well of the New Year, reminding him, despite his shyness of jubilees, that with 1929 now upon us, it was twenty years since he had begun his ballet career.

'Yes,' he said. 'It's a long time, during which we've grown old.'

'Not old,' said I. 'Wise. *You* will always be young, Sergey Pavlovich.'

Diaghilev smiled. 'Of all the people I started with on my "ballet career," as you call it, only two are still with me: you and Valechka'—that is, Nouvel. 'So let me congratulate *you* on *your* jubilee!'—on which we all, in the Russian fashion, embraced.

★   ★   ★

According to our regular time-table we had to be back in Monte Carlo some time in January. On our way from Paris, however, we went to Bordeaux, where we gave some performances at the *Grand Théâtre de l'Opéra*, attracting large audiences. Diaghilev did not wish us to arrive in Monte Carlo much before the opening of the opera season; so he also arranged for us to perform at Pau, the winter health resort. Pau being not far from Lourdes, we also paid Lourdes a visit—as tourists, not dancers! So by the time we at length reached Monte Carlo there was only time for us to perform twice before the operas began.

★   ★   ★

Our participation in the Monte Carlo operas became simpler and easier every year, since the incidental dances once composed were repeated season after season. This was just as well from Balanchine's point of view, since this year he had two new ballets to compose for the summer in Paris, one of which had to be presented first at Monte Carlo. The score of the first of these ballets was by Vittorio Rieti, the composer of *Barabau*, from whom Diaghilev had ordered it during his last visit to Italy. The score of the second was being written by Prokofiev. The scenario in each case was again to be by Kochno.

These two new ballets would not, however, be enough, so Diaghilev considered, since we were to give quite a large number of performances in Paris this year; and so for a third he bethought him of Stravinsky's *Renard*, which had last been done in 1922. This, it is true, would not be a new work. But Nijinska's choreography had by now been forgotten and would have to be replaced by a new version. Nijinska herself could not very well be invited to undertake this, since she was now working for Ida Rubinstein; Massine had gone to the United States; and Balanchine already had the other two new ballets to cope with. Diaghilev therefore decided to see once again what Lifar might be capable of in the way of choreography. The drawback to this, however, was that his personal interest in Lifar was now a thing of the past, and that their relations had grown positively cold. By way of a preliminary experiment he asked Lifar to try composing one or two dances. But even for these Diaghilev was so reluctant to have more to do with Lifar than he need that, as before in turn with Massine and Slavinsky, he appointed Larionov to supervise and guide him.

Meanwhile *Le Bal*—for such was the name of the ballet for which Rieti had composed the music—had also been put into rehearsal. In the course of its composition Diaghilev had asked Rieti so often to make alterations in the score that when finally sending this to Diaghilev, Rieti had written:

Cher Monsieur Diaghilev,

 Voici Le Bal. Il vous est dédié; il est à vous; faites-en ce que vous voulez, mais surtout n'espérez pas que j'y travaille encore!

       Toujours à vous,
        Vittorio Rieti

Paris 27.2.29.

The Diaghilev Ballet

* * *

Not long after our arrival in Monte Carlo, Diaghilev went off to Paris to see Prokofiev and hear the score of *his* new ballet, which was to be called *Le Fils Prodigue*. He seemed to like it, and hardly asked Prokofiev to alter anything!

This final year of the Ballet's existence was marked by an abandonment of what I may call the *divertissement* type of ballet and a return to the ballet of plot and character—a change for which I had longed for years. What brought this about it is hard to say. Perhaps it was that the more Diaghilev lost interest in the Ballet, the more Kochno was left to do as he wished; and that Kochno grew tired of devising mere successions of scenes and dances and preferred to invent coherent themes. If so, in my estimation he certainly did us a service. In any case, our two last new ballets were to be more dramatic than any we had produced for many a long day. This change in the character of the ballets naturally affected both the dancers and the choreographer. But whereas it was easy for the dancers to adapt themselves to this change, it was by no means equally so for a choreographer such as Balanchine; and the difficulties he encountered in the attempt so to adapt himself were reflected in his composition of *Le Fils Prodigue*.

The title role in this ballet was to be taken by Lifar. But Diaghilev was anxious that the chief male part in *Le Bal* should be taken by someone else, since, in view of their somewhat strained relations, he thought it wiser not to rely on Lifar exclusively. The departure of Massine, however, had left us with only two leading male dancers, Lifar and Woidzikowsky; and Woidzikowsky did not possess the right personality for this part. Diaghilev therefore conceived the idea of inviting Dolin to return to us, since Dolin, he considered, was exactly suited to it. It thus came about that Dolin rejoined the company, and that by his reappearance a situation was created the precise opposite of an earlier one. For the re-engagement of Dolin was as much a cause of resentment to Lifar as the favour shown by Diaghilev to Lifar five years before had been to Dolin. However, unlike Dolin then, Lifar, if he ever contemplated leaving us, thought better of it—possibly because of the opportunity afforded him by the choreography of *Le Renard*.

* * *

By the time that Diaghilev returned to Monte Carlo, Dolin had already rejoined us; Balanchine and Lifar were hard at work on their respective

254

ballets, and the rest of us were engaged in preparations for the forthcoming seasons. Diaghilev appeared to be agreeably surprised by what
could so far be seen of *Le Renard*, but was rather ungenerously inclined
to put down its best features to Larionov. As for *Le Bal*, with the music
of which he was so well acquainted, he made a number of suggestions
and alterations, and, as was all to the good, he, Kochno and Balanchine
frequently discussed the whole production together. Then, hardly was
Le Bal complete before Prokofiev arrived and a similar process had to
be gone through with *Le Fils Prodigue*.

Our season in Monte Carlo opened in April; and one of its notable
features—which reminded us of the glorious days of Karsavina and
Nijinsky twenty years before—was the revival, among many of the
other Fokine ballets, of *Le Spectre de la Rose*, which had not been danced
since Dolin had left the company in 1923. He now danced it again—
with Tchernicheva—and though a trifle mannered, was remarkably
good in it.

Le Bal turned out a great success. Diaghilev's hand in it was very
evident. The *décor* was by the Italian painter Giorgio de Chirico. There
were two scenes. The first, which was set down-stage, represented the
façade of a house with three doors in it, which were very cleverly used
by Balanchine for entrances and exits. The second was a hall, in which
the actual ball of the title took place. Its walls were marbled, and so was
the material of the costumes, which gave their wearers an air of animated statues. The leading characters were three: the Lady, beautifully
danced by Danilova; the Young Man—Dolin; and the Astrologer,
taken by a dancer named Bobrov, who was tall and elegant. *Le Bal* was
a ballet of action, with choreography based on classical steps somewhat
modernized by Balanchine.

We continued to give *Le Bal* up to the end of our season at Monte
Carlo, where the last programme ever to be presented by the Diaghilev
Ballet consisted of *Le Tricorne* and two ballets that had figured also in
the programme of our very first season there in 1911—*Schéhérazade* and
Cléopâtre.

★   ★   ★

For our last season in Paris we were once again—for the fourth year in
succession—at the *Théâtre Sarah Bernhardt*. It seemed to have become
our summer resort, just as the *Opéra* was wont to open its doors to us at
Christmas.

The Diaghilev Ballet

Diaghilev had left Monte Carlo before the end of our engagement. When seeing him off, I noticed that he was looking far from well: he seemed tired and depressed. I asked him how he was feeling.

'Oh, I'm all right,' he said. 'I've been getting boils, though; and with a diabetic like me it's a bad sign!'

I duly commiserated with him, but I did not attach any great importance to what he had said. He had suffered from boils before, I knew, and had got over them without any grave alarms.

We arrived in Paris this summer rather later than usual, and did not give our first performance till May the 21st, when we showed *Les Fâcheux*, the Polovtsian Dances, *Le Fils Prodigue* and *Le Renard*. The latter in its finished state was a mixture of dancing and acrobatics, which were rather in fashion at that time. Lifar had 'doubled' the various roles, so that parts of each were performed by dancers and the rest by acrobats: what the dancer could not do being done by the acrobat and vice versa. As the dancer and acrobat in each pair were of the same height (as near as might be) and wore similar costumes and masks (for they all represented animals), the public could scarcely tell the two apart. Yet for all this ingenuity *Le Renard* had no real value beyond its ephemeral 'art-snob' appeal.

The serious interest of the evening was centred on *Le Fils Prodigue*—the third ballet to be composed by Prokofiev for Diaghilev (the others being *Chout* and *Le Pas d'Acier*). When I first heard the music, I was sorry that the choreography should not be by Fokine: it seemed so eminently suited to his talent. Gifted though Balanchine undoubtedly was, his approach was almost exclusively intellectual, and any manifestation of emotion was foreign to him. Throughout the years he spent with Diaghilev the other ballets for which he composed the choreography were almost entirely devoid of drama and feeling, whereas *Le Fils Prodigue* was full of both. Prokofiev immediately felt that Balanchine was not the choreographer the subject demanded; and Diaghilev himself must have shared this opinion, since he insisted with the whole cast, including Lifar, on the importance of their interpreting their parts to the full, with a display of all the emotion appropriate. It was odd to hear Diaghilev extol in this way what for so many years he had been wont to condemn.

The *décor* of *Le Fils Prodigue* was by Georges Rouault and was extremely striking and effective. Prokofiev's score was the best he composed for us. The dancers, too, all interpreted their parts most excellently, especially Lifar as the Prodigal and Doubrovska as the Seductress, though they were both slightly lacking in dramatic force. Whatever its shortcomings, accordingly—and they were few—*Le Fils Prodigue* was greeted in Paris with great enthusiasm and Diaghilev was highly praised for the production.

Le Bal, our third *première*, went equally well, with Dolin and Danilova again in the chief parts. Nevertheless the production of these ballets was the occasion for renewed accusations on the part of certain Russian critics in Paris that Diaghilev was neglecting to maintain the classical tradition; and this time Diaghilev lost patience with them and replied in a lengthy article in a Russian-language paper, defending his point of view and explaining why he could not stand still but was impelled always to explore new possibilities in choreography. Diaghilev would often expatiate on this theme. Every age possesses its own creators, he would say. The problem is to find them. One of the most difficult tasks is to discover a choreographer: a choreographer is the rarest of birds. A good choreographer must be a person of wide culture. In the existence of a Ballet his emergence is of paramount importance.

★   ★   ★

At the close of this our last season in Paris, instead of moving straight to London, we went to Berlin, where we had an engagement to give several performances of our latest works (*Le Fils Prodigue*, *Le Bal* and *La Chatte*), our Stravinsky ballets, and that evergreen favourite the Polovtsian Dances. The ballet that evoked most enthusiasm was *Le Sacre du Printemps*, which Berlin had never seen before. It was conducted by Ansermet, whom Diaghilev engaged specially for the purpose. This time, mysteriously enough, our visit to Berlin went off triumphantly: the theatre was always full and the press most laudatory. The contrast with our unhappy season of 1926 could not have been more complete. Diaghilev left Berlin well satisfied; and we followed a few days later, stopping on our way to London at Cologne.

★   ★   ★

Highly satisfactory in every respect though our last three seasons in London had proved, Diaghilev's ambition was to return to Covent Garden, where the Ballet had not appeared since 1920; and, thanks yet again to Sir Thomas Beecham, he now achieved it. Our programme, as in Berlin, was to include our latest creations and *Le Sacre*; and special attractions were to be the reappearance of Karsavina in *Petrushka* and of Spesivtseva in *Le Lac des Cygnes*. The interest of the season was to be further enhanced by the performance, as symphonic interludes, of works as yet unheard in London—one of Diaghilev's motives in making this decision being a wish to exhibit his new discovery, Markevich.

I feel sure that Diaghilev half realized at least that it was too soon as yet for Markevich to make his *début*. But Diaghilev was impatient by nature and could not endure any delay before showing the world his latest find; moreover, to perform at Covent Garden with the Diaghilev Ballet was an opportunity for Markevich which might not recur.

However—our season opened on Monday, July the 1st, when we included *Le Fils Prodigue* in the programme. Prokofiev's music was thought even more highly of here than in Paris; the *décor* by Rouault was much admired; and the ballet as a whole was well received. Only Balanchine's choreography met with some hostile criticism, and some of the action was even considered shocking! Diaghilev—always a cunning arranger of programmes—created the most favourable atmosphere possible for the reception of *Le Fils Prodigue* by placing it between two 'London particulars': *The Gods Go a-Begging* and *Le Mariage d'Aurore*.

The reappearance of Karsavina in *Petrushka* was greeted with rapture by her innumerable devotees; and then, on July the 8th, we presented *Le Bal*. This was a far greater success than *Le Fils Prodigue*: all the elements of the production—music, *décor* and choreography—were thought to be most happily combined, and Dolin's brilliant performance was in particular warmly applauded.

At the beginning of the season Diaghilev exhibited all his usual energy. But he was not looking at all well. It was all too clear that illness was undermining his strength, and that he was in constant pain. His Paris doctor took a grave view of his condition and urged him to take care of himself: he must as far as possible avoid all fatigue and excitement, and, as soon as the season in London was over, go into a clinic for a cure. But Diaghilev declined to listen to these admonitions—which, considering how nervous of his health he had always been, was strange.

He was already in this disturbing state when the moment arrived for Markevich to make his *début*. On the day before, Diaghilev arranged a semi-public *répétition-générale* of *Le Renard*, at which Markevich was also to play his piano concerto. At this performance Markevich was introduced to certain friends and acquaintances of Diaghilev and to some members of the press. But it was noticeable that, though they were all very kind to the young composer, they were more inclined to discuss *Le Renard* than his composition. Then on the next night, Monday, July the 15th, there followed its public performance, which was placed in the programme after *Le Carnaval* and *L'Après-Midi* and before *Le Renard* and *The Gods*. The concerto was advertised on the programme in the following terms:

First performance in London. Concerto for Piano and Orchestra in F by Igor Markevich. *Allegro Vivace—Andante—Allegro Risoluto.* Executed by the Composer. Conducted by Roger Desormière. Igor Markevich was born at Kiev in 1912. He studied counterpoint under Nadia Boulanger and orchestration under Vittorio Rieti.

That evening Diaghilev was in a terrible state of agitation. His belief in Markevich's talent was unbounded, and he was bent on making him immediately famous. But, alas, his hopes were entirely disappointed. Markevich had no success whatever. His playing was insufficiently accomplished, and whether from inexperience or nerves he failed completely to make any special impression. There was some applause at the end of the concerto, but it was no more than polite, and carried no message of admiration. Markevich, it was evident, was not yet ready for a public performance, especially one so loudly heralded and before so critical an audience as that of Covent Garden.

Nor, except for Stravinsky's music, was *Le Renard* much better liked. But Diaghilev scarcely minded that; whereas Markevich's failure was a terrible blow to him—so terrible that his illness at once took a turn for the worse. He now retired to bed and never appeared at the theatre. Only Nouvel and Kochno were permitted to see him. They told us daily how he was, assuring us that his illness was taking its normal course and that all he required was rest and quiet. But despite their assurances we were all very worried, till—a week before the end of the season— Diaghilev unexpectedly reappeared. That evening we were giving *Le Sacre* and Spesivtseva was dancing *Le Lac des Cygnes*. The performance went well; and it was a comfort to see Diaghilev about again. I remember his speaking of *Le Sacre* on this occasion. 'So the public accept this at last,' he said. 'It has taken us sixteen years to persuade them!'

Diaghilev paid several more visits to the theatre. But he always remained on the stage. He would not venture into the auditorium. He usually sat on my chair in the prompt corner, and during the intervals we were able to talk. He was beginning gradually to feel a little better, and said that as soon as the season was over he hoped to go to Germany, where it was his intention to see Hindemith about a new ballet he had in mind. He often referred to Markevich, saying how gifted he was and how before long he too would compose a ballet for us. He was full of plans for the following year.

Our last performance took place on July the 26th. Diaghilev asked me to assemble the company on the stage to say goodbye, as we were leaving the next morning for Ostend without him. He walked on to the stage slowly, looking very pale and very dark under the eyes, which had a feverish glint in them: he was clearly in pain. We all stood up; and he greeted us quietly, speaking in a low voice. 'You are leaving tomorrow; and I shall not see you again until the autumn. I wish you all to have a good rest and return to work refreshed and invigorated. We have a busy year before us. All my contracts are signed; and for the first time in our whole career we have an uninterrupted series of engagements already fixed. I thank you for the excellent work you have done, which has been largely responsible for any success we may have had. Goodbye— and good luck!' He then shook hands with everyone; and he and I embraced. We little imagined that we were not to see him again. His illness no longer much perturbed us, and we hoped that, by the time we met again, a rest and his cure would have fully restored his health.

The next morning we left, as arranged, for Ostend; and Diaghilev went to Paris.

★   ★   ★

This last season of ours in London had been exceptionally successful; and the company accordingly left London in a cheerful and contented mood. Before we began our holidays, however, we had another engagement to fulfil: we were to appear for a week at Vichy. We there encountered a number of old friends, including Chaliapine, who came to see us every night. Our last performance took place on August the 4th, when we gave *Cimarosiana*, *Le Tricorne* and *La Boutique Fantasque*, with Danilova, Tchernicheva, Balanchine, Woidzikowsky and Lifar. At the end we received a tremendous ovation—and so it came about that, amid this applause, the Diaghilev Ballet took its final curtain.

★   ★   ★

On reaching Paris, instead of following his doctor's advice and taking a cure, Diaghilev went off first to Munich and then to the Salzburg Festival with Markevich. In both places he went to concerts and round picture galleries; he pursued his eternal search for books; he visited not only Hindemith but also other composers. These activities in no way improved his health and on again feeling worse he consulted other doctors. He wrote to his cousin Korebut-Kubatovich at Monte Carlo, telling him that he was suffering from acute pains in the back, which he supposed were rheumatic. Markevich remained with him only for some ten days. They then parted company; and Diaghilev went to Venice.

After closing at Vichy the company broke up for the holidays; and my wife and I went to Monte Carlo. It was there that at 11 A.M. on August the 19th a telegram was handed to me. It was from Venice and read: 'Diaghilev died this morning. Inform company. Lifar.'

I read this terrible telegram over and over again. I could not take it in. Diaghilev dead! The idea seemed nonsensical. And then, as the truth was borne in on me, I grew dizzy, and for the first time in my life I fainted.

An hour later there arrived another telegram. I hoped against hope it might be a denial. But all it too said was: ' *Terrible nouvelle. Diaghilev est mort ce matin.* Kochno.'

Diaghilev was buried where he died, in Venice. To add to my distress, the Italian Government refused me a *visa*; so I was unable to be present at his funeral.

EPILOGUE

EIGHT years passed before I at length had a chance to return to Italy. I went straight to Venice, to the cemetery where Diaghilev is buried. During all these years the desire to visit it had never left me. The memory of Diaghilev was always alive in me, as it will be to the end of my days.

I crossed the lagoon in a gondola, and involuntarily pictured to myself how, slowly and with splashing oars, they had borne across this water the remains of that great Russian personality and creator, who had so deeply loved his country and life and the arts. And then, standing by his grave, I remembered the many years I had spent in his company; and there flooded over me again the grief and pain I had suffered on that dreadful morning, when I received the news of his death. I stood with my eyes shut and my head bowed, murmuring his name as if in prayer.

It was a wonderful sunny day. A deep silence reigned, the silence of all cemeteries on still, fine days. Opening my eyes after a minute, I read the words cut on his tombstone:

Venise, l'Inspiratrice Éternelle de nos Appaisements.
Serge de Diaghilev.
1872–1929.

APPENDIX

LIST OF BALLETS

1909

1. *Le Pavillon d'Armide*, ballet in three scenes. First performance: 25th November 1907 at the *Mariinsky* Theatre, St. Petersburg. First performed by the Diaghilev Ballet on 19th May 1909 at the *Théâtre du Châtelet*, Paris. Libretto by Benois. Music by N. Tchérépnine. Choreography by M. Fokine. *Décor* by Benois. Principal dancers: A. Pavlova, M. Fokine, V. Nijinsky, A. Bulgakov. *Conductor*: N. Tchérépnine. *Régisseur*: S. Grigoriev.

2. The Polovtsian Dances from the opera *Prince Igor*. First performance: 19th May 1909 at the *Théâtre du Châtelet*. Music by A. Borodine. Choreography by M. Fokine. *Décor* by N. Roerich. Principal dancers: E. Smirnova, S. Fedorova, A. Bolm. Conductor: E. Cooper. *Régisseur*: S. Grigoriev.

3. *Le Festin, suite de danses*. First performance: 19th May 1909 at the *Théâtre du Châtelet*. Arranged by S. P. Diaghilev. Music by Glinka, Tchaikovsky, Moussorgsky, Glazounov and Rimsky-Korsakov. Choreography by Petipa, Gorsky, Fokine, Goltz and F. Kchessinsky. *Décor* by C. Korovine. Costumes by Bakst, Benois, Bilibine, Korovine. Conductor: E. Cooper. *Régisseur*: S. Grigoriev.

4. *Les Sylphides*, ballet in one act. First performance, under the title *Chopiniana*: 6th April 1906 at the *Mariinsky* Theatre, St. Petersburg. First performance by the Diaghilev Ballet: 2nd June 1909 at the *Théâtre du Châtelet*, Paris. Music by Chopin. Choreography by Fokine. *Décor* by Benois. Principal dancers: Pavlova, Karsavina, Baldina, Nijinsky. Conductor: Tchérépnine. *Régisseur*: S. Grigoriev.

5. *Cléopâtre*, choreographic drama in one act. First performance: 2nd June 1909 at the *Théâtre du Châtelet*. Music by Arensky, Taneev, Rimsky-Korsakov, Glinka, Glazounov, Moussorgsky, Tchérépnine. Choreography by Fokine. *Décor* by Bakst. Principal dancers: Pavlova, I. Rubinstein, Karsavina, Fokine, Nijinsky, Bulgakov. Conductor: Tchérépnine. *Régisseur*: S. Grigoriev.

1910

6. *Le Carnaval, ballet-pantomime* in one act. First performance: 20th May 1910 at the *Theater des Westens*, Berlin. Libretto by Bakst and Fokine. Music by Schumann, orchestrated by Rimsky-Korsakov, Liadov, Glazounov, Tchérépnine. Choreography by Fokine. *Décor* by Bakst. Principal

dancers: Karsavina, Piltz, Nijinsky. Conductor: Tchérépnine. *Régisseur*: S. Grigoriev.

7. *Schéhérazade*, choreographic drama in one act. First performance: 4th June 1910 at the *Grand Opéra*, Paris. Libretto by Bakst. Music by Rimsky-Korsakov. Choreography by Fokine. *Décor* by Bakst. Principal dancers: I. Rubinstein, Nijinsky, Bulgakov. Conductor: Tchérépnine. *Régisseur*: S. Grigoriev.

8. *Giselle, ballet-pantomime* in two acts by Saint-Georges, Théophile Gautier and Coralli. First performance: 1841 at the National Academy of Music, Paris. First performance by the Diaghilev Ballet: 18th June at the *Grand Opéra*, Paris. Music by Adolphe Adam. Choreography after Coralli and Perrot. *Décor* by Benois. Principal dancers: Karsavina, Nijinsky. Conductor: Paul Vidal. *Régisseur*: S. Grigoriev.

9. *L'Oiseau de Feu*, Russian fairy-tale in two scenes. First performance: 25th June 1910 at the *Grand Opéra*, Paris. Libretto by Fokine. Music by Stravinsky. Choreography by Fokine. *Décor* by Golovine. Principal dancers: Karsavina, V. Fokina, Fokine, Bulgakov. Conductor: Gabriel Pierné. *Régisseur*: S. Grigoriev.

10. *Les Orientales, esquisses chorégraphiques*. First performance: 25th June 1910 at the *Grand Opéra*, Paris. Arranged by S. P. Diaghilev. Music by Glazounov, Sinding, Arensky, Grieg, Borodine. *Décor* by Korovine. Principal dancers: Gheltzer, Karsavina, Fokina, Nijinsky, Volinin, Orlov. Conductor: Tchérépnine. *Régisseur*: S. Grigoriev.

1911

11. *Le Spectre de la Rose*, choreographic tableau from a poem by Théophile Gautier. First performance: 19th April 1911 at Monte Carlo. Libretto by J. Vaudoyer. Music by Weber. Choreography by Fokine. *Décor* by Bakst. Dancers: Karsavina, Nijinsky. Conductor: Tchérépnine. *Régisseur*: S. Grigoriev.

12. *Narcisse*, mythological poem in one act. First performance: 26th April 1911, at Monte Carlo. Libretto by Bakst. Music by Tchérépnine. Choreography by Fokine. *Décor* by Bakst. Principal dancers: Karsavina, Nijinska, Nijinsky. Conductor: Tchérépnine. *Régisseur*: S. Grigoriev.

13. *Sadkó*—'*Au royaume sous-marin*'. First performance: 6th June 1911 at the *Théâtre du Châtelet*. Music by Rimsky-Korsakov. Choreography by Fokine. *Décor* by B. Anisfeldt. Conductor: Tchérépnine. *Régisseur*: S. Grigoriev.

14. *Petrushka*, burlesque scenes in four tableaux. First performance: 13th June 1911 at the *Théâtre du Châtelet*. Libretto by Igor Stravinsky and Alexandre Benois. Music by Stravinsky. Choreography by Fokine. *Décor* by Benois. Principal dancers: Karsavina, Nijinsky, Orlov, Cecchetti. Conductor: P. Monteux. *Régisseur*: S. Grigoriev.

15. *Le Lac des Cygnes, ballet-pantomime* in two acts and three tableaux. First performance: 17th February 1894 at the *Mariinsky* Theatre. First performed by the Diaghilev Ballet in October 1911 at the Theatre Royal, Covent Garden. Libretto by M. Tchaikovsky. Music by P. Tchaikovsky. Choreography by Petipa. *Décor* by Korovine and Golovine. Principal dancers: Kchessinska and Nijinsky. Conductor: P. Monteux. *Régisseur*: S. Grigoriev.

1912

16. *Le Dieu Bleu*, Hindu legend in one act. First performance: 13th May 1912 at the *Théâtre du Châtelet*. Libretto by Jean Cocteau and de Madrazo. Music by Reynaldo Hahn. Choreography by Fokine. *Décor* by Bakst. Principal dancers: Karsavina, Nelidova, Nijinsky, Frohman. Conductor: D. Inghelbrecht. *Régisseur*: S. Grigoriev.

17. *Thamar*, choreographic drama in one act. First performance: 20th May 1912 at the *Théâtre du Châtelet*. Libretto by Bakst. Music by Balakirev. Choreography by Fokine. *Décor* by Bakst. Principal dancers: Karsavina, Bolm. Conductor: P. Monteux. *Régisseur*: S. Grigoriev.

18. *L'Après-Midi d'un Faune, tableau chorégraphique*. First performance: 29th May 1912 at the *Théâtre du Châtelet*. Music by Claude Debussy. Choreography by Nijinsky. *Décor* by Bakst. Principal dancers: Nelidova, Nijinsky. Conductor: P. Monteux. *Régisseur*: S. Grigoriev.

19. *Daphnis et Chloë*, ballet in one act and three tableaux. First performance: 8th June 1912 at the *Théâtre du Châtelet*. Music by Maurice Ravel. Choreography by Fokine. *Décor* by Bakst. Principal dancers: Karsavina, Nijinsky, Bolm. Conductor: P. Monteux. *Régisseur*: S. Grigoriev.

1913

20. *L'Oiseau d'Or, pas de deux classique*. First performance: January 1913 at the Vienna Opera House. Music by Tchaikovsky. Choreography by Petipa. Dancers: Karsavina, Nijinsky. Conductor: P. Monteux. *Régisseur*: S. Grigoriev.

21. *Jeux, poème dansé*. First performance: 15th May 1913 at the *Théâtre des Champs-Élysées*, Paris. Music by Claude Debussy. Choreography by Nijinsky. *Décor* by Bakst. Principal dancers: Karsavina, Schollar, Nijinsky. Conductor: P. Monteux. *Régisseur*: S. Grigoriev.

22. *Le Sacre du Printemps*, tableau of pagan Russia in two acts. First performance: 29th May 1913 at the *Théâtre des Champs-Élysées*. Libretto by Stravinsky and Roerich. Music by Stravinsky. Choreography by Nijinsky. *Décor* by Roerich. Principal dancer: M. Piltz. Conductor: P. Monteux. *Régisseur*: S. Grigoriev.

23. *La Tragédie de Salomé*, after a poem by Robert d'Humières. First performance: 12th June 1913 at the *Théâtre des Champs-Élysées*. Music by Florent Schmidt. Choreography by B. Romanov. *Décor* by S. Soudeikine. Principal dancer: Karsavina. Conductor: P. Monteux. *Régisseur*: S. Grigoriev.

The Diaghilev Ballet

1914

24. *Papillons*, ballet in one act. First performance: 16th April 1914 at Monte Carlo. Music by Schumann, orchestrated by Tchérépnine. Choreography by Fokine. Scenery by M. Doboujinsky. Costumes by Bakst. Principal dancers: Karsavina, Schollar. Conductor: P. Monteux. *Régisseur*: S. Grigoriev.

25. *La Légende de Joseph*, ballet in one act. First performance 17th May 1914 at the *Grand Opéra*, Paris. Libretto by Count Harry von Kessler and Hugo von Hofmannsthal. Music by Richard Strauss. Choreography by Fokine. Scenery by José-Maria Sert. Costumes by Bakst. Principal dancers: M. Kouznetsova, L. Massine, Bulgakov. Conductor: Richard Strauss. *Régisseur*: S. Grigoriev.

26. *Le Coq d'Or*, opera in three tableaux by Rimsky-Korsakov. First performance: 24th May 1914 at the *Grand Opéra*. Arrangement suggested by Alexandre Benois. Production and choreography by Fokine. *Décor* by N. Goncharova. Principal singers: Dobrovolska, Petrenko, B. Getrov, Alchevsky, Belianin and Nikolaeva (in title role). Principal dancers: Karsavina, Jezierska, Bulgakov, Cecchetti, Kovalski. Conductor: P. Monteux. *Régisseur*: S. Grigoriev.

27. *Le Rossignol*, opera in three tableaux by I. Stravinsky, after a fairy-tale by Hans Andersen. First performance: 26th May 1914 at the *Grand Opéra*. *Mise en scène* by A. Benois and A. Sanine. *Décor* by A. Benois. Dances arranged by B. Romanov. Conductor: P. Monteux. *Régisseur*: S. Grigoriev.

28. *Midas*, mythological comedy in one act by L. Bakst. First performance: 2nd June 1914 at the *Grand Opéra*. Music by Maximilien Steinberg. *Décor* by M. Doboujinsky. Principal dancers: Karsavina, Bolm, Frohman. Conductor: René Baton. *Régisseur*: S. Grigoriev.

1915

29. *Le Soleil de Nuit*, Russian scenes and dances. First performance: 20th December 1915 at the *Grand Théâtre*, Geneva. Music by Rimsky-Korsakov. Choreography by L. Massine. *Décor* by M. Larionov. Principal dancers: L. Massine, N. Zverev. Conductor: E. Ansermet. *Régisseur*: S. Grigoriev.

1916

30. *Till Eulenspiegel*, 'comico-dramatic' ballet by Nijinsky. First performance: 23rd October 1916 at the Manhattan Opera House, New York. Music by Richard Strauss. Choreography by Nijinsky. *Décor* by Robert E. Jones. Principal dancers: F. Revalles, Nijinsky. Conductor: A. Goetz. *Régisseur*: N. Kremnev.

31. *Las Meninas*, pavane by L. Massine. First performance: 21st August 1916 at the Eugenia-Victoria Theatre in San Sebastian, Spain. Music by Gabriel Fauré. Scenery by Carlo Socrate. Costumes by J.-M. Sert. Principal dancers: Sokolova, Khokhlova, Massine, Woidzikowsky. Conductor: E. Ansermet. *Régisseur*: S. Grigoriev.

32. *Kikimora*, Russian fairy-tale. First performance: 25th August 1916 at the Eugenia-Victoria Theatre, San Sebastian. Music by Liadov. Choreography by Massine. *Décor* by Larionov. Principal dancers: Shabelska, Idzikovsky. Conductor: Ansermet. *Régisseur*: S. Grigoriev.

1917

33. *Fireworks*, symphonic poem by I. Stravinsky. First performance: 12th April 1917 at the *Costanzi* Theatre, Rome. *Décor* by M. Ballo. Conductor: Ansermet. *Régisseur*: S. Diaghilev.

34. *Les Femmes de Bonne Humeur*, choreographic comedy after Carlo Goldoni (1707–1793). First performance: 12th April 1917 at the *Costanzi* Theatre, Rome. Music by Domenico Scarlatti (1685–1757), orchestrated and arranged by Vincenzo Tommasini. Choreography by Massine. Principal dancers: Lopokova, Tchernicheva, Madame J. Cecchetti, Massine, E. Cecchetti, Idzikovsky, Woidzikowsky. Conductor: Ansermet. *Régisseur*: S. Grigoriev.

35. *Les Contes Russes*, suite of scenes and dances on Russian folklore themes, including *Kikimora* (see 32 above). First performance: 11th May 1917 at the *Théâtre du Châtelet*, Paris. Music by Liadov. Choreography by Massine. *Décor* and curtain by Larionov. Principal dancers: Tchernicheva, Sokolova, Woidzikowsky, Jazvinsky, Idzikovsky. Conductor: Ansermet. *Régisseur*: S. Grigoriev.

36. *Parade*. First performance: 18th May 1917 at the *Théâtre du Châtelet*. Theme by Jean Cocteau. Music by Eric Satie. *Décor* by Picasso, by whom curtain was not only designed but also painted. Choreography by Massine. Principal dancers: Lopokova, Shabelska, Massine, Zverev. Conductor: Ansermet. *Régisseur*: S. Grigoriev.

1919

37. *La Boutique Fantasque*, ballet in one act. First performance: 5th July 1919 at the Alhambra Theatre, London. Music by Giacomo Rossini, arranged and orchestrated by Ottorino Respighi. Choreography by Massine. *Décor* and curtain by André Derain. Principal dancers: Lopokova, Massine. Conductor: Henry Delfosse. *Régisseur*: S. Grigoriev.

38. *Le Tricorne*, ballet in one act by Martínez Sierra. First performance: 22nd July 1919 at the Alhambra. Music by Manuel de Falla. Choreography by Massine. *Décor* and curtain by Picasso. Principal dancers: Karsavina, Massine, Woidzikowsky. Conductor: Ansermet. *Régisseur*: S. Grigoriev.

The Diaghilev Ballet

1920

39. *Le Chant du Rossignol*, ballet in one act, adapted from the opera *Le Rossignol* (see 27 above). First performance: 2nd February 1920 at the *Grand Opéra*, Paris. Music by Stravinsky. Choreography by Massine. Principal dancers: Karsavina, Sokolova, S. Grigoriev. Conductor: Ansermet. *Régisseur*: S. Grigoriev.

40. *Pulcinella*, ballet in one act, with song in one scene. First performance: 15th May 1920 at the *Grand Opéra*, Paris. Music by Stravinsky on themes by Pergolesi. Choreography by Massine. *Décor* by Picasso. Principal dancers: Karsavina, Tchernicheva, Nemchinova, Massine, Idzikovsky, Cecchetti, Zverev, Novak. Conductor: Ansermet. *Régisseur*: S. Grigoriev.

41. *Le Astuzie Femminili*, opera-ballet in three tableaux. First performance: 27th May 1920 at the *Grand Opéra*, Paris. Music by Domenico Cimarosa. Recitatives after Cimarosa, orchestrated by Ottorino Respighi. Choreography by Massine. *Décor* by J.-M. Sert. Principal singers: Mafalda de Voltri, Romaniza, Rozovska, Angelo Masni-Pieralli, A. Anglada, G. de Weech. Principal dancers: Karsavina, Tchernicheva, Nemchinova, Sokolova, Idzikovsky, Woidzikowsky, Novak. Conductor: Ansermet . *Régisseur*: S. Grigoriev.

1921

42. *Chout*, Russian legend in six scenes. First performance: 17th May 1921 at the *Gaieté-Lyrique* Theatre, Paris. Music by Serge Prokofiev. Choreography by Larionov and T. Slavinsky. *Décor* by Larionov. Principal dancers: C. Devillier, T. Slavinsky, J. Jazvinsky. Conductor: Ansermet. *Régisseur*: S. Grigoriev.

43. *Cuadro Flamenco*, suite of Andalusian dances. First performance: 17th May 1921 at the *Gaieté-Lyrique*, Paris. *Décor* by Picasso. Principal dancers: Maria Dalbaicin, La Rubia de Jerez, La Gabrielita del Gorrotín, La López, El Tejero, El Moreno.

44. *The Sleeping Princess (La Belle au Bois Dormant)*, ballet in four acts, after Perrault. First performance: 2nd November 1921 at the Alhambra, London. Music by Tchaikovsky. Choreography by Petipa, reproduced by M. Sergeev. *Décor* and whole production by Bakst. Principal dancers: O. Spesivtseva, Lopokova, Carlotta Brianza, Tchernicheva, B. Nijinska, P. Vladimirov, A. Vilzak, Idzikovsky, Woidzikowsky. Conductor: Gregor Fitelberg. *Régisseur*: S. Grigoriev.

1922

45. *Le Mariage de la Belle au Bois Dormant (Aurora's Wedding)*, classical ballet in one act (taken from 44 above). First performance: 18th May 1922 at the *Grand Opéra*, Paris. Music by Tchaikovsky. Choreography after

Petipa. *Décor* (taken from 1 above) by A. Benois. Principal dancers: Vera Trefilova, P. Vladimirov. Conductor: G. Fitelberg. *Régisseur*: S. Grigoriev.

46. *Le Renard, ballet burlesque avec chant.* First performance: 18th May 1922 at the *Grand Opéra*, Paris. Libretto and music by Stravinsky (French version by C. F. Ramuz). *Décor* by N. Goncharova. Choreography by La Nijinska. Principal dancers: La Nijinska, Idzikovsky, Jazvinsky, Federov. Conductor: Ansermet. *Régisseur*: S. Grigoriev.

1923

47. *Les Noces*, Russian choreographic movements in four continuous scenes. First performance: 13th July 1923 at the *Gaieté-Lyrique*, Paris. Words and music by Stravinsky. Choreography by La Nijinska. *Décor* by N. Goncharova: Singers: N. Smirnova, M. Davidova, D'Arial, G. Danskoy. Principal dancers: Tchernicheva, F. Doubrovska, Woidzikowsky, N. Semenov. Conductor: Ansermet. *Régisseur*: S. Grigoriev.

1924

48. *Les Tentations de la Bergère, ou l'Amour Vainqueur*, ballet in one act. First performance: 3rd January 1924 at Monte Carlo. Music by Montéclair (1666–1737), restored and orchestrated by H. Casadesus. *Décor* and curtain by Juan Gris. Choreography by La Nijinska. Principal dancers: Nemchinova, Tchernicheva, Woidzikowsky, Vilzak. Conductor: Édouard Flament. *Régisseur*: S. Grigoriev.

49. *Les Biches*, ballet in one act. First performance: 6th January 1924 at Monte Carlo. Music by Francis Poulenc. Choreography by La Nijinska. *Décor* and curtain by Marie Laurencin. Principal dancers: Nemchinova, Nijinska, Tchernicheva, Sokolova, Vilzak, Woidzikowsky, Zverev. Conductor: E. Flament. *Régisseur*: S. Grigoriev.

50. *Cimarosiana*, suite of dances (taken from 41 above). First performance: 8th January 1924 at Monte Carlo. Music by Cimarosa. *Décor* by Sert. Choreography by Massine. Principal dancers: Nemchinova, Tchernicheva, Sokolova, Idzikovsky, Woidzikowsky, Vilzak. Conductor: E. Flament. *Régisseur*: S. Grigoriev.

51. *Les Fâcheux*, ballet in one act by Boris Kochno, from the comedy-ballet of Molière. First performance: 19th January 1924 at Monte Carlo. Music by Georges Auric. Choreography by La Nijinska. *Décor* and curtain by Georges Bracque. Principal dancers: Tchernicheva, Vilzak, Dolin. Conductor: E. Flament. *Régisseur*: S. Grigoriev.

52. *La Nuit sur le Mont Chauve, tableau chorégraphique.* First performance: 13th April 1924 at Monte Carlo. Music by Moussorgsky. Choreography by La Nijinska. Principal dancers: Sokolova, Fedorov. Conductor: E. Flament. *Régisseur*: S. Grigoriev.

The Diaghilev Ballet

53. *Le Train Bleu, opérette dansée* in one act. First performance 20th June 1924 at the *Théâtre des Champs-Élysées*, Paris. Scenario by Jean Cocteau. Music by Darius Milhaud. Choreography by La Nijinska. Scenery by H. Laurens. Costumes by Chanel. Curtain by Picasso. Principal dancers: La Nijinska, Sokolova, Dolin, Woidzikowsky. Conductor: P. Monteux. *Régisseur*: S. Grigoriev.

1925

54. *Zéphire et Flore*, ballet in three tableaux by Boris Kochno. First performance: 28th April 1925 at Monte Carlo. Music by Vladimir Dukelsky. Choreography by Massine. *Décor* by Georges Bracque. Principal dancers: Nikitina, Dolin, Serge Lifar. Conductor: M.-C. Scotto. *Régisseur*: S. Grigoriev.

55. *Les Matelots*, ballet in five tableaux by Boris Kochno. First performance: 17th June 1925 at the *Gaieté-Lyrique*, Paris. Music by Georges Auric. Choreography by Massine. *Décor* and curtain by Pruna. Dancers: Nemchinova, Sokolova, Woidzikowsky, Lifar, Slavinsky. Conductor: M.-C. Scotto. *Régisseur*: S. Grigoriev.

56. *Barabau*, ballet with vocal chorus. First performance: 11th December 1925 at the Coliseum Theatre, London. Book and music by Vittorio Rieti. Choreography by Georges Balanchine. *Décor* by Utrillo. Principal dancers: Woidzikowsky, Lifar, Tatiana Chamié. Conductor: Roger Desormière. *Régisseur*: S. Grigoriev.

1926

57. *Roméo et Juliette*, 'a rehearsal, without scenery, in two parts'. First performance: 4th May 1926 at Monte Carlo. Music by Constant Lambert. Curtains and scenic adjuncts by Max Ernst and Joan Miro. Choreography by La Nijinska. Choreography of the *entr'acte* by G. Balanchine. Principal dancers: Karsavina, Lifar, Slavinsky. Conductor: M.-C. Scotto. *Régisseur*: S. Grigoriev.

58. *La Pastorale*. First performance: 29th May 1926 at the *Théâtre Sarah Bernhardt*, Paris. Scenario by B. Kochno. Music by G. Auric. *Décor* by Pruna. Choreography by Balanchine. Principal dancers: F. Doubrovska, A. Danilova, Lifar, Woidzikowsky. Conductor: R. Desormière. *Régisseur*: S. Grigoriev.

59. *Jack-in-the-Box*. First performance: 3rd July 1926 at the *Théâtre Sarah Bernhardt*. Music by E. Satie. Choreography by Balanchine. *Décor* by Derain. Dancers: Danilova, Tchernicheva, Doubrovska, Idzikovsky. Conductor: R. Desormière. *Régisseur*: S. Grigoriev.

60. *The Triumph of Neptune*, English pantomime in twelve tableaux. First performance: 3rd December 1926 at the Lyceum Theatre, London. Book by Sacheverell Sitwell. Music by Lord Berners. Choreography by Balanchine. *Décor* adapted and scenery executed by Prince A. Sher-

vashidze from prints by G. and R. Cruikshank, Tofts, Honigold and Webb, collected by B. Pollock. Principal dancers: Danilova, Tchernicheva, Sokolova, Lifar, Balanchine, Tcherkass. Conductor: H. Defosse. *Régisseur*: S. Grigoriev.

61. *La Chatte*, ballet in one act by Sobeka, based on one of Aesop's Fables. First performance: 30th April 1927 at Monte Carlo. Music by Henri Sauguet. Choreography by Balanchine. Architectural and sculptural constructions by Gabo and Pevsner. Principal dancers: Spesivtseva, Lifar. Conductor: M.-C. Scotto. *Régisseur*: S. Grigoriev.

62. *Mercure*, '*poses plastiques*'. Originally presented on 15th June 1924 at the *Soirées de Paris* organized by Comte Étienne de Beaumont. First performed by the Diaghilev Ballet on 2nd June 1927 at the *Théâtre Sarah Bernhardt*, Paris. Music by E. Satie. Theme and choreography by Massine. *Décor* by Picasso. Principal dancers: Petrova, Massine, Lissanevich. Conductor: R. Desormière. *Régisseur*: S. Grigoriev.

63. *Le Pas d'Acier*, ballet in two tableaux by S. Prokofiev and G. Yakoulov. First performance: 7th June 1927 at the *Théâtre Sarah Bernhardt*. Music by S. Prokofiev. Choreography by Massine. Constructions and costumes after designs by G. Yakoulov. Principal dancers: Tchernicheva, Danilova, Petrova, Massine, Lifar, Woidzikowsky. Conductor: R. Desormière. *Régisseur*: S. Grigoriev.

1928

64. *Ode*, spectacle in two acts. First performance: 6th June 1928 at the *Théâtre Sarah Bernhardt*, Paris. Scenic book by B. Kochno. Music by N. Nabokov to a text by Lomonosov. Decorative contributions by P. Tchelichev in collaboration with Pierre Charbonnier. Choreography by Massine. Principal dancers: Ira Beliamina, F. Doubrovska, A. Nikitina, Massine, Lifar, Efimov, Tcherkass. Conductor: R. Desormière. *Régisseur*: S. Grigoriev.

65. *Apollon Musagète*, ballet in two scenes by Igor Stravinsky. First performance: 12th June 1928 at the *Théâtre Sarah Bernhardt*. Choreography by Balanchine. *Décor* by A. Bauchant. Principal dancers: Danilova, Tchernicheva, Doubrovska, Lifar. Conductor: R. Desormière. *Régisseur*: S. Grigoriev.

66. *The Gods Go a-Begging*, *pastorale* by Sobeka. First performance: 16th July 1928 at His Majesty's Theatre, London. Music by Handel, arranged by Sir Thomas Beecham. Choreography by Balanchine. Principal dancers: Danilova, Tchernicheva, Doubrovska, Woidzikowsky, Tcherkass. Conductor: Sir Thomas Beecham. *Régisseur*: S. Grigoriev.

1929

67. *Le Bal*, ballet in two tableaux by B. Kochno. First performance: 9th May 1929 at Monte Carlo. Music by Vittorio Rieti. Choreography by

The Diaghilev Ballet

Balanchine. *Décor* by G. de Chirico. Principal dancers: Danilova, Doubrovska,P. Lipkovska, Dolin, Bobrov, Woidzikowsky, Balanchine, Lifar. Conductor: M.-C. Scotto. *Régisseur*: S. Grigoriev.

68. *Le Fils Prodigue*, scenes in three tableaux by B. Kochno. First performance: 21st May 1929 at the *Théâtre Sarah Bernhardt*, Paris. Music by S. Prokofiev. Choreography by Balanchine. *Décor* by Georges Rouault. Principal dancers: Doubrovska, Lifar, Woidzikowsky, Dolin, Fedorov. Conductor: R. Desormière. *Régisseur*: S. Grigoriev.

INDEX

The Diaghilev Ballet

Carnaval, Le, 30, 32, 33, 263; performed in Berlin, 34, 61; in Paris, 35, 41, 52; in London, 56, 259; at Monte Carlo, 65; at Deauville, 73; in Rio, 89; Nijinsky appears in, 97; performed at Geneva, 107; in Madrid, 112

Cecchetti, *Maestro* Enrico, 45, 49, 58, 76, 86, 96, 116, 139, 214; living in Lausanne, 103; leaves company, 169; dances in *The Sleeping Princess* on his fiftieth anniversary as dancer, 172; appointment in Milan, 211-12; recommends Tchernicheva as ballet-mistress, 216-18; meeting with company in Milan, 232; death, 249

Century Theatre, New York, 109

Chabrier, E., 193

Chaliapine, F., in *Boris Godounov*, 2, 83, 85, 100; in *Prince Igor*, 20, 21, 100; in *Ivan the Terrible*, 22, 100; in *Khovanshchina*, 73, 84, 85; first appearance in London, 85; acting ability, 94; attends ballet performances at Vichy, 260

Chamié, Tatiana, 212

Chanel, 198

Chant du Rossignol, Le, 268; performed in Paris, 152, 153; in London, 157; new version, 205, 206; performed in Paris, 209, 212

Châtelet (Paris): *see under* Paris

Chatte, La, 233, 234, 271; performed at Monte Carlo, 234, 235; in Paris, 237, 240; in London, 239; in Vienna, 240; in Berlin, 257

Chausovsky, 17, 112, 127

Chirico, Giorgio de, 255

Chopin, 7, 23

Chopiniana, renamed: *see Sylphides, Les*

Chout, 163, 164, 165, 268; performed in Paris, 166; in London, 167

Chu Chin Chow, long run in London, 167

Ciacchi, 77

Cimarosa, Domenico, 153, 157, 161

Cimarosiana, 193, 249, 269; performed in London, 199-200, 247; at Monte Carlo, 203; at Milan, 232; at Vichy, 260

Cléopâtre, 7-8, 9, 10, 13, 15-17, 30, 32, 199, 263; performed in Paris, 23-5, 32, 41, 99; in Berlin, 34, 61, 76; in London, 56, 139, 150; in Madrid, 122; scenery destroyed by fire, 127; performed in

Cléopâtre (continued): Switzerland, 188; at Barcelona, 196, 208; at Monte Carlo, 243, 255

Cochran, Charles, 167

Cocteau, Jean, 61, 117, 118, 195

Coliseum (London): *see under* London

Colombe, La, 191

Concurrence, La, 187

Connaught, Duke of, 204, 226, 239, 247

'Constructivist' style, 233, 234, 235

Contes Russes, Les (Kikimora ballet), 114, 118, 267; performed in Paris, 121; in Madrid, 122; new version for London performance, 141; performed in Madrid, 164-5; popular in Germany, 199

Cooper, Émile, 20, 84, 85

Coppélia, 168

Coq d'Or, Le, 94, 97, 266; performed in Paris, 99, 100; in London, 100

Covent Garden: *see under* London

Cuadro Flamenco, 165, 268; performed in Paris, 166; in London, 167; Picasso paintings on *décor* sold, 219

Dalbaicin, Maria, 165-6, 167

Dalcroze, Jacques, 61-2, 78

Danilova, Alexandra, joins company, 200; in *Zéphire et Flore*, 207; progress, 214; in *Jack-in-the-Box*, 222; appearance in London, 224; in *Le Lac des Cygnes*, 226; in *L'Oiseau de Feu*, 228; in *The Triumph of Neptune*, 228; in *Turandot*, 232; in *Apollon Musagète*, 246; in *Le Bal*, 255, 257; performances at Vichy, 260

Daphnis et Chloë, 47, 50, 58, 66, 97, 265; performed in Paris, 69; in London, 100; rehearsal in Lisbon, 134; proposed revival (1920), 158, 159; (1923), 188-9; revived at Monte Carlo, 191; last performance at Barcelona, 196; scenery used for *The Gods*, 248

Da Rosa, 128, 129, 130

Davidov, 23

Deauville, performances at, 72-3

Debussy, 61, 66, 73, 81, 82-3

Defosse, Henri, 228

Degas, 34

Delaunay, Robert, 139

Delibes, 1

Démon, Le, 205

Derain, André, 144, 222

The Diaghilev Ballet

The Diaghilev Ballet